Songwriting
and The Creative Process

Suggestions
and starting
points for
songwriters

by Steve Gillette

SingOut!

A Sing Out! Publication

Editor: *Mark Moss*
Publications Director: *Eric Nemeyer*
Art Director: *Ed Courrier*
Additional Text Editing: *Rich Kerstetter*
Music Typesetting: *Eric Nemeyer*
Cover Design: *Christine Ronan*, Ronan Design, Chicago IL

ISBN: 1-881322-03-3

Library of Congress Cataloging-in-Publication Data

Gillette, Steve
    Songwriting and The Creative Process : Suggestions and Starting Points for Songwriters / by Steve Gillette.
        p.   cm.
    Includes bibliographical reference and index.
    ISBN 1-881322-03-3 : $14.95
    1. Popular music--writing and publishing.   I. Title.
MT67.G46 1995
782.42164'13--dc20

94-17026

CIP

MN

A Sing Out! Publication

Sing Out Corporation
P.O. Box 5253
Bethlehem, PA 18015-0253
610-865-5366

For all of us.

Table of Contents

Foreward

Steve Gillette tells it like it is, and this wonderful book is going to help you write songs. It's already helped me, and I've written songs for a long time – about 25 years.

I knew Steve's songwriting is very, very good. What was surprising is that Steve, as well as being a fine songwriter, is a fine teacher of the craft of writing. And songwriting *is* a craft.

There are tools to use in writing songs. I once wrote a song a day, good or bad, for 90 days. Anything can change if you do it for 90 days. If you work on a regular basis, and use what you learn from this great book, you will get better as a songwriter: You can't fail.

One of the most important things that you will find here is that you *can* write songs. Writing is a matter of knowing some simple things, knowing yourself, getting comfortable with a feeling that you have something to say. Steve talks you through the essentials like rhyme and time, syntax and color, contrast and beat, shape and texture. He tells you what to listen to and lets you know you are capable of being inspired even when you don't feel inspired. There is a lot to be said for writing on a schedule, whether you want to or not, whether you feel like it or not. Steve will show you how to do that.

I didn't start out as a songwriter. I was raised on Rodgers and Hart and started studying classical piano at 5 years of age. At 13 I played Mozart with an orchestra, also listened to the great Broadway songwriters, as my dad had his own radio shows in Denver, Seattle and Los Angeles. I was raised listening to the great songwriters of that era – from Cole Porter to Irving Berlin. You might say that I didn't have the "habit" of songwriting; on the other hand, I *did* have the habits of "song-listening" and "song-loving." That was a good start. And my father, for his radio shows, looked for and found the best of what was being written in Broadway and the musical theatre. So I learned to "hear" a good song.

Folk music came into my life like an explosion, and at 14 I began to play the guitar and sing folk songs enthralled, delighted, moved and urged by the great stories one could tell in song. Folk music gripped my imagination, turning my focus away from classical music and my father's rich heritage of Broadway. Now, in the vast gathering of traditional music as embodied at first on the radio by the popularity of Harry Belafonte, The Kingston Trio and Peter, Paul and Mary, there was a new, vital, rich language. These folk songs had a broad scope, a deep plumbing of emotions and range, and a very different voice that rang in their melodies and words. At that time I didn't consider myself to be a singer, but a teller of stories. And on the coffeehouse circuit, I heard magnificent tales – "Plane Wreck at Los Gatos," "Gypsy Rover," "The Great Sulchie," as well as songs collected by Alan Lomax, and those written by John Jacob Niles and Burl Ives – "Black is the Color," "Scarlet Ribbons," "Go Down You Red Red Roses," "The Greenland Fisheries," "The Water is Wide") songs of heartbreak and a day's work on the sea; songs of pain and laughter, songs of healing, songs of terror. There were the great mythical traditional ballads, full of dramatic stories of murder and revenge, passion and poison, lovers and leaders. I searched and listened, studying songs now as I had read books, eager to hear the ring of the truth in their fiber.

By the early '60s, I had signed a record contract with Elektra that was to go on for 24 years. *Sing Out!* was already on the scene, and I searched every issue for new singers, new writers, newly discovered versions of folk songs. The "folk movement" was in full swing. I found Dylan ("Tambourine Man," "The Lonesome Death of Hattie Caroll," "Pity the Poor Immigrant") and Paxton ("Bottle of Wine"), Eric Andersen ("Thirsty Boots") – the songs of the city writers with their joy, their rage, their sorrow. These songs appealed to my singer's soul and, along with the traditional songs I loved, were rounding out the enormous canvas on which I wanted to paint as a singer.

There was so much music that I never thought of writing my own songs. Of course, there were often advantages to not being a songwriter. I was not under the kind of pressure to come up with all my own material. I could search for the perfect story for my voice, the perfect solace for my soul. Part of the reason was that I never really thought of writing as something I did.

One terrible experience probably contributed to that status, my non-writer status. I had been wild to write in high school. Not songs, but prose. I read a great deal, and had since I was a child – *Moby Dick, The Brothers Karamazov, Les Miserables*. And in my writing classes, I wrote a ton of short stories and papers, articles, and short fiction. I had mostly good teachers who believed I had talent and encouraged me.

In my senior year of high school I ran into a tight-mouthed, mean-spirited woman teacher. After reading what I knew was good and might possibly be a brilliant three-page interpretation of T.S. Eliot's "Cocktail Party," she accused me of plagiarizing the piece. I was heartbroken, sick, shamed, hurt, and I believe, silenced. For 10 years. Of course, I understood T.S. Eliot. We read in my family, we talked, we thought, we read poetry out loud, we fought about what Eliot meant, what Dostoyevsky meant, what Melville meant. We loved books, and we loved language.

I've heard many writers who have had this terrible experience over the years. It is a great trauma. This teacher probably kept a lid on my songwriting as well as my prose writing for a long time.

But not forever.

In the mid '60s, after having released half a dozen records, I found my own songwriting voice. By that time I had made six albums, two of traditional material, then a couple of albums of the "city-writers." By 1966, when I was looking for the material for *In My Life*, I wanted to stretch, to change, to be challenged. There was a new wind blowing in popular music. The '50s and '40s music, on which I had been weaned by my father's singing, was being enriched by what amounted to a revolution in songwriting. Since the beginning of the '60s, when the folk movement had swept the United States, England and many other parts of the world, the kind of music being written and performed had dramatically changed. I recorded songs from Peter Brook's great musical about the French Revolution, *Marat/Sade*. I recorded "Pirate Jenny" from *Three Penny Opera* by Brecht and Weill. I recorded the Beatles song "In My Life." I wanted drama. I wanted change.

At that time I met Leonard Cohen who told me I should be writing songs. Leonard said, "If I can do it, you can do it." It cut right through that nasty teacher's critical, unjust, hurtful shadow, the one that I realized must have been cast across the years for far too long.

At first I kept a journal of "writings" – musings, thoughts, ideas, some from the journals I had by now kept for a few years. I think journal-keeping is fundamental to the life of any songwriter. I showed the journal to an old friend who read it and said, "It is full of dark thoughts." By the way, some of those dark thoughts probably would have been just the thing to start me out. But my friend did something brilliant. He gave me a simple instruction. He said, "I want you to go home and write five songs about a love affair. The beginning, the middle, and the end of the affair."

My first song was "Since You've Asked." I was so happy I could hardly breathe. Singing was great. This was better. Thrilling. I wrote a song about my father, then a big, strangely-structured song called "Albatross," whose shape came more from my classical training and opera singing than from folk music.

Or did it? Often there is a movement between "classical" themes and folk music. Think of the big pieces of Aaron Copland, not to compare myself with such a genius, but just think of all the "big" themes, the major works, which have a simple, three-minute, memorable folk melody as their inspiration and often their major substance.

I wrote songs that sometimes took an hour – like the song for my father. Then I wrote songs on major themes, like the life of "Ché Guevara," which took five years. I often went to my journals to find a line, a beginning, a theme. That is where the journal-keeping is essential. I like what Jimmy Webb says about writing songs: "The job of the songwriter is to remember everything."

I like simplicity, direction. You'll find a great wealth of that in Steve's book. To learn to use it in songwriting will be a continuing lesson. To write a good love song is amazing.

A good songwriter is a national, no, a worldwide treasure. Capturing the essence of an experience in a melody and words is a great gift. To take a theme of social significance, like the tragedy at Attica, and do what Tom Paxton did with "The Hostage," is nothing short of miraculous.

There is no wrong way to write songs, just as there is no wrong way to love someone. Songwriting is about discipline. And it is about letting go of your "projections."

I liked the experiences I have had collaborating. They were very different than writing on my own and took me to places I hadn't been able to go as a writer before. They opened doors that could be reopened on my own. And collaborating is fun!

I strive to put whatever is in my heart at the moment into the song I am writing. I believe the best of my work is always inspired by a comment, a feeling, a vision, if you will, of something I love or someone I love. A quirk. A comment.

I plan to be writing for the rest of my life. One of my most recent songs, "The Blizzard," is a big, dramatic story, the kind I have always been attracted to, only this time, I wrote the song. I think that is what Steve will give you in this great book on writing, a sense that your very deepest desires as a songwriter are possible.

You will learn a lot from this book.

I already have.

Judy Collins
Spring, 1994

Introduction

Can songwriting be taught? Yes, of course it can. You might just as well ask if driving can be taught. You can learn to drive by watching others and by experimenting, but a friend can save you a lot of trouble by suggesting that you let a boiling radiator cool down before you take the cap off, or that you might consider shifting into a lower gear before you start down Six Mile Grade.

When songwriters talk about their craft they discover that they've encountered many of the same problems, but often have different ways to explain the lessons that this work has taught them. This book owes its beginnings to the "Courting the Muse" columns which are a regular feature of *Sing Out! Magazine*. In these columns songwriters have found a very enlightened forum for just such a discussion, and gives them a chance to talk about their craft and approach to writing.

"Courting the Muse" has given the rest of us a chance to read the words of some of the most interesting songwriters of our time. They represent a wide range of musical experience and each writes for varying reasons. Some have sold millions of records, some have written for Broadway, some have written for children, and some have actively taught songwriting. There are insights and valuable advice in all their articles and each has given freely of his or her best ideas. All of the columns to date are included here.

As students of the art and craft of songwriting, we already know a lot about songs. This knowledge comes from our very early and mostly unconscious enjoyment of music over a lifetime. Much of the job of the writing teacher has to do with helping us to codify and access what we already know. To suggest that there are principles of songwriting, or that songs follow rules, is only an attempt to give the writer a working frame of reference. The good songs all bend or break the rules in interesting ways.

Can thinking be taught? Can self-expression be taught? Yes and yes again. But it begins to become clear that there is an aspect of all these endeavors that depends on the abilities and the determination of the individual. Ability is a relative term, but it must be obvious that anyone reading and understanding these lines has at least the verbal ability to write good song lyrics. The musical talent involved in songwriting can also be developed and improved upon and with simple practice, progress can be made.

Determination is a much more interesting and productive area of discussion. Educators and artists alike have recognized that motivation is inextricably linked to passion and joy. Because music is an emotional activity and is in itself very enjoyable, we as listeners can make the transition to being composers fairly naturally. And if as songwriters we can connect with the immense energy of emotional truth in the heart of each of us waiting to be expressed and acknowledged there is no limit to what a song can accomplish.

Many books that talk about songwriting present the subject in the context of the commercial music business. There are good reasons for this, of course. Most writers wish to have the opportunity to participate in the music industry and earn its rewards of wealth and celebrity. Also, the songs which are used as examples are widely known.

The limitations of the music industry as a source of inspiration for the serious considerations of artistic life, however, should be obvious. If a thought, no matter how insightful does not lend itself to the radio or the video, it is not likely to have much of a chance to be heard. So much depends on how well the work endorses the values and the issues of the programmer and the sponsor. There is the opportunity to reach a great number of people but the window can be an extremely narrow opening.

There are many very good reasons for the existence of art and creative activity which cannot be justified in terms of the top forty charts. This book attempts to help the songwriter to explore the paths of creative process and to connect with his or her best energy and insight – to have the experience of being in touch with this gift and to be confident and open enough to speak directly to the needs and loves of our greater society for the reasons of the heart and the soul.

Special Note

I strongly encourage the reader to follow along through the music examples. They progress from the very simple to the more complex in a gradual and understandable way. If you do not have a piano or electronic keyboard you might wish to purchase one. Inexpensive battery operated keyboards are available in stores everywhere, but even a child's xylophone would be adequate to play the examples in the book.

If you do purchase a xylophone, especially for a child, make sure that you get one that has been made to a high standard of accuracy in pitch. This will make a big difference in the development of a good sense of musical intervals. It's important to be able to hear the notes ring together and hear the subtle relationships of dissonance and consonance.

1.

To Begin With ...

1.1 A Conspiracy of Romance

One of my first vivid memories of the power and excitement of music is of a time when I was 5 years old. I do remember many happy times before then singing silly songs with my grandfather, or singing on car trips, or just listening, but this one particular moment stays with me.

My dad plays the piano, and over the years our family has had a succession of usually old, upright pianos. On the occasion I remember my parents had some friends from their college days over for dinner and afterwards they gathered around the piano to sing some of the old famil-iar songs.

I remember standing with my arms wrapped around the leg of the piano with my jaw tight against the wood at one end of the keyboard. My dad's powerful playing and the ringing of the frame of the piano were particularly hypnotic, and as I listened to these four people sing, "Shine on, shine on harvest moon" and "Only a shanty in old shanty town," and "There's a long, long trail a-winding," and "I'll be down to get you in a taxi, Honey," it occurred to me with the vivid realization reserved for five year olds and Brahmans that they were making love.

Love and music were the language that was being spoken. These two activities were the same activity. Without apology, or embarrass-ment, these two young couples were celebrating a form of public joy, a romantic conspiracy of song. I too felt the romance of the moment, al-though I was also aware that between the four adults there was a special bond that had to do with the songs and common experiences.

Since that time I've noticed that same conspiracy of romance on many occasions, in a concert hall, sometimes in a living room or around a campfire. And I know that it's the songs and the regard for the songs, and the willingness to let the songs work their magic that is the basis of this wonderful thing that we all share.

It's the mother's reassuring heartbeat. The dream language and the subliminal pulse of peace and rest. It's the wind in the trees just before a light rain. It's the call of birds at the time around sunset when they are settling in for the night. It's the enchantment of crickets and the urgency of the cicada.

Songs have the power to change our mood, to allay anxiety, to awaken our sense of joy. There is a synergy in words and music that can lift us and disengage us from tedium. There is the whole aspect of spirit in songs. An undeniable magic.

The only memory of past kingdoms in some cases has come down to a piece of music. The ancients accorded great celebrity to their musicians and that is no less true today. I'm not only referring to the opulent homes of the stars when I say that a great deal can be had "for a song."

When the prisoner on his way to the gallows in Merle Haggard's classic "Sing Me Back Home" makes that request of his buddy with the guitar in the next cell, we understand just what it might mean. I believe that deep within us all are many such epiphanal points of reference which are touched on by songs.

The next five words you put on paper really could change everything.

Many of the emotional experiences to which we aspire we only know from songs. Many things which we have been capable of doing and coping with as a society we might not have been able to do without songs. I'm thinking of the Civil Rights Movement, although many would say the same thing about the Great Depression, World War II and even their own teenage years.

There are no songs without songwriters. Many have been forgotten, many have been simply those who passed the song along and made some small change in the process. Today we live in a time when we have tremendous access to the world through our songs. There is a thrilling sense of rejoinder. We can listen to the ideas of others and respond and there is the possibility, although somewhat subject to the tariffs of the industry, of a true dialogue, a true tribal culture on a world scale. There are many examples of songs which communicate basic truths which are well known in virtually every corner of the earth.

A song can be recorded hundreds of times. Songs are routinely translated into many languages, and can go out much farther in the world than any person could travel. Songs can live almost forever, at least they can survive on a scale that approaches true immortality. It is not just the name or the idea of the songwriter which survives, there is in each song a kind of spiritual DNA that is evident and reassuring to people of distant places and times.

A well-formed thought or a timely message can reach and resonate with an amazingly large audience. In Tiananmen Square, at the Berlin Wall, and in the halls of Congress, songs have been quoted and sung. The next five words you put on paper really could change everything.

1.2 Songwriters & the Muse

What does a songwriter do? A songwriter is, first of all, a lover of songs. Someone who has an emotional stake in music. In the title of Pete Seeger's biography, *How Can I Keep From Singing?*, the author expresses Pete's idea that joy and love are linked in song and that there is nothing more natural than that song finding its voice in us. This basic impulse has been channeled into glistening constellations of intricate artistry by some gifted practitioners, but even the lowly lullaby or the anonymous work song are made of the same magic stuff.

Can you whistle? Can you keep from whistling? I think we all must know what it is to be enchanted with a song. We've all found ourselves humming or whistling at unexpected times. Some have even suggested that this event may represent a clue to our own unconscious processes and may even be a sign of what we are "really" thinking. I don't go along very far with this theory except to agree that there is some connection between that part of us that just feels things and may or may not be able to verbalize those feelings and the emotional wisdom of ordinary songs.

When we decide to take on the job of helping this event along or to initiate some new example of homemade magic, we begin to ask the questions that need to be answered with our own growth as writers.

There are so many good reasons for creating more beauty and music in the world. Some of them are simply inexpressible, and none need to be justified. One of my favorite ways of looking at this issue is to think of this process as the same kind of happy, unselfconscious banter we participate in when we're out with a few friends, laughing and acting silly and taking our turn at risking humor and good natured fun.

> *There are so many good reasons for creating more beauty and music in the world.*

It almost seems wrong to intrude on the spirit of that kind of moment with analysis, but it seems to me that the best writing takes place in just this kind of spontaneous and unrestrained atmosphere, when the moment is right and we just say what's funny, or what perpetuates the spirit of good times.

Where does it come from? Where inside do we go for that gift of the perfect thought? Well, maybe it's not always such a perfect thought. Maybe if we listened to a tape recording of our wild times, we'd have a hard time convincing anybody that this is great humor. But what about those times when things really were wonderfully funny? Didn't you ever say, "I wish you could have been there?" I contend that the only difference between our kidding around and the great writers of humor or great songs is just a matter of sustaining that moment of unrestrained creative joy and letting the work grow and improve under the best kind of nurturing practice and circumstance.

Doesn't it seem that there is a voice that comes to us, or through us at those times? What is that voice and where does it come from? Can we listen for that voice? Can we cultivate a relationship with that wise voice? Can we ask for and receive guidance and wisdom from that voice?

The name given to that voice by the ancient Greeks was the **Muse**. The Greeks believed that the muses were nine sister goddesses, daughters of Zeus and Mnemosyne. Each presides over her special artistic pursuit; poetry and song, painting, dance, drama, astronomy, etc. Their names, which should sound somewhat familiar, are Calliope, Clio, Erato, Euterpe, Melpomene, Polyhymnia, Terpsichore, Thalia and Urania. It's not important that we remember their names, only that to the Greeks this was a way to visualize and understand this special voice. We have come to think of the muse as the goddess or the hidden power which inspires the poet. There are other ways of expressing this and every culture has its equivalent of the muse.

The verb "to muse" means (according to Webster) "To reflect or meditate in silence, as on some subject, often as in a reverie." That should provide some clues about this process. If it is true that we can think of the muse as a voice or a spirit or a goddess, how can we approach this goddess? Can we really think of "courting the muse." What would be the nature of this courtship? How can we prepare ourselves, how can we make ourselves worthy? What kind of a relationship are we asking for?

If it seems like I'm taking this to an extreme, consider the serious nature of our need to find some way to approach this special voice or gift within us. It seems to me that sincerity is the first thing and openness the second. And from there we'll have to see where true dialogue leads us.

1.3 "Courting the Muse" by Michael Smith

I like the way it sounds on the guitar when you go from a D chord to a G chord. I like D-minor to B-flat too, and E-minor to D has a wonderful feeling, as in "What Shall We Do With A Drunken Sailor?" When you hear an A-minor with a B note in it for the first time it's a big thrill. I remember getting chills the first time I heard that chord at a Weavers concert. An old friend in Miami, Bob Ingram, used to work in a group with David Crosby – they had three twelve-strings and a standup bass. When all four of them sang this one harmony and played all those twelve-strings at the same time in E-minor, I got the same chills. I think that the sensations you get from hearing chords change, from hearing harmonies stacked, are indescribable. They are sensations very much in the moment, suspended in time. It's nice that some things are indescribable, isn't it?

I started to write songs because I wanted to plan similar moments for myself, and incidentally for other people. I have fun digging the ways chords go together. I like it when it's simple with just a little complication. That why I love the Beatles. It seems to me that they were very thoughtful about their chord progressions and they used their knowledge with joy and calmness and sureness. You can learn a lot by playing Beatles songs.

It's such a personal thing, writing. A lot of what goes into it is unconscious and not under my control. I want to trust that "It" will be there without fail, and I don't always trust, and that's my koan to figure out: how to let my child be. The child does the creating, the adult keeps the help to a minimum; ideally, lets it happen. It's so much fun, so engrossing, to write a song when I have no results in mind. My best songs are always about my life, the thing I know best, the only thing I know. Here no one can come in and say: "You've got it wrong there, it's really not like that." It's a place where I get to be King, only without the beheadings. Every time I've started a song to please someone other than myself, the song has kind of lain there. It's like the song knows you're not really in it for the emotion and it says: "OK, I'm not coming to life for you." The nuns at Our Lady Of The Valley used to say: "Don't do it for the reward. Do it for the sake of doing it."

Don't do it for the reward. Do it for the sake of doing it.

People I love are in my songs. When I first started writing about people I loved, the songs weren't very good, and I thought maybe I shouldn't be autobiographical. Now I see there's no deciding about that, it's all autobiographical. I was just starting and I had to get rid of the "poetry" and the imitations. Only four of us get to be Beatles, only one of us gets to be Dylan. I'm sure it's more fun to listen to the Beatles when you aren't one, anyway. I must say that now, when Dylan or McCartney writes a tune that doesn't thrill me, it's a bit of a relief. I think: Bless their hearts, everybody has ups and downs.

I have an opinion about everything. I think this condition fuels writing, which is after all the art of saying in an explicit way: I hear a song that goes like this. I aspire to a state of having less opinions, though, and when the songwriting is going well, I have no opinions at all and am perfectly happy. What comes first?

I like the thought of not being musically critical too. Mr. Krishnamurti would say it's just because I am. Sure took me a long time to arrive at this: when you criticize and put down you're doing it to yourself too. Who's your favorite musician of all time? Somewhere someone thinks that musician is awful, has no talent. It's so subjective that I've come to think, "Ah, the hell with it, everybody's great."

When I hear music that turns me off, I find if I imagine it's being played by my favorite cousin, Anne Marie, it always starts to sound good. Always. Sometimes I hate it so much I can't bring myself to imagine Anne Marie playing it; then I know that music has something to teach me. I'm not necessarily thrilled to know this. Everyone is very good in some way, probably, and it's up to you to allow your ears to hear that. Not easy, but go, go, go.

To an alien, we'd all sound alike anyway. "Those Earth players, they all sound like Ravi Shankar, or who's the other one? Julius La Rosa? No, Bea Lillie. They're all really doing Bea Lillie."

Some of us are wonderful from the beginning, and some of us have to take a little time. There is really nothing we can do about how long it takes, but we still have to act as if what we do to contribute is important. I, for instance, am having to take a little time. I know when I'm casting bread on the water, and you know when you're doing it too. The nuns would say: "Offer it up." I would say: "Don't sit there waiting for a statue to move."

Writing songs is so selfish, too. It's me saying I want a song to go like this; furthermore I want to put my name on it. If the Pope knew how much fun this was there'd be a brand new mortal sin. Is that a lyric or what?

It seems to me now that I write songs with the expectation that every once in a while one will turn out better than I planned. God knows a lot of them turn out worse. How fortunate that no one can write my songs but me, nobody can elbow in with a better idea.

I've heard D go to G now a million times. It's still great. I'm glad I didn't have to make it up, though. I never would have thought of it.

Advice: you're on your own. How does it feel?

2.
Songwriting Mechanics
Part 1: The Music

2.1 A Survey of Musical Elements

"Music is the space between the notes."
— CLAUDE DEBUSSY

The essential elements of music are fairly easy to learn. Our songwriting will be limited by our knowledge in this area, but by learning just a little bit more, or by getting just a little more facility on an instrument, we can experience a breakthrough in the quality of our writing. There is, of course, no end to what can be learned in the field of music, but it is never too late to begin. Some more experienced readers may be able to skip ahead at this point. What follows is an outline of the basics of music.

Notes

Notes are the basic units of music and each note designates a single musical event. The pitch of the note depends on the position of the note on the staff, and the type of note (eighth note, quarter note, etc.) determines its duration. One way we can represent the different notes is by singing do, re, mi, fa, sol, la, ti, do, etc. This method of ascribing syllables to the notes of the scale has been traced to a Benedictine monk named Guido of Arezzo in the year 1020. Some still don't have it down.

The Staff

The notes of the musical scale are written on or between the five horizontal lines of the staff and may extend above or below on ledger lines. The first thing you will see at the far left of the staff is usually a treble clef. Also known as the "G" clef, this symbol looks like an ornate letter "S" and sits on the line for the note **G**.

Sometimes when sheet music has a pair of staff lines as in a piano arrangement, the lower of the two sets of staff lines will have another kind of clef called a bass clef. This clef looks like a large comma and is centered on the note **F** and shows the part to be played by the left hand. There are several other clefs which are used for specific instruments and orchestral parts.

Treble Clef   **Bass Clef**

From bottom to top, the lines of the treble clef represent the notes, **E, G, B, D,** and **F**. A mnemonic device taught to help remember these notes goes *"every good boy does fine."*

The spaces, again from bottom to top, are **F, A, C,** and **E**, or "face." If a note falls above or below the range of the staff, small lines called "ledger" lines are added.

A B C D E F G A B C D E F G A

These notes correspond to the white keys of the piano and with them songs can be played in the keys of **C**, and **A minor** (at least, in the Aolean minor mode; more about modes to come).

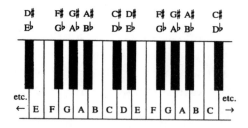

If a song is written in any other key it becomes necessary to alter some of the notes slightly upward or downward, and mark them with a sharp (♯) or a flat (♭). The reason for this is that our ear is used to a certain pattern of whole steps and half steps which give a scale its identity, and if the scale begins on any note other than **C** we have to alter some of the notes to make the relationships of whole steps and half steps seem correct.

Tetrachords

If we divide the eight notes of the scale into two groups of four, called tetrachords, we find that each group is made up of identical patterns of intervals. Between **C** and **D** there is one whole step or two half steps (each move to the next adjacent key is a half step) and there is a black key (**C♯**) between **C** and **D**.

The interval from **D** to **E** is again one whole step or two half steps and again there is one black key, **D♯**, between them. The next step, however, is only one half step, from **E-F**. On the piano there is no **E♯** or **F♭**. This is the pattern of intervals which our ear accepts as the familiar *"do, re, mi, fa."*

Lower Tetrachord

After allowing one whole step between the first and second group of four, we see that the second tetrachord is structured exactly the same way with whole step, whole step, half step between **G** and **A**, **A** and **B**, and **B** and **C**. This order of intervals sounds to our ear like *"sol, la, ti, do"* and is what we recognize as the last four ascending notes of the major scale.

Lower Tetrachord   **Upper Tetrachord**

Modes

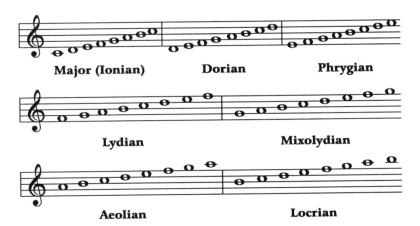

Major (Ionian)   **Dorian**   **Phrygian**

Lydian   **Mixolydian**

Aeolian   **Locrian**

A pattern of intervals can be called a "mode." If we play from **D** to **D** using the white keys only, the intervals will be in a different order and have a very different, more minor sound to our ear. This is called the Dorian mode. **C** to **C**, the mode we think of as normal, is called the

Ionian mode. From **G** to **G** on the white keys only is called the Mixolydian mode. From **E** to **E** is the Phrygian mode, From **F** to **F**, is the Lydian mode and from **A** to **A**, the Aeolian.

The Aeolian mode is the basis for most minor scales, although some minor scales are altered in the seventh or sixth and seventh scale degrees to give a sense of resolution more like a major scale. These points will be more fully explained later in the book.

Sharps & Flats

If we sing do-re-me, etc. starting on the **G** note we find that the first group of four notes falls nicely on the first four white keys but the next group of four needs one slight change to make it sound right. When we get to the sol-la-ti-do, we find that the *"ti,"* if we play it on the **F** key, sounds wrong. It is a half step too low. We must change this note up to the **F♯** which is the black key between **F** and **G**. This change restores the whole step, whole step, half step pattern our ear needs to hear to sound "right."

This is why when a song is written in the key of **G**, there is a sharp sign (♯) written over the **F** line at the beginning of the first measure of the song. This is called the key signature and tells the musician to change every **F** note to **F♯**. This also applies to songs in the key of **E minor** since the **E minor** scale uses the same notes as the **G** scale. **E minor** is the "relative" minor of **G**.

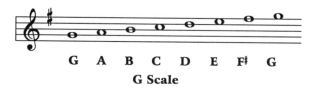

G   A   B   C   D   E   F♯   G
G Scale

If we started the scale on the note **F**, and sang do-re-mi-fa, we would run into a problem when we got to the fourth note, the **B**. This note would not sound right because it is too high to fit the sound we are used to when we get to *"fa."* In the key of **F** we have to lower the **B** notes to **B flat** or **B♭**. So if we see a ♭ on the line for **B** in the key signature, we know that the song is in the key of **F Major** or **D minor**.

If a note altered by the key signature, either by a sharp or flat, needs to be heard in its "natural" or un-sharped or un-flatted tone at some point in the song, then the natural symbol, ♮, is used. This symbol only applies to the measure in which it appears and affects all notes of that pitch for the remainder of the measure.

In **D**, the **F** and the **C** both have to be raised a half step to **F♯** and **C♯** and so the key signature for **D** has two sharps in it. Three sharps designate the key of **A** and the third sharp is **G♯**. You can see that in this way we can account for all the keys and that a sharp is added every time we go down four notes or up a "fifth." Going up five notes in the scale, of course, we land on the same note we would find if we went down four notes, and we can say that the one interval is an "inversion" of the other. A circle of fourths or fifths can be created which will demonstrate not only the relationships of all the keys but their relative minor keys as well.

The scale of a minor key is built on the sixth scale degree of its relative major key. The key of **A minor** is built on the **C** scale starting from the **A** or the sixth note, **E minor** is built on **G**, starting from **E**, its sixth, **D minor** on the scale of **F**, and **G minor** on **B♭**, etc.

It is said that Irving Berlin had a piano specially constructed so that he could move the keyboard to the right or the left so that the hammers would strike different strings. This enabled him to play in any key without having to learn the fingering for any key but **C**.

The Circle of Fifths

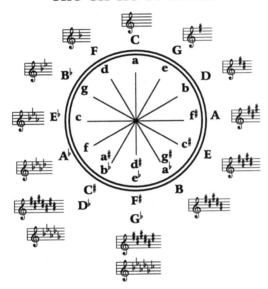

It is helpful to have an understanding of the circle of fifths. It explains the order of sharps and flats, major and minor keys, and is helpful when transposing or moving a song to a different key, or when a capo is used on the guitar to raise the key. If one player has a capo on the fifth fret of his guitar and another player is playing on a guitar with no capo, the first must play the chords which are a fifth above or a fourth below, the other must play the chords which are a fifth below or a fourth above the other. That is the guitar with the capo on the fifth fret will have to play a **D** chord to be in tune with a the guitar with no capo playing a **G** chord.

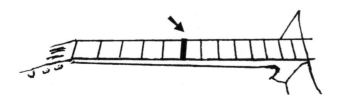

C♭ has the same sound as **B**, and **F♯** has the same sound as **G♭**. It is possible to go into double sharps and flats but these are not often encountered.

Just as a color wheel shows the harmonious relationships of colors, the circle of fifths shows the relationship of harmony elements used in songs. When a song is in the key of **C**, the **C** chord is called the tonic chord. The **G** chord is the dominant chord, which is based on the fifth degree of the **C** scale and **F** is the sub-dominant, based on the fourth scale degree. In the chord progression of most blues songs, the tonic, fourth, and fifth chords are played in a fixed pattern that repeats continuously until either the song ends or another pattern is encountered in a chorus or bridge.

Musicians playing an unfamiliar song or improvising on stage might say, "It's a simple one, four, five song" or, "It goes to the two minor in the bridge" or "stay on the five chord for two bars in the turnaround."

All of this implies that there is a logic to keys, chords and numbers which can facilitate playing and can help to avoid getting stuck in predictable changes. It is said that the balance between what is expected and what is not expected is the secret of a successful work of art. Study the circle of fifths until you can apply its resources to your music.

Intervals

The distance between two notes is called an interval. Intervals are most often expressed as the number of notes between the lower and the upper note. The distance between **C** and **F** is a fourth. Counting up the keyboard from **F** to **C**, the distance is a fifth. If the distance is expressed as between the upper and lower it is called an inverted interval.

A second, can be a minor second, that is just one half step, as from **C** to **C♯**, or a major second, two half steps, as from **C** to **D**. A third can be a minor third or a major third depending on how many half steps it contains.

| Minor 2nd | Major 2nd | Minor 3rd | Major 3rd |

From **C** to **E** is a major third because it is made up of four half steps. Another way to think about a major third is that between **C** and **E** there are two black keys and one white key. The interval between **A** and **C** is a minor third. There are only three half steps or one white key and one black key between **A** and **C**. The interval between **C** and **A** is a sixth, a major sixth. The interval between **E** and **C** is a minor sixth and you can see that the inversion of a major third is a minor sixth, and the inversion of the interval of a minor third is a major sixth.

The octave always has the same number of half steps in it so these intervals will always have their complement. The fourth and fifth are "pure" and always contain five half steps and seven half steps respectively. The only exception to this is the interval between **F** and **B**, and its inversion **B** to **F**. This is known as an augmented fourth or a diminished fifth and only occurs once in each scale. Other intervals and their inversions are the minor and major second, and their complements, the major and minor seventh. From **C** to **D** is a major second but from **E** to **F** is a minor second. Conversely, **D** to **C** is a minor seventh, but **F** to **E** is a major seventh.

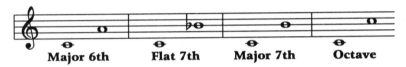

Chords

A chord is made up of three or more notes. All chords are created by stacking intervals. Depending on the intervals, the chord can be major or minor, or augmented or diminished. A **C Major** triad is a chord which contains the notes **C**, **E**, and **G**. The **C** to **E** interval is a major third, which determines that the chord will be a major chord. If the **E** were an **E♭**, then the chord would be a **C minor** triad. The **G** is the fifth of the chord and completes it. The interval between the **E** and the **G** is a minor third. If the **E** were an **E♭**, then the interval between the **E♭** and the **G** would be a major third since the **C** to **G** interval must be a "perfect" fifth in order have the stability of a major or minor triad.

If we were to raise the **G** to a **G♯**, the chord would then be a **C augmented** chord and would have a very different and unstable sound and a different effect in the song. The augmented chord is made up of two major thirds; if we stack two minor thirds we get a **diminished** chord.

C Augmented **C Diminished Triad**

Diminished chords are most often seen as a stack of three minor thirds and are named for any of the four notes in the chord. For instance if we start with **C** and add the note which is a minor third above **C**, that would be **E♭**. Then a minor third above **E♭** would be **G♭**. These three notes would give us a **C diminished** chord, but in most cases we would also find the **A** added since it is a minor third above **G♭** and a minor third below **C**. These four notes make up a chord which could just as easily be called a **C dim**, an **E♭ dim**, a **G♭ dim**, or an **A diminished** chord, and could be played in several positions on the guitar.

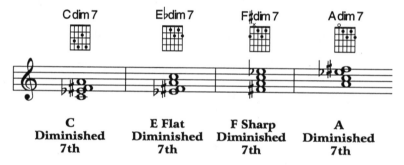

C Diminished 7th **E Flat Diminished 7th** **F Sharp Diminished 7th** **A Diminished 7th**

The Seventh Chords

The major seventh chord, the minor seventh chord and the dominant seventh chord are all chords which use the seventh note above the letter note of the chord, but each has a different sound. A major seventh chord is a major triad with a fourth note added, which is a major seventh above the chord letter note. A **C Major seventh** chord would therefore have a **C**, an **E**, a **G**, and a **B♮**. Another way to think about this is that the fourth note is just a half step below the octave of the chord letter note.

The minor seventh chord is a minor chord with a fourth note added and this note is again the seventh note up from the chord letter note, but in this case it is a minor seventh. In a **C minor seventh** chord the notes would be **C**, **E♭**, **G**, and **B♭**.

The dominant seventh chord is the chord built on the fifth scale degree of the key and contains a fourth note, which is always a minor seventh. This is what distinguishes it in sound from the major seventh chord. In the key of **C**, the dominant chord is **G** and the **G dominant seventh** chord would consist of **G**, **B**, **D**, and **F♮**. Another way to remember this is that the **F** is the same as it is in the normal **C** scale. The dominant seventh is still just one of the chords made up of elements of the scale of the key the song is written in.

An Augmentation of Voicings

Chords and melodies may be enhanced by the choice of how the notes are placed in relation to each other. The guitar is somewhat limited as to where the notes of a **G** chord can be played, and yet, playing the chord in a closed, barred position as if it were an **E** chord with the bar of the first finger across the third fret will give a different sound from the normal **G** chord played on three fretted and three open strings. The difference is a matter of voicing the chord. The same chord can be played as a **D** chord played above a bar at the fifth fret, or as an **A** chord with a bar at the tenth fret, and so on. Each gives a choice of which notes are present and in what positions or voicings.

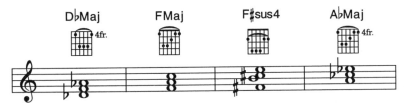

Inversions

The keyboard is much more versatile since the fingers can play any of the notes in just about any combination. Given the possibilities, the writer can make a choice of which order of intervals sounds best for the song. When a chord is "voiced" so that the tonic note is the lowest note, this is the normal way to hear the chord. If we are playing a **C** chord, then the **C** would normally be the lowest note and the **E**, the **G**, and if the chord is a seventh chord, the **B**♭, will all be stacked above the bass **C**. But if we put the third of the chord, the **E**, on the bottom, the chord has a different sound.

This is known as the first "inversion" of the chord and the chord doesn't sound quite as solid, or resolved. It may be that this is the appropriate voicing for the chord when it is heard in a less stressed position in the song, but usually not on the final resolution at the end of the song. If we place the **G** on the bottom of the chord, this is called the second inversion and again has a less substantial but an interesting sound. The **F** chord with a **C** in the bass is quite common on the popular music charts. By experimenting with these inversions we can achieve many subtle effects and still be using relatively simple chords.

If we place the seventh, the **B**♭, at the bottom of the chord, we have a very dark, brooding chord which has been used to great effect in popular music. The Righteous Brothers song "You've Lost That Lovin' Feeling" is a good example.

There is no formula for the placement of the rest of the notes in the chord. Sometimes the fifth will be doubled in the left and the right hand and the third will only be present in one note of the chord. This is especially true of choral singing where the major or minor tonality of a chord can be established by only one voice and may not need to be doubled.

You really have to rely on your ear in this question of voicing as in other considerations of songwriting. There are many possibilities. Try some of these and experiment with others:

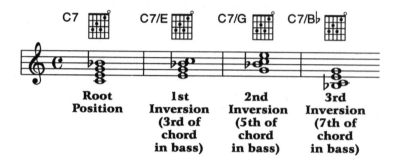

(Instead of **C, E, G, B♭** for the **C7** chord, try **C, F, G, B♭**, which replaces the third of the chord with a fourth for a "suspended" effect, or **C, F, B♭, E**, or **C, G, E, F, B♭**, and for a minor example, **Cmin7**, try **C, G, B♭, E♭, G, B♭**, others including suspensions and ninths, thirteenths, etc.)

The "Nashville" Chord Number System

Nashville is famous for the high standard of its studio musicians. Players from all over the country migrate to Tennessee and strive to become studio sidemen. Competition is fierce and only a handful of the best musicians are thought of as the "A" team. Still, although Nashville has its own brand of virtuosity it's not based on the same skills that are found in the great orchestras of the world. Chet Atkins, who has been one of the most successful producers and record company executives in all of country music, is often quoted as saying about his musicians, "Sure they can read music, but not enough to hurt their playing."

It's true that most of the time in the studios of Nashville the players are not using sheet music per se. Instead they use what are known as "Nashville" chord charts. Before the recording begins, the players will listen, usually just once through the song, either on tape or sung live. Each musician will make a simple chart listing the chords and with other markings to help him to play the song. The chords will be designated by simple numbers, sometimes Roman numerals but usually just regular numbers 1, 4, 5, 3, 6, etc. And where a chord has a different note in the base or the inversion needs to be noted, this will be shown by making a slash

"/" with the bass note written as a scale degree, such as 4/3 or 5/5. A suspension will be designated with "sus," or just an "s."

Any other information such as coda, first and second endings, intro, outro, crescendo, decrescendo, and so forth is written down in a system of arrows and lines sometimes only decipherable to the musician who wrote it. These charts are amazingly infallible.

An added advantage is that if the producer or the singer should decide at the last minute to raise or lower the key, the same chart works without any amendments since the chords are all designated in their relative position in the scale and those positions remain true no matter what the key.

This method of shorthand is ideal for the songwriter. It is only when the song is finished that a proper lead sheet needs to be made for purposes of showing the song and for copyright.

Triads

To build all the triads in the key of **C**, start with **C, E,** and **G.** This one, three, five pattern is the basis of all triads. This first chord called the tonic, is **C Major. D, F,** and **A** give us the two minor or the submediant, the **D minor** chord. **E, G,** and **B** make up the three minor, or mediant, an **E minor** chord. **F, A,** and **C** the four chord or sub-dominant chord, **F Major.** Then **G, B,** and **D** the five chord, the dominant chord, **G Major. A, C, E** the six chord, **A minor.** Notes **B, D,** and **F** give us the only diminished chord in C scale, the seven chord, the **B dim.** There are no naturally occurring augmented chords since the interval of the augmented fifth does not occur in the normal scale.

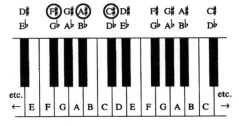

Here's an example of an F# major triad. The notes to play are circled.

Check the intervals with the keyboard and study this method of building chords. You will find a lot of chords in songs which are not based only on the notes in the key of that song. Often chords are "borrowed" from a related key, for instance an **A major** chord might be found in a song in the key of **G** where one would expect to find an **A minor**, which is the normal chord constructed on the second degree of the scale. The reason for the **A Major** is that it is related to the key of **D** and in the song it functions to give a stronger weight to the **D** chord by making it seem like it is the home or tonic chord in the key of **D** where **A Major** would be the fifth or dominant chord. This **A Major** chord is called a borrowed dominant or V/V chord since it is the five chord of the key of **D** which is the key of the five chord of **G**.

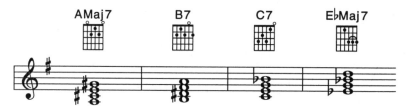

Borrowed chords in the key of G

There are many other ways that chords are borrowed or interposed and some of these can be discovered by trial and error. It is good to listen for examples of these creative breakings of the rules. Sometimes, interesting chords can be arrived at by harmonizing root movement by steps or other intervals. Sometimes simply changing the expected minor chord to a major chord or vice versa is effective. More about this later.

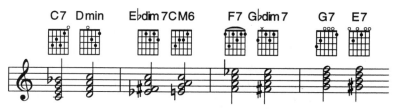

The following chords in this progression are considered borrowed chords in the key of C (except CM6 and G7 which occur naturally in this key)

A chord may contain almost any combination of notes but most can be understood by starting from the triad and adding or taking away notes to create the desired effect. A chord with no third is called a modal chord since it is neither major nor minor. Intervals which are commonly added to a chord to give it a more specific sound are the sixth, the seventh, the ninth, and thirteenth, again, always counting from the do or the root of the chord.

Triad with added 9th, 11th, 13th

Time

The final aspect of musical notation has to do with the duration of the note. The symbol for a musical tone is a note. The symbol for a pause or silence between notes is a rest. The time signature is written as a fraction in the first bar of a song. The top number, the numerator, shows the number of notes of a given time value contained in each measure and the bottom number, the denominator shows the kind of note the top number is based on.

Time signature

The total of notes and rests in one measure must be equal to the fraction of the time signature. If a song is in 4/4 time, this means that there are the equivalent of four quarter notes per measure. In a waltz, there are three quarter notes in each bar and the time signature is 3/4. A whole note is held for the full duration of one bar of 4/4. Six eighth notes or 6/8, and two quarter notes or 2/4 are also common time signatures.

The "shuffle" is a common rhythm form and is in 6/8 time. So many songs in the rhythm and blues and country music tradition are shuffles including many of Elvis Presley's hits, like "Teddy Bear" and "Now and Then, There's a Fool Such As I."

Below are a whole note, half, quarter, eighth, sixteenth and thirty-second notes.

| Whole note | Half note | Quarter note | Eighth note | Sixteenth note | Thirty-second note |

Rests are the quiet spaces that occur in music and are also divided and added together in the same way;

| Whole rest | Half rest | Quarter rest | Eighth rest | Sixteenth rest | Thirty-second rest |

A note can be held through a longer time by being tied to another note. Rests also can be combined for longer pauses. A note can begin at the end of one measure and be tied over into the next or beyond. A dot next to a note means that it is held for half-again its normal time.

Home on the Range

Oh,   give   me   a   home where the   buf - fa-lo   roam,   andthe

2.2 Hearing Musical Intervals

Another way to talk about intervals is to give examples of each interval in the context of a well-known song. Since the study of intervals is such an essential part of writing good melodies, it is directly helpful to see how these elements work in songs that we know.

Here are one or two for each interval, ascending and descending. Be sure to sing them to yourself to get a feel for the notes and think of other examples from the music of your own experience.

Ascending Intervals

Second:

HapPY BIRTH day to you   (**notation of each interval**)
Good King WEN-CES-las went out
ARE YOU sleeping?

Minor Third:

WHAT CHILD is this?
The WORMS CRAWL in ...

Major Third:

The Marine Hymn - FROM THE halls
KUM BA ya, kum ba ya
IF I loved you ...

Fourth:

HERE COMES the bride
A-MAZ-ing grace, how sweet the sound
The Mexican Hat Dance, DA DUM, DA DUM, DA DUM,

Fifth:

TWINKLE, TWINKLE little star
Bah, BAH BLACK sheep have you any wool?
DON'T THROW bouquets at me,

Sixth:

> <u>MY</u> <u>BON</u>-nie lies over the ocean
> <u>IT</u> <u>CAME</u> upon a midnight clear,
> <u>BE</u>-<u>YOND</u> the blue horizon

Minor Seventh:

> <u>THERE'S</u> <u>A</u> place for us,

Major Seventh:

> All at <u>ONCE</u> <u>AM</u> I, several stories high

Octaves:

> <u>SOME</u>-<u>WHERE</u> over the rainbow,
> Hap-<u>PY</u> <u>TRAILS</u> to you,
> <u>YOU</u> <u>GO</u> to my head ...

Descending Intervals

Second:

> <u>MEM</u>-<u>RIES</u>, light the corners of my mind
> <u>THREE</u> <u>BLIND</u> mice

Minor Third:

> Sixteen Tons and what <u>DO</u> <u>YOU</u> get?
> <u>SOME</u>- <u>DAY</u> I'LL <u>WISH</u> <u>UP</u>- <u>ON</u> <u>A</u> <u>STAR</u>
> <u>WHEN</u> <u>EV</u>- er I feel afraid ...
> <u>HEY</u> <u>JUDE</u>,

Major Third:

> <u>NOW</u> <u>IS</u> the hour,
> <u>GOOD</u> <u>NIGHT</u> ladies ...

Fourth:

> <u>BORN</u> <u>FREE</u>
> Seventy-<u>SIX</u> <u>TROM</u>- bones led the big parade,

Fifth:

> <u>YOUNG</u> <u>AND</u> foolish
> From the <u>MOUN</u>- <u>TAINS</u> ... (to the prairies)
> ...<u>AS</u> <u>TIME</u> goes by.

Sixth:

> From the mountains, to the <u>PRAIR</u>- <u>IES</u>
> <u>MEAN</u> <u>TO</u> me, why must you be mean to me?
> <u>BYE</u>-<u>BYE</u> blues

Major Seventh:

Up a lazy riv-<u>ER</u> <u>BY</u> the old mill stream

Octaves:

<u>YOU</u> <u>ARE</u> my lucky star
<u>WIL</u>-<u>LOW</u> weep for me

2.3 Intervals & Melody

Intervals are the backbone of melody. The combinations of intervals and their relationships melodically and harmonically are what make a song recognizable and memorable. There are only a limited number of these intervals and yet, they have been combined in thousands of creative ways and each of these songs is recognizable. Some are so distinctive that the song can be named after hearing only two or three notes.

Harmony can be described as the vertical distribution of intervals, stacked one above the other, and melody as the horizontal placement of intervals. The one other factor that determines melody is time. Each note has a duration and the spaces between the notes have duration and it is the combination of these that gives us a melody.

Motif or Motive

Often, strong melodies are created with phrases or groups of phrases called "motives" or "motifs." In many cases these motive phrases are altered slightly in repetition or shift in their timing or emphasis. Sometimes phrases are even inverted to create portions of the melody that seem to reflect or answer other parts of the melody.

In the song "Fly Me To the Moon," the unique melody is actually made up by linking certain five-note phrases. Each starts high and ends low, but each starts on a different note. The first note of each phrase is emphasized partly by the length of the note and partly by leaping up from the previous note. This song is a good example of a repeating motive.

Fly Me to the Moon (In Other Words)
Words and Music by Bart Howard

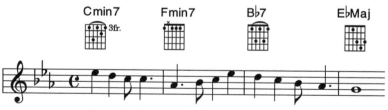

Fly Me To The Moon and let me play a-mong the stars;

Repetition

Echoes and repetition are very common devices in melody. So much so that you probably wouldn't notice many of the ways that they are used. *"Yesterday, all my troubles seemed so far away,"* is an example of one form of repetition. Different notes are used, but each group of three notes is similar in that the first is emphasized, falling on a strong beat, and the other two are lower and double up on the same note.

Yesterday
Words and Music by John Lennon and Paul McCartney

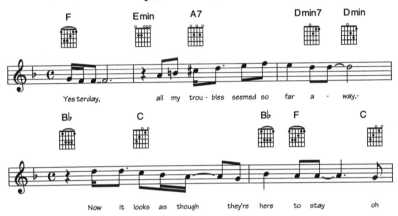

In the song "Stand By Your Man," the repetition effect is used in a different way. The phrase that is repeated comes later after a few notes to set it up. The repetition, in turn, sets up the cadence at the mid point of the verse, and later the same effect is used to build to the ending of the song. In a more subtle way, the linking phrases are themselves repetitions of the pattern established by the "hook" phrase. Think of the song as made up of two phrases: da, da, da, dum, as in bars one and three, and da, di, da, da, as in bars four and six.

Stand By Your Man
Tammy Wynette and Billy Sherrill

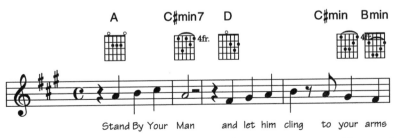

Melodic Skips

Melodic skips or leaps can be used to create strong and recognizable melodies. By using leaps of larger intervals in contrast to movement by adjacent single notes, we can bring a certain excitement into our melody writing. This is another one of those balancing acts since every song is a matrix of tones and textures and has a cumulative effect on the listener. This effect is most satisfying when it's not too heavy-handed.

There are many good examples of leaps and skips to be found and they may come from all types of music. Some follow regular patterns like the notes of a chord as in the folk songs "Kum Ba Ya," and "Michael Row the Boat Ashore." Others take chances by leaping to a radical or unstable interval, like "Maria" from *West Side Story*, or "Born Free." In "Maria," the second note is so striking, leaping up as it does to such an unexpected place. This interval is an augmented fourth, a very unstable interval. It is a note that holds a certain amount of tension. It "wants" to resolve. In this case, it wants to resolve upward by a half step to the fifth and come to rest in a nice comfortable major chord.

Tension & Release

The **ti-do** resolution is very common in songs and by landing on the seventh, the "ti," the melody benefits from the tension inherent in the relationship of these two notes. An example of this is the familiar *"Shave and a haircut, two bits."* Similar tension is created when the second degree of the scale is present and also the fourth and the sixth. It depends on how each of these is used, but there are several ways in which these tensions can create a satisfying effect.

Suspensions

One of the most common is the suspension. A suspension occurs when a note that is dissonant to the chord is held for a strong beat and then allowed to resolve to a note that is in tune or consonant with the chord. For instance, if we play a **C** chord and hold the note **F** for a moment through the first strong beat or longer and then let it resolve down a half step to **E** we have what is called a 4-3 suspension. Another suspension which is often used is the 2-1 suspension and is the same except that if we use our example of a **C** chord, the suspended note would be the **D** and would resolve downward to the **C**. The other common suspension is the 7-8 suspension. This suspension is unique because it resolves upward.

There are many examples of suspensions in well-known songs. Any time you have a note falling on a strong beat which is not in the chord, you are hearing the effect of a suspension. Stravinsky used the minor second to great effect, although this interval is too grating for most kinds of music. All of these devices rely on the dynamic of tension and release.

As you can see, tension can be created by the words or the music. In the music, tension is created by the relationship of the intervals, vertical or horizontal, and by their occurrence in time.

Valences

All notes by virtue of their position relative to the other notes in the song have what might be called tendencies, or valences. This property is almost like the valences which are spoken of in chemistry. Some of the effects of these tendencies are the result of what comes before the note in question, what expectation has been established. If notes are repeated, even though there has been no movement up or down, a tension has been created and something new is expected.

It is this emotional energy that is the stock in trade of the songwriter. The best way to gain some facility with these elements is to learn to play and sing a great many songs. In a way this is the writer's musical vocabulary. The secret is to get to the point with songs where we don't just think in terms of notes and words, but in more complex terms of mood and meaning. I suppose this is similar to learning any language where we hope to get past just one word and the next and think in concepts.

Originality

It's all right to talk about what has been done in other songs, but what about creating something new? How "new" does it have to be? If there are only twelve notes, how can I do something that has never been done before? And if writing songs is like learning a language, don't I have to create my songs using elements that are somewhat familiar?

This is a topic that comes up often in writing workshops. At those times I'm fond of saying that it's not so much a question of doing and saying something that has never been done or said before as it is a matter of being "authentic" in the writing. Being original doesn't mean writing something that could only have come from another planet, but is more a matter of the writer being truly present in a creative way in the song.

Intent

You would never think of using lines you heard in a movie with someone you have just met. You might make a joke, or speak a "line" just to be cute, but you would never insult your partner by not taking the chance of being yourself. And yet, many of the things people say have been said before. Couples on their honeymoons must say the same things that couples have said for centuries and yet what they say is still authentic and original. I believe that imitation and originality in this context are really a matter of intent.

Plagiarism

Plagiarism, or the stealing of someone else's work, is pretty common, but should not be the concern of any serious writer. If someone borrows from you there is not much that can be done unless you can demonstrate that whole sections of the song are virtually identical. It is surprisingly common to see ideas migrate from your best work and show up in unexpected places. The best policy in these cases is to consider it a form of flattery. Somebody thought enough of your idea to borrow it.

It may be that you will do some borrowing without being aware of it. This is also quite common but shouldn't cause you too much concern. As you become more conversant with the elements of songwriting and have more songs of your own and others in your mental reference library, there will be less need to worry about it. The right attitude should be that, as a writer, you are willing to tune into your own emotional understanding and focus on the listener with confidence that if you are true to yourself, your music will be as authentic and original as it needs to be.

This doesn't mean that if you or anyone else hears something in your new song that sounds uncomfortably close to someone else's song you don't have to do some work on it. You may wake up some night and realize that you have just re-written "Hard Day's Night." There is always time to rethink your approach as long as the promo copies of your new CD haven't gone out in the mail.

All songs are still part of a great ongoing oral tradition. You may wish to call attention to a song that has gone before. Many times this is done out of respect, or to make a comment on some part of our communal understanding that was established by an earlier song. There are many examples of this in country music, which seems to build on themes week after week with each new generation of top 20 songs.

Some of these are a tip of the hat and some are an outright rip-off. "On the Other Hand," a great example of double meaning in songs, inspired "On Second Thought" and "I Put the Ring On the Right Left Hand" and many more. Some have more of their own thought to bring to the dialogue than others. Some are thinly disguised attempts to capitalize on the success of the earlier song.

Each of us must decide how close is too close. It's important to believe in your own voice and to say what's true. Remember, your song may be around a lot longer that any of the others and should stand on its own.

Variation

Songs achieve variation in a number of ways. There are really only twelve notes, four or five note values, and a few different rests, but by using different variations of interval, time, and harmonic combinations, there seems to be no limit to the possibilities for new songs. How much variation, and how much repetition? Are there principles for arranging songs so as to make them more memorable, or more accessible?

> *"A good style in literature, if closely examined, will be seen to consist in a constant succession of tiny surprises."*
> — FORD MADOX FORD

2.4 Elements of Composition

Dick Goodwin is a composer and arranger who lives in Columbia, South Carolina, and has been on the staff of Kerrville Songwriter's School for many years. The following discussion of the musical elements of songwriting is taken from his lectures and demonstrations.

Melody (Pitch)

1. Try starting your melody on each possible scale degree. Most writers have a tendency to begin in the same way or to repeat the things that have worked in the past. Listen to songs with this question in mind. Check the songs currently in the top 20 in your favorite place on the dial.

2. Try each possible opening interval or group of intervals. Try the upward movement and the downward use of each interval or intervals. Try out the intervals that make up the chord or chords and alternatively try intervals that challenge the chord or take another approach, even if this causes you to question the chords you have. The objective is to write strong melodies that are harmonized in a satisfying way. Don't be limited to melodies that are written to accommodate the chord progression.

3. Invert all or part of your melodic figure. This is also a good way to find melody ideas for other sections of the song. Use "mirror writing" by using your existing melody ideas to write sections of the melody either backwards or upside down.

4. Derive melodic materials by assigning notes to phone numbers or the letters of someone's name. There are many examples of this even in classical music. The name of Bach was often set in music, "H" is German for **B (natural)**. **B** is what the Germans use for **B(flat)** So literally – Bach's signature tune is **B(flat) - A - C - B**. Find other chance combinations that can give you a new

direction – lottery tickets, a deck of cards. "I was having a bowl of alphabet soup the other day and your name came up."

5. Add or cut out certain pitches for pleasing combinations. Once you have a new idea, let the "editor" of your ear go to work on it. This is especially helpful when you have developed an approach to harmonizing your melody. You can let the chords do some of the work of the melody and leave out some notes, and conversely you can help the chords in their effect by tailoring your melody.

6. Try your melody ideas in different scales like major or minor. Explore the possibilities of different modes and scales like pentatonics, etc. This technique might help to delineate between verse and chorus and bridge by changing modes in mid-song.

7. Can you use "**accidental**" notes? These are the notes outside the scale – those in the cracks. Sometimes these can be derived by changing a minor chord to a major, as in changing the **A minor** chord in the key of **C** to an **A major**. This can give the song a much more interesting harmonic foundation. "**Blue**" notes can give another profound effect. These "blue" notes are derived by flatting the third, fifth and seventh scale degrees. In the key of **C** these notes would be **E-flat**, **G-flat**, and **B-flat**.

Another way to discover these elements is to explore the area of borrowed chord stepwise bass. Using inversions here gives infinite possibilities for fresh harmonies. Again find notes in chords from related keys to make interesting sense out of the bass progression.

Melody (Rhythm)

1. Move a melodic figure backward or forward in time in the measure. Anticipate, or wait to sing the phrase, giving a different rhythmic emphasis to the phrase. Sometimes a song will use two different phrasings of the same words.

2. Elongate or shorten certain values. Usually this will have to be consistent with the conversational sense of the phrase, but there is often wide latitude to experiment. Consider the difference if the Rolling Stones sang "I can't get no satisfaction" as straight eighth notes.

Harmony

1. Consider at random other scale degrees of root movement. The most common are up a fourth, or up a fifth, or down to

the six minor. What about up to the second, or down to the seventh? It may be that some of these places are best visited on the way to somewhere else.

2. Try the strong progressions. One step to anywhere, up two, up four, down three, down two, including chromatic (half step) motion.

3. What else is possible? (up five?, up three?)

4. Alter chord types. A major chord can become a minor chord, or a seventh chord, etc. Try inversions of the chord. Try added notes like a flatted fifth, sixth, seventh, ninth, eleventh, thirteenth, etc.

5. Let the harmony be controlled by stepwise bass. Using inversions here gives infinite possibilities for fresh harmonies. Again find notes in chords from related keys to make interesting sense out of the bass progression.

6. Let the harmony be determined by a **thumb line**. In this case, with both hands on the keyboard, the thumbs explore the middle ground between the two hands and the rest of the fingers change to make the best use of the notes suggested by the thumbs. Often this will be stepwise movement in either direction but there are numerous possibilities.

7. Is your harmonic rhythm logical? Does there seem to be an appropriate number of rhythmic beats per chord? Is there a satisfying balance of these rhythmic elements in the different sections of the song? For instance, the verses might be more harmonically "busy" than the choruses.

8. The bridge might depart from patterns created in verses and choruses. In a bridge, it might be acceptable to "go off on a tangent," or find a new path to or back from a different harmonic place. Also, if there is a point in the song where things come to a momentary halt, this is likely to come at the beginning or at the end of the bridge.

Rhythm

1. Experiment with different meters: 4/4, 3/4, 6/8, 12/8, hemiola, etc. **Hemiola** usually refers to time values in the relationship of 3 to 2, as in three half notes instead of two dotted half notes. Brahms' Symphony no. 2 is an example of the use of this rhythmic device. In the music of Motown there are examples of quarter note triplets used for a similar effect. Dick

Goodwin uses the example of "America" from *West Side Story* to illustrate hemiola.

Hemiola

Hemiola in six/eight

2. Try different "feels" or "grooves." See how a waltz differs from a bolero, a shuffle, a polka, and so on.

3. Listen for the differences between short and long **articulations** (staccato vs. legato etc.). One way to differentiate verse and chorus is by having shorter note values in one and longer in the other. A chorus is more likely to have plainer more slogan-like phrases which are repeated.

4. Shift the tempo up or down. See how phrasing is affected. Is there still time to breathe? If the song is a lot slower, does it need a more rhythmic expression of the phrasing?

As the tempo increases, does the pulse of the meter change?

Texture

1. **Boom-chuck.** This is a familiar alternating left hand, right hand piano style similar to the pick-strum "Carter Family" style of guitar, also known as the "church lick." In more rock-oriented songs, the boom-chuck often becomes boom-pa chuck-a, boom-pa chuck-a, ala Buddy Holly.

2. **Pedal points.** Sustain a single note through a phrase (most often this is a bass note, but it could be elsewhere in the texture). This also impacts on harmony and can create some interesting suspensions and other kinds of tensions.

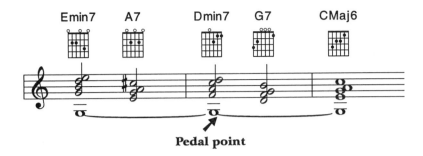

Pedal point

3. **Breaks** (*G.P.* the grand pause) an absolute halt in the motion of a song, and holds (**fermata**). Sometimes it takes courage to resist the impulse to fill up the song with continuous sound.

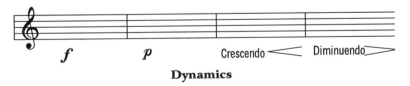

Grand pause   **Fermata**

4. **Bass alone**. A device that often begins an arrangement of a song but can be effective at any point.

5. A great effect can be achieved by exploring the differences between letting the song get up into the energy of the higher range and coming back down to the lower ranges of melody. This is especially true when beginning a second verse or coming back down after a climactic point late in the song for a dramatic ending.

Dynamics

Dynamics is the use of the range of loud and soft. Notice how seasoned performers take advantage of the dramatic implications of volume. It gives a performer a chance to make the most of his or her ability to generate energy, but requires a subtlety and sensitivity to the audience.

On a musical score these dynamic considerations are designated by the terms -**subito** (suddenly), f (forte or loud) or p (piano or soft), **cresc.** (getting louder), **dim.** (getting softer), etc.

f p Crescendo   Diminuendo

Dynamics

Song Form

Analyze tunes to learn standard practices and write at least one song in each of the following forms: verse/chorus, aaba, abac, ababcb, 12 bar blues, etc. Make special note of bridges that you hear and notice how many ways writers have found to break up the expected patterns and keep things interesting.

Timbre (Often Related to Texture)

1. Vary instrumental combinations (particularly backup fills, snare vs. rim, etc). This is especially important to distinguish between verses and choruses and to allow the song to build from a more sparse beginning to reach a peak of energy at a later point.

2. With the guitar there are many options for whether to strum or to pick on the individual strings, or to snap, slap, thump, or drum on the strings. Many effects are produced by the right hand and others by the left or by both in combination. The string will produce a noticeably different sound depending upon whether you strike it with your fingernail, or with a flat pick, a finger pick (steel or brass), or with the bare skin of your finger, or whether you pick or strum closer to the bridge or the fingerboard.

    There are also dampening effects which can be achieved by using the heel of the right hand or the extra fingers of the left hand. Also, picking up the fingers of a chord, or just releasing some of the pressure, which gives a good clear note to the fretted string, and letting the finger tips dampen the strings – this produces an effect similar to lifting the sustain pedal of a piano.

    A solo guitar player will have a harder time differentiating between rhythm and lead playing than would two guitarists or a guitar and bass. Guitar tunings can suggest a different sound and use other resonances and timbre.

3. Remember that **tessitura** has dramatic tension-release implications. Different voices have different qualities and as you explore the range of your own voice or write for other voices you will become aware of the dramatic effects of stretching or reaching for higher notes or coming down for those low notes.

    Special care needs to be taken so that singers are not discouraged from singing or wanting to sing your song. But again, to use "You've Lost That Lovin' Feeling" as an example, Bill Medley's first notes make a very dramatic beginning for the song, almost unbelievably low. This is even more impressive later in the song as Bobby Hatfield wails up into the higher reaches. Few songs can be expected to be produced with anywhere near that wide a range.

Are you getting all you can from melodic curves or peaks or from a carefully prepared dramatic climax in the song? Are there considerations in the area of melismatic vs. syllabic repeated notes? Melismatic means more than one tone is sung for a given syllable, as in *"I am calling you-oo-oo-oo-oo-oo-oo."*

Is there a different word rhythm or chord rhythm that gives a clear distinction to a new section in the form? Does the chorus lift? Are sections prepared for or set up? Is there anything that might help to set the song apart from what has been done before while still making the song stronger?

Don't feel that you have to tackle all of these principles at once. Take them on one at a time and experiment until you feel you understand the effect of each consideration.

* * * * * *

"Lead Belly" was Huddie Ledbetter, writer of "Irene Goodnight," "The Midnight Special," and "Rock Island Line." He was a legendary, self-taught twelve-string guitarist and songwriter. When he was asked to explain how he learned to play the way he did, he said, "First you have to learn to tap with both feet."

2.5 Alternative & Non-Standard Guitar Tunings

By adopting one or another of these non-standard tunings, the guitar can take on a whole new character. A little experimentation can create some interesting effects.

The most common altered tuning is the **"Dropped D Tuning."** The notes on the guitar would be: **D, A, D, G, B, E.** For this tuning, start in standard tuning, then lower the sixth string one whole step from **E** to **D**. This tuning is most often used for playing in the key of **D**. Its strength is that the bass "D" string makes the tonic **D** chord very strong.

Remember that since the sixth string is tuned down two frets, the fingering for any chord using that string must be adjusted "up" two frets, so a "G" chord, for instance, would need the bass string to be fretted at the fifth fret instead of the third fret where it would normally be. Players in **"dropped D"** usually play a **"G"** chord with the third and fourth fingers of the left hand fretting the "G" on the sixth string at the fifth fret and the "D" on the fifth string at the fifth fret and letting the second string be the only "B" in the chord.

Some **"open chord"** tunings, named for the chord that the strings are tuned to, are easier to play since a straight bar across all six strings is a major chord no matter where it is fretted. This has been employed by many singers who have a limited ability with the guitar, as well as many expert slide or bottleneck players. It's a little harder to get minor chords in an open chord tuning, although some players like Richie Havens have found ingenious ways of doing that.

For **open G Tuning**: **D, G, D, G, B, D**, start in standard tuning. Lower both the first and sixth strings one whole step from **E** to **D**. then lower the fifth string one whole step from **A** to **G**. For **open D tuning: D, A, D, F♯, A, D**, start in standard tuning, lower both the first and sixth strings one whole step from **E** to **D**. Lower the second string one whole step from **B** to **A**, and lower the third string one half step from **G** to **F♯**.

One of the most useful and prevalent tunings is a **modified D tuning** (often called "dadgad"): **D, A, D, G, A, D**. For this tuning, start with an open **D** tuning. Raise the third string one half step from **F♯** to **G**. If you fret the third string anywhere along its length the melody on this string will be accompanied by all **D** and **A** notes droning along like a mountain dulcimer or bagpipes.

Another version of the **modified D tuning** you might want to try is **D, A, D, G, C, D**. Yet another variation is **D, A, D, G, A, B**. For another **modified G tuning, D, G, D, G, A, D**, start with an open **G** tuning. Lower the second string one whole step from **B** to **A**. Another variation on modified **G** is **D, G, D, G, C, D**.

For a **modified A tuning** try **E, A, C♯, E, A, E**. Start in normal guitar tuning. Lower the second string one whole step from **B** to **A**. Lower the third string a minor third from **G** to **E**, and lower the fourth string a half step from **D** to **C♯**.

For an **open C tuning, C, G, C, G, C, E**, start in standard tuning. Lower the sixth string two whole steps from **E** to **C**. Lower the fifth string one whole step from **A** to **G**. Lower the fourth string one whole step from **D** to **C**, and raise the second string one half step from **B** to **C**.

Experiment with your own special tunings. Some are more adapted to slide and bottleneck playing. Some need another guitar part. You will notice that some tunings are more versatile and some are only good for one song since everything played in that tuning tends to sound like the same song.

Try playing in cross keys, that is, play in **C** in a **G** tuning, or **A** in a **D** tuning, etc. You will discover by going farther up the neck, these tunings help you to find different inversions or voicings of the chords in combination with the open strings.

You can even try different gauges of strings. The Nashville or hi-strung guitar uses the strings that would remain from a twelve-string set if you removed the six regular strings of a normal six-string set. That is, they are the octave higher strings of the bass **E, A, D, G,** and then regular gauge **B** and high **E**. The octave **G** makes it sound very much like a twelve-string and yet the sound is more transparent without all the deep bass. This makes a great rhythm guitar or second rhythm guitar sound and is heard on many recordings.

2.6 Improvisation, Discovery & Accident

Victor Borge does a wonderful stage routine with many musical jokes and pranks. One of them is based on playing a brief unrecognizable musical phrase. While the audience listens patiently, he plays a series of descending notes, then two groups of staccato triplets. The phrases are not familiar and don't really seem like music.

At this point he gets a puzzled look on his face and turns the sheet music over and plays the first phrases of the William Tell Overture, and needless to say everyone recognizes the tune and laughs. But what of the other "melody." Many people have used this upside down idea for inspiration and some have even settled on turning the music over as an improvement of their original melody.

There is some part of our awareness that will not hear notes as a melody until we play them with some conviction. It's as if we have to think things through, then come up with an experimental idea, write out the part, check it for correctness, and then learn it and play it and ask ourselves if it works in a subjective way. What if this complicated process were swept away and we were forced to compose "on the run" as we performed the piece for the first time? This question of improvisation in songwriting is a controversial one.

I really love to have a lot of time to write. If I could just sing and play the song for hours and hours, and make the smallest adjustments to melody and chord and lyric ideas, it would be the most comfortable way for me to work. But some people really like to break loose and let improvisation take a central role in composition. Many stage performers have become so at home with thinking on their feet that they can ask the audience for ideas and compose a song on the spot. It's a balance that each writer needs to find for himself.

In any case, there is a real thrill to having new music unfold out of some mysterious place. Even if we do a lot of editing later, there is nothing like going with the flow and catching what we can of it with our pen while it lasts. This ability can be cultivated like any other aspect of songwriting. Even if we are not stage performers skilled on a lead instrument or used to jamming, we can experience the same magic occurrence.

This is one man's description of the event:

"... In the first state, I am improvising consciously, forcing the music rather than becoming one with it. This improvisation, if we can call it that, is a matter of editing rather than creating; I am simply picking out riffs from past improvisations and placing them in some order that satisfies the requirements of the melodic line and the harmonic progression. My movements in this state are studied and awkward. The music is stilted and joyless.

"Then, if all goes well, there is a transformation of state. It is not a gradual change, but a sudden shift, marked for me by an unmistakable physical sign: Whatever the room temperature, I feel a flush of perspiration on my forehead. At this moment, the improvisation becomes effortless. I take no thought of what I am going to play; I simply allow my consciousness to stay in the time and place from which the music emerges."

— GEORGE LEONARD, *THE SILENT PULSE*

This effortless, inspired playing must be one of the things that is most satisfying for musicians performing on stage. But improvisation and inspiration are also very much a part of the writer's process. It may be that Leonard's description is similar to what happens when we write, although in songwriting, my experience is that the process occurs on several levels and at several different times. Some of it is "in the moment" as above, and much of it is a matter of assembling little inspirations and then editing and rewriting to create a balanced work which has in it the best of both the flash and the form.

2.7 Song Structure

The Verse

The verse is the first and most common element of song structure. The verse is the place where the story unfolds.

If the chorus is the sing-along part, the verse is where we get all the background, all the stage directions. It's where we get our ideas of who is speaking, where they are, what has happened, and it is the place where we have room for explication. Verses can be more wordy. All of these thoughts are generalizations and there are exceptions to every one of them, but this should give you a rough idea of how the verse functions in the song.

In the old Tin Pan Alley tradition of songwriting, verses were spoken and were hardly ever heard again once the song passed into the piano bars and the fake books and people only sang the chorus. George Burns is a great source of these long forgotten verses and I've seen him stump the band with quite a few of them.

The Chorus

The chorus is the part of the song which will come back in the same form time and again. Where the verse is explication and stage setting, the chorus is the slogan and the simple phrase which can be repeated over and over. A chorus may be as simple as "Let it be, let it be, let it be, let it be." The chorus is the place where everybody joins in, even if they are just singing along in the car in traffic. Sometimes the chorus will be repeated over and over and fade in to the distance at the end of the song.

Verse-Chorus Songs

Verse-chorus songs are the most common and are simply songs in which either one or two verses are sung and then one or two chorues are sung and so on. In most cases this can be represented as an ABAB structure or AABAB, or even AABABABBB, depending on how many of each section is sung.

Folk songs may have dozens of verses and the chorus will be repeated usually after each verse. Choruses are usually written to be as simple and memorable as possible so that everyone can join in singing. Sometimes the chorus will reflect some change suggested by the verse such as an accumulation of objects: "There Was An Old Lady Who Swallowed a Fly" or "The Rattlin' Bog" are good examples. These songs are called cumulative songs.

Usually the verse and the chorus will be of equal length, the preponderance of cases being sixteen bars, although many songs vary from this drastically. In contemporary "chart" music, the tendency is for the verses to be exceedingly short or for there to be two very short verses, so that the chorus comes in after only a very short time into the song. I used to think in terms of a minute or so, but these days it is seldom more than twenty seconds to the "hook."

The Bridge

A bridge is like a distant cousin to the verse and the chorus. Seldom heard more than once in a song, it is the strange breeze which blows through the song usually after the verse and chorus have each been heard twice, and rather than go back to another verse or to another chorus, the bridge comes in like a breath of fresh air and takes us to another level of the song.

At the end of the bridge we may come right back into another chorus in a way that sets us up to hear it one more time, or we may go through a modulation of some kind, either a true key change or just the illusion of a key change so that the next section seems to be fresh and familiar at the same time.

The bridge is often the place where the language of the song becomes either extremely candid and plain, as if to say, "Look, no more fooling around, this is what I've been trying to say." Or, it may introduce a different tone from the rest of the song and may become more poetic or artistic. The bridge surprises us and plays off of the expectations created by the structure of verse and chorus leading up to it. If there is to be a key change in the song, it usually occurs either at the beginning or the ending of the bridge.

Sections of a Song

Songwriters often speak of the different sections of the song in terms of letters. A verse-chorus song would be a simple **ABAB** song and if two verses were followed by one chorus and another verse it would be an **AABA** song. Two verses, a chorus, verse, bridge, chorus would be an **AABACB** song. Other common forms are **ABA, ABABCB, AABBAACB**.

One of my favorite song forms uses the first half of the verse and the last half of the chorus. This may occur after the bridge or in some songs, this innovation is enough to take the place of a bridge. Another variation of this form is to have a third section doing some of what a bridge does, but only occupying the first half of this combined verse form where the second half is the second half of the chorus. There are many examples of both of these techniques and many other variations in popular music.

"Give me two A's, a B, then modulate and fade on the chorus."

Intros

When songs are arranged for performance or recording, it is fashionable to have some sort of introduction. Often this is very simple. It may be just four clicks of the drum sticks and go right into the song. Some songs take a great deal of time, I'm thinking of "A Day In the Life," from "Sergeant Pepper," but today's style is to do only short intros, two or four bars. The car radio has had its effect on intros, usually the less time you give the listener to get bored and push the button to change the station, the better.

Musically speaking, the intro may be simply the last four bars of the chorus, or may start on the VI chord of the song and simply walk to the I chord. Intros may have some vocals, but usually the intro is sparse in order to set itself apart from the beginning of the song. Some record producers have seen the intro as a chance to grab the attention of the audience; a song like "Wipe Out" comes to mind where the only vocal is the maniacal laugh and the title words in the intro.

Outros

In a similar way, the few bars of music at the end of the song can be an opportunity for a creative statement. Listening to the radio, it's surprising how many songs have faded endings. This is a lot easier to accomplish in the studio and gives the producer some options in mixdown, but in contrast, a well-thought-out (and well-played) ending can be very effective.

Many times the outro will just be a repeat of the last phrase of the song. Sometimes one note will be held for a longer value, maybe to emphasize a particular thought, or to allow the singer one more chance at a thrilling high note. The message here is to leave the listener with a vivid impression of the song.

Turn-arounds

A turn-around is a feature of the song that joins sections of the song and gives the listener a break from the lyric. Often based on the last two bars of a verse or chorus, the typical turn-around is usually a simple walk most often through the five chord, although it may involve the three or six minor, or perhaps a suspension. It is a sort of window dressing in many arrangements.

The blues has a tradition of turn-arounds and blues players pride themselves on the originality of their use of this device. Typical blues turn-arounds are **E, A, E, B7,** or **E7, A, Amin, E, B7.** Another possibility is **C, C7, C6, C♭6, C, G7.** There are literally thousands of possibilities.

Cadences

The Cadence refers to an ending, although it may not be limited to the ending of the song. Any time a section of the song comes to an end there is a cadence, but it is at the end of the song where the opportunity to create an interesting ending presents itself. A typical cadence is V7, I, as in *"Shave and a haircut ... two bits."* There are many standard cadences. The *"Amen"* cadence uses the IV chord. Rather than end on the expected tonic or I chord, the ending lands on the surprise IV chord and then resolves to the I.

Cadences

In a sense this is a "false" cadence because it plays off our expectations and slips in the surprise chord. There are many possibilities for false cadences. Minor chords are very useful in false cadences. For instance instead of ending the song, I, IV, V, I, you might find I, IV, V, VImin. Other common false cadences are I, V, IImin, I, and V, V, IV, I. In a minor key, a false cadence might involve going to a major chord when a minor chord was expected, although any unexpected chord makes a good false cadence if it allows you to resolve the song gracefully.

Musical "Hooks"

When we talk of hooks, most of the time we are talking about lyric hooks. Double meanings and trick phrases make good lyric hooks and catch our attention. There are two ways of thinking about musical hooks.

One is that they support the lyric hook. It's important that the music be supportive of any lyric device, but there are many examples of hooks that are strictly musical. In the Rolling Stones song "Satisfaction," before we hear the distinctive and memorable opening line, we have already been jostled, by the introduction, in a very satisfying way by the strictly musical phrase played on baritone saxophone.

Now as it happens, this musical hook is the same as the lyric hook and the title of the song. This is most often the case. But, there are hooks that are simply musical and are in many cases more memorable than the rest of the song. A good example of this is the guitar intro to the Beatles, "Day Tripper":

Day Tripper
Words and Music by John Lennon and Paul McCartney

© 1965 Northern Songs Ltd. (Copyright Renewed) All Rights Controlled and Administered by EMI Blackwood Music Inc. under license from ATV Music Corp. (Maclen Music) All Rights Reserved International Copyright Secured Used by Permission

As in other considerations of good songwriting, choices should support the best energy of the song. The hook should have more in common with a graceful hookshot than a meat hook.

2.8 Writing for Singers, An Article by Anne Hills

There is little that can rival the thrill of hearing your song performed by a great singer. And hearing an audience harmonize on a chorus you have written makes all the hours spent struggling with a phrase well worth it. What is it that makes a song a joy to sing, and how do we make a song singable?

One of the first considerations in writing for others is the subject of the song. If a song is too specifically personal it could feel as uncomfortable as an ill-fitting suit of clothes. There are wonderful writers whose work will never be covered by other artists because of its idiosyncratic nature.

All singers are in search of a haunting melody, but the range of notes covered in a song will determine who will be capable of singing it. When composers write for the orchestra they have to consider the range and tonal quality of the various instruments. It is wise to understand the voice and its limitations when you write a song. Try to imagine the singer of your choice singing the song. Sing the song yourself and listen for those places where other singers might have trouble.

If the song is very difficult to sing, then only the few, best singers with be able to work with it. If the melody follows the natural lilt of the spoken phrase, it will be learned more quickly and remembered more easily. If the melody is too unpredictable, an audience will not be able to master it for a sing-along. But you may be looking for a startling melodic line to emphasize the emotion. Be aware of the difficulty this may present. Try to avoid things like an octave jump in the melody or a very high part on a closed vowel sound. You want to make it easy for the singer to sound natural.

If you want to know which vowel sounds work best in the upper register, try yodeling. Usually in yodeling the upper note will open up to a full "a" or "e" vowel sound. It's hard to yodel into a sound like the "i" in tin or the "ion" in fashion. Consider how good it feels to sing a long high note on an "oo" or on an "oh" as opposed to an "i" as in "it." It is easier for the singer to carry emotion on this sound because, as you see if you try it, you have to think about technique on the harder sounds.

Most of the songs you hear in pop music have a limited range. There are lots of reasons for this, but if you look at songs written in the classical field you will often find a range of at least an octave and a half. Mostly this is because the singers are trained in breath control and focus. The songs are written to show this off. In the folk/country field, we write more in the speaking range in part to keep a more personal and conversational feeling. A classical-style vocal sound in a folk song would be quite alienating and pull the listener away from the common-man storytelling stance that distinguishes traditional music.

When writing a musical phrase that holds a note for a long time, it is wise to once again consider the vowel sound within the word. Only the pure, open vowel sounds are beautiful and easy when held for a long time, so you should weigh this consideration against your natural lyrical choice. Be sure that you are leaving room for the singer to breathe even if the breath has to come in an unconventional place. It may be that the sense of the lyric will be affected by stopping for a breath. Be sure that half a line doesn't say something you don't want to say.

The singer's first priority is always communication of emotion and though technical challenges can be exciting, they should never be so excessive that they take away from communication. As writers we need to be sure that these vocal challenges are there for a reason that works in favor of the message.

If you are working on a melody first, then an "oo" sound or a hum can be most soothing while you decide on content. But if your lyrics come first and you are in search of a melody, you can begin in the most organic place by speaking the phrases. Our voices move up and down to emphasize our thoughts. If the melody moves in a way that's similar to the speaking voice it will feel natural and be easy to sing. Audiences will quickly join in a chorus that follows the natural cadence of the speaking voice.

It could also be said that some of the finest singers do not have the finest voices. Artists like Tom Waits and Dr. John are great singers because of their phrasing, putting emotional energy ahead of beautiful tone. This is very encouraging for those of us who wish to focus almost entirely on the second half of singer-songwriter. But to get your songs heard and to eventually make a living from them it's wise to pay attention to the phrasing of the best singers. Listen to good singers and you are more likely to become one yourself. If you choose to work on your own voice there are some very safe and simple exercises that you can put to use on a regular basis and it is wise to seek out a vocal coach to help keep your voice healthy.

3.

Songwriting Mechanics
Part 2: The Words

3.1 Words, Words, Words

Colorful Language

In his book *Wordstruck*, Robert MacNeil offers most of a page of examples of common expressions that come down to us from the time when we were so dependent on the sea and sea travel. There are dozens of familiar phrases like "when our ship comes in," or "we're all in the same boat," "get to know the ropes," "keep a weather eye open," "down the hatch," "three sheets to the wind," "keeled over," "lower the boom," "take the wind out of his sails," "come hell or high water," "clear sailing," "hit the decks," "from stem to stern," and "shipshape."

Similarly, there are many examples of songs which use the special language of a particular field. Guy Clark has written a great song which uses the language of the professional carpenter. "He was true as a level, straight as a rule ..." Guy does a similar thing in "Desperados Waiting For a Train." Railroad workers, miners, cowboys, loggers, card players, gangsters and auto mechanics all have rich jargon. Many of these terms have become figures of speech in much wider use.

In traditional music there are hundreds of songs about weaving and spinning and songs which use the language of that industry, sometimes with wonderful double entendre. Any field which is familiar to you may offer its own special language and give your song a unique point of view.

Imagery

"Among the twenty snowy mountains, the only moving thing was the eye of the blackbird."
— WALLACE STEVENS

Good imagery gives a powerful lift to a song. Most writing teachers emphasize the importance of being observant. It is good to develop an eye for the telling detail, and it is worth the time and the effort if you can capture that one little picture in a word or two that will bring another dimension of verisimilitude and interest to your song. "Red Sails in the Sunset," "Fire and Rain," "Silver Wings," and "Cool Water" are all songs that use good imagery.

Mining the Mother Tongue

Part of developing a songwriter's style is learning how to make observations that ring true with the listener. It's only necessary to say important things some if the time. Usually, more progress is made by observing unimportant but cogent or interesting things which contribute to the atmosphere of the song.

These ways of seeing the world may just relax the listener almost as casual conversation would serve to relax someone with whom you wished to have a serious talk. As in the case of true rhyme, this area of sensible observance is one way you can establish credibility with the listener.

Sometimes this is a matter of words of wisdom as in Don Schlitz's song "The Gambler." "You got to know when to hold 'em / Know when to fold 'em / Know when to walk away / Know when to run." Or it may be just some inconsequential observation that sets the stage or the mood for the song. With songs, there is plenty of opportunity to demonstrate that you are curious about the world and like to ask interesting questions about it even if they don't take the form of a question.

"The trouble with light bulbs is that the shadows don't dance."
— Judy Benson

Tuning Your Ear

Many writers keep notebooks for just this kind of phrase. It may not have a place in the song you are working on, but it's worth hanging onto. I write things in the margins of my work pages and go back and copy them to another page for later consideration.

You will undoubtedly hear things in conversation and in the world in general and it's good to keep your ear attuned to these little verbal glimpses of the way things are – or seem – to someone. This unusual pairing or grouping of words may be a good clue to character, or may have just the right amount of understatement, or any number of special qualities that makes it a gem.

Things We Said Today

Every day the mail is filled with good song ideas. The windows of stores and ads in the newspaper offer many catchy phrases. I remember seeing a sign in a hardware store window that said, "Cast Iron Sinks."

That one made me laugh but I don't think it suggests a song unless it is a song that puts together a lot of silly sayings.

If we keep our eyes and ears open we may find song titles, or we may hear things that will make our songs more interesting. Paul Simon got the title for "Mother and Child Reunion" from the menu of a Chinese restaurant. These found objects can help the process of songwriting immeasurably. The rest may just be a matter of understanding how the idea fits in the song and what the song is about.

3.2 The First Line: The Best Defense Is a Good Offense

"Have something to say, and say it as clearly as you can."
— MATTHEW ARNOLD

If the first thing we hear is a strong, captivating idea, it makes us want to continue listening. If the writer honors our consideration we feel grateful and let down our guard. We will go along with a thoughtful premise and see how we feel about what we hear.

I remember one joke session aboard the Clearwater among the volunteers during the annual fund-raising pumpkin sail. The jokes seemed to get more and more preposterous until just as a new joke began, someone yelled out "Premise alert, premise alert" and we all realized how willing we were to take for granted any ridiculous situation just to see where the joke went.

That may be fine in good company, but when the listener is fighting traffic on the interstate or just not sure the next song is going to be worth the candle, so to speak, that first line can present your case.

Sometimes we may recognize in a great line the potential for this first line status. More often, though, the first line is the last line to be written. It may take considerable thought about what the song is saying and just what we want the first line to accomplish. The best approach may be a form of misdirection or it may be a matter of card stacking, or the first line may begin in the middle of a conversation. We may have to try many different approaches to find the line that works just right. This is another one of the places in the process of songwriting where a little thought can make a big difference.

Some examples of good first lines in a few of these categories are:

Setting the scene:
"A long steel rail and a short cross tie"
"Almost heaven, West Virginia"
"As I walked out in the streets of Laredo"
"From the halls of Montezuma"
"I come from Alabama with my banjo on my knee"

"I dreamed I saw Joe Hill last night, alive as you and me"
"I gave my love a cherry that had no stone"
"I know an old lady who swallowed a fly"
"In 1814 we took a little trip"
"In a cavern, in a canyon, excavating for a mine"
"In Scarlet Town where I was born"
"In the Blue Ridge Mountains of Virginia"
"In the early morning rain"
"In the town of Springhill, Nova Scotia"
"Last night I had the strangest dream"
"Moon river, wider than a mile"
"Once a jolly swagman camped beside a billabong"
"Ridin' on the City of New Orleans"
"Sittin' in the mornin' sun"
"Somewhere over the rainbow"
"Summertime, and the livin' is easy"
"Ten years ago on a cold dark night"
"The first time ever I saw your face"
"There is a house in New Orleans, they call the Rising Sun"
"There is a tavern in the town"
"There's a bright golden haze on the meadow"
"Trailer for sale or rent, rooms to let, fifty cents"
"Up a lazy river by the old mill run"
"Way down upon the Swanee River"
"Well I woke up this morning"
"When I first came to this land"

Please do this for me:
"All of me, why not take all of me?"
"Come all ye (faithful, fair and tender ladies, bold fishermen, rounders, etc.)
"Come on and hear, come on and hear, Alexander's Ragtime Band"
"Follow the drinkin' gourd"
"Give my regards to Broadway"
"Hang down your head Tom Dooley"
"Hear that lonesome whippoorwill, he sounds too blue to fly"
"Hush little baby, don't you cry"
"Take this hammer"
"Wake up, wake up, darlin' Corey"
"Well, come along boys and listen to my tale"
"When the storms of life are raging, stand by me"
"Won't you come home, Bill Bailey?"
"You get a line, I'll get a pole, Honey"
"You who are on the road"

Tell me:
"Ain't she sweet?"
"Are you going to Scarborough fair?"

"How many roads must a man walk down?"
"How many times have you heard someone say?"
"What shall we do with the drunken sailor?"
"Where have all the flowers gone?"

What you are to me:
"Oh Shenandoah, I long to see you"
"You ain't nothin' but a hound dog"
"You are every woman in the world"
"You are so beautiful"
"You are the sunshine of my life"
"Your feet's too big"

If:
"If a picture paints a thousand words"
"If ever I would leave you"
"If I had wings like Noah's dove"
"If I were a rich man"

Here's my philosophy:
"Amazing grace, how sweet the sound"
"Free at last, free at last"
"Good news, chariot's a-comin' "
"I don't want your millions, mister"
"I'm a little cookie, yes I am"
"I'm a little teapot short and stout"
"I'm in the mood for love"
"I'm just a typical American boy"
"Inch by inch, row by row"
"Just a closer walk with thee"
"Let it rain, let it pour"
"Life is like a mountain railroad"
"Love is but a song we sing"
"Oh, freedom, oh, freedom"
"Should auld acquaintance be forgot"
"Some people say a man is made out of mud"
"Spanish is the loving tongue"
"The hills are alive with the sound of music"
"There's a dark and a troubled side of life"
"Viva la Quince Brigada"
"What the world needs now"

What I'm gonna do:
"Gonna jump down, turn around, pick a bale o'cotton"
"I'm going to leave old Texas now"
"I'm gonna buy a paper doll that I can call my own"
"I'm gonna wash that man right out of my hair"

As you can see, the categories are only the crudest suggestion of a way to think about the things the first line may accomplish. Almost all are exceptional in some way. Listen to each of the songs of these first lines and notice how quite a few repeat the first line or answer its premise with a similar line. Go through your own songbooks and CD collection and see how first lines function in good songs.

Needless to say, many times the first line and the title of the song are the same thing. Sometimes it's hard to say which came first. Many traditional songs become known by the first line, which became the title as it was handed down.

3.3 Rhyme

Another area where thought and respect for the listener can make the difference is the whole issue of rhyme. Rhyme is sacred. The spoken word, of course, predates all written language. The sound of the human voice speaking the words has given language its dimensions. In some cultures the ability to speak in rhyme is respected as a gift. Ours is certainly one of those cultures.

All day long, radio and TV assault our ears with slogans, sales pitches, and all sorts of promotional information and it's hard to find even one of these that doesn't rely on rhyme to make its message more memorable. Almost everyone who works in communication or education is aware of the power of rhyme.

As songwriters, we expect to make use of rhyme and are always discovering new things about it. From our first nursery rhymes we develop certain expectations about words which become more and more subtle and sophisticated the more we work with them.

There are several types of rhymes and several places they can show up. Some fall in subtle, almost unnoticed places in the song, in the middle of lines, in lines separated from one another and in the middle of words, diphthong and triphthong sounds and are hardly there at all. Some are as obvious as a hammered thumb. All rhymes have magic and are worthy of careful thought.

The most common rhymes are single or masculine rhymes and occur at the end of sequential lines:

"In fourteen hundred and ninety-two
Columbus sailed the ocean blue."

An example of double or feminine rhyme would be:

"Back in the winter of nineteen-eighty
She did a picture with Warren Beatty."

Triple rhyme would be:

"If you want to keep the brass from tarnishing,
Somebody's got to do some varnishing."

or,

"If you want to keep the brass from demolishing,
Somebody's got to do some polishing."

True Rhyme

There are really only two requirements for a rhyme. One is that it have exactly the same vowel sound or sounds as the word it rhymes. And, the consonant that precedes the rhyme must be different from that of the rhyming word.

For instance "say" and "play" are rhymes, but "sublimate" and "consummate" are not because the same consonant precedes the rhyme. "Pendant" and "independent" are not technically rhymes but might still work in a song. Of course, there are many examples of rhymes which do not conform to these criteria in a variety of ways and still may be found in good songs.

Usually by this point someone has raised the question that the sense of what is being said in the song may take precedence over how well the words rhyme. Or, at least there is some reason for discussion of the relationship between these two issues. The answer is thoughts must all be brilliant and rhymes must all be perfect. Wherever you stop short of that is up to you.

... it's important to respect the listener's sensibilities.

I think the listener is willing to give you the benefit of the doubt, and even indulge you to some extent. If your rhymes are interesting or humorous they can add a lot of life to the song. Here again, the tone of the song and the character of the singer need to be taken into consideration. If it really works for the song you can rhyme things like "Adam" with "had 'em," and "Birth of a nation" with "versification."

If you think about the person hearing a song for the first time, just as it is with you or me, there is a certain amount of skepticism or inertia to overcome. It's not that we have to do more than just say what is true in a good way, but if we are interested in establishing a clear channel of communication it's important to respect the listener's sensibilities. One of the ways we can do that is with rhymes that ring true.

Even though examples of sloppy or casual rhymes can be found among the most successful popular songs, it is my belief that by taking a little more trouble and being a little more innovative and original with your rhymes you can show your consideration for the listener. Rhyme is one of the few tangible ways you can demonstrate that you are willing to do what it takes to do a good job. Recording artists who might sing your song also have a weakness for great rhymes.

Inner Line Rhyme

An inner line rhyme is an occurrence of rhyme or near rhyme which is not at the end of the lines but somewhere in the middle. This may be in between adjacent lines, but is much more effective and likely to be found within a single line. An example of this kind of rhyme is:

"I'm a little lost sheep, I can't sleep,
I keep tryin' to forget ...

An example of compound rhyme used in this way is:

"There was an old lady who swallowed a spider,
It wriggled and jiggled and tickled inside her."

3.4 How to Use a Rhyming Dictionary

I recommend using a rhyming dictionary. Some people have developed tricks for finding rhymes by mentally going through the alphabet or modified alphabets, which include common combinations of consonants like b, bl, br, etc. When you don't have a rhyming dictionary handy, this is a useful practice, but I find that there is an advantage to having the list of rhymes in front of me without having to create it.

Most rhyming dictionaries will give you several types of rhyme for each word. Sometimes they are organized according to single rhymes – ordinary masculine rhymes like ache, bake, fake. And double rhymes or feminine rhymes like aching, baking, faking. And triple rhymes like breakable and unmistakable.

Any number of syllables may precede the rhyme, and words in the dictionary are organized by the number of syllables in each of the single, double, and triple rhyme sections. These possibilities may include some words which may or may not be exact rhymes depending on pronunciation, which may vary according to region of the country, or near rhymes. These are listed in italics in my rhyming dictionary.

Be sure to look at all the examples of words that rhyme even if they have fewer or more syllables than you need. You can always add a word or two before or use the rhyming word in a phrase that gives you the right number of beats. It is in this area of word context that I think you will find the greatest advantage to using a rhyming dictionary.

I will write down all the words which I feel may be of use in the verse I am working on and as I write down each word I try to be conscious of any phrase or expression the word might suggest. For instance, breaking might suggest heartbreaking, or my heart is breaking, the dawn is breaking, or the news is breaking. Many of these phrases will be worthy of writing down even if they are only useful to suggest other paths of thought or other ways in which to structure the verse.

There is a technique that is similar to clustering that is particularly useful with the help of a rhyming dictionary. As an example, I will use a song I've been working on about Johnny Appleseed. The chorus I have is:

"Hey, Johnny Appleseed
You really are a friend indeed.
And I will follow where you lead,
Johnny Appleseed."

Note that the word "indeed" at the end of the second line is a good example of friendly ambiguity. More about ambiguity later.

In the course of developing the chorus and a double-length version of the chorus which occurs at the end of the song, I explored and wrote down many possibilities for the "eed" rhyme.

Although I ended up using different rhymes for the verses, I can demonstrate this rhyme clustering with some of the ideas which came up out this search.

This technique can really help you to come up with ideas that are related to your central theme, and by starting with rhyme, you have some of your final language already locked in.

I begin by writing down all the rhyming words and the phrases they suggest to me:

Indeed ... in deed ... guaranteed ... need ... you taught me everything I need ... we all agreed ... disagreed ... speed ... freed ... growin' like a weed ... bright as a bead ... there for all the world to read ... before I could read ... plead ... must concede ... trusty steed ... proceed ... succeed ... from a tiny seed ... etc.

Many of these will be eliminated as soon as they are written down, but no matter. Useful in a number of ways, they sustain the rhythm of my thinking, they generate ideas which I can go with or not, and they suggest ways in which they come from similar language.

That is, there are different ways in which words are alike, and I can get a lot out of evaluating their properties. The idea of rhyme clustering is that we take these considerations to the next level.

We start with words that have some inherent similarities. Weed, reed, and seed are all growing things. Seed is already less useful, because it is so prominent in our chorus, but for the purposes of the example we can build on these three words.

In a sense, we have a metaphorical relationship in these words. This suggests that if we chose to explore the lyric possibilities of these three rhyming words, the idea of young and growing things is right there before us.

If we take a quick step backward, we can see that other combinations from the same list of rhyming words suggest other metaphors. Steed, speed, freed, might have something to do with horses, or an escape, or an episode of adventure that we could develop as a part of our story.

Again, it takes only a moment to see if there is anything here which is worth working on. Bright as a bead, before I could read, likely to succeed, all work together in a similar way. Of course, only one of these groups of ideas would necessarily be used in any one verse, but you can see how easy it is to generate a lot of ideas this way.

The next consideration in this idea of rhyme clustering is to find another rhyming word or words which will give us a second polarity for our verse structure. Bear in mind that this practice is only one way of generating ideas.

Coming from the direction of our basic story line would be a much more conventional way to start with ideas for verses, but as you can see, when we are in the thick of things, these elements are all flying fast and it helps to have an orderly approach to them. Recognizing the need for another rhyme scheme for our "eed" rhymes to play off of leads us to the next step.

This is a process I like to call engendering. If we take the first of our group of rhyming words, seed, weed, reed, and we name the words which are engendered by their common properties, we may come up with flower, bloom, stalk, etc. Flower could engender hour, tower, shower, etc. And stalk could engender walk, talk, etc.

We can proceed until we have come up with rhyme possibilities which play off of our original idea in a good way. Similarly, speed, steed, freed would engender their own groups and subgroups of rhyming words and associated ideas.

This may seem at first to be a lot of trouble to go to, but after working with these kinds of word issues for a while this goes very quickly, and as we mentioned, this is a practice which may be useful when we are stuck or need to come up with an idea, but which may not be necessary most of the time.

Just as playing cards may have numbers and suits and faces, words have rhyme, literal meaning, figurative meaning, and associative properties which are tricky to work with. Organizing them by rhyme is only one way to sort them out. It's true that after working with words for a while, the method becomes less visible and more intuitive but it's good to have a place to start. Many times whole lines and rhyme structures will occur to us in the shower, or at the supermarket, but we're more likely to have these experiences the more we are used to working with words.

I have faith in strong phrases. If I'm looking for a rhyme for "when," I may write down fifteen rhyming words but I'm most likely to believe in the ones that give a strong sense of character and resolution of thought like "every now and then," or "the best laid plans of mice and men," "bearding the lion in its den," "nine times out of ten," well, I guess you must see what I mean. Assuming that these phrases scan correctly and hang together melodically in a satisfying way, I always feel better when the last few words in a line sound as if they just rolled off my uncontriving tongue.

Get Out Your Crayons

In her book *How to Write a Hit Song*, Molly-Ann Leikin writes, "In my first songwriting workshop, the instructor underlined each single rhyme (joke, Coke) in red, each double rhyme (jingle, mingle) in green, each triple rhyme (banana, Havana) in blue. He circled all the picture words (Porsche, pig) in yellow. Intense feelings were circled in orange. His theory was the more colorful and illegible the lyric after you went through it with your crayons, the better. If you just have a series of red underlines and your song doesn't feel or sound terrific yet, perhaps you need to add a color – a picture or a double rhyme. I like to shoot for at least three colors in each song."

3.5 Alliteration, Assonance & Consonance

Alliteration is the use of similar sounds in order to make the overall sound of a line more pleasing. Assonance refers to the use of like vowel sounds, and consonance refers to the use of the sounds of similar consonants. An example of assonance is;

"Along the hollow halls, on I walked and walked alone."

The classic country song "Cool, Clear Water" uses a lot of very clever assonant phrases, like:

"All day I face the barren waste without a taste of water."

This is also a good example of inner line rhyme since the words with alliterative sounds also end in rhymes.

An example of consonance is:

"The clickity clackity clamor of the first fast freight."

Also, the "s" sounds of "face," "waste," and "taste" in "Cool, Clear Water" are good examples of the use of consonance.

Alliteration is a very powerful tool and can be used with great subtlety. Here, again, a little goes a long way. What we are usually striving for is conversational believability without calling attention to our own cleverness. Alliteration is a device, but as our ear becomes sensitized to it, we begin to hear it everywhere.

3.6 A Survey of Poetic Terms (Simplified)

Meter is the basic pattern of beats which repeats throughout a verse of poetry or the lyrics of a song. It corresponds to the beat of the music. One out of every two or three syllables is normally accented. Unlike normal speech, which has a random pattern of weak and strong beats, verses use a regular system of meter with predictable accents.

There are four kinds of meter in English. Each unit of meter is called a foot, or a metric foot. In **iambic meter**, each foot has two syllables and the accent falls on the second syllable. One iambic foot is called an **iamb**, pronounced "I am."

An example of iambic meter might be:

"My horse has got a broken leg"

Trochaic meter is made up of units of two syllables also, but the accent falls on the first syllable. One trochaic foot is called a **trochee**, pronounced "tro-key." An example of trochaic meter might be:

"Never have I ever given so much time away for free."

Anapestic meter is made up of three syllable feet where the accent is on the third syllable. An example of anapestic meter might be:

"When the weight of the car settled down on my foot, it brought tears to my eyes in a flash."

Any example of anapestic meter will bring to mind lines from the poem that begins "'Twas The Night Before Christmas."

Dactylic meter of three syllables has the accent on the first syllable, as in:

"Merrily, merrily, merrily, merrily, life is but a dream."

As you can see, these last two meters lend themselves naturally to three/four or waltz time.

There is one other type of foot which is known as a **spondee**. A spondee is a two-syllable form with both syllables accented as in "fresh fish." There really is no such thing as **spondaic meter** since it would be impossible to impose all strong accented syllables on the sense of a verse. The spondee is used to give a break to the monotony of any of the other meters.

The number of metrical feet in a line determines how that line is described. The most common number of iambic feet in a line, for instance, is five and the familiar name for this is **iambic pentameter**.

If a line has only one foot of any kind of meter it is called **monometer**. If it has only two feet, **dimeter**. Three feet, **trimeter**, four feet, **tetrameter**, five feet as we have noted is called **pentameter**. If the line has six feet it is called **hexameter**, seven, **heptameter**, eight, **octometer**.

Iambic pentameter is by far the most common and seems to be the most conversational. In the blues, this is the most common meter. In a discussion of the blues, Leonard Bernstein recited lines from Macbeth to demonstrate that the twelve-bar blues served as a perfect setting for the poetry of Shakespeare's plays.

Once we have set up a regular pattern of meter we have created an expectation in the ears of the listener. If this is honored, a hypnotic and pleasing effect can be the result. If we break from this pattern awkwardly by accenting the wrong syllable of a word, thereby breaking the "chant," we may disenchant the listener.

This principle is referred to as **scansion**. It is said that a poem or a song or a line **scans** well, or doesn't **scan**. This is another area where it's better for the songwriter's craft to be invisible and inaudible.

According to Tony Barrand:

There once was a man from Sudan
Whose poems would never quite scan.
When asked why he did it,
He said to his credit,
"I like to try to get as many words into the last line as I possibly can."

3.7 Rhyme & Meter

The meter of English hymns is classified according to the kind of feet used, iambic, trochaic, or dactylic. In iambic meter, the most often encountered, the term "Common Metre" (C.M.) applies to lines with 8, 6, 8, 6 syllables per line. "Long Metre" (L.M.) applies to lines of 8, 8, 8, 8 syllables per line. "Short Metre" (S.M.) designates lines with 6, 6, 8, 6 syllables per line.

These forms of English hymn usually have four stanzas, but when eight stanzas are used the forms are called by the names "Common Metre Double" (C.M.D.), "Long Metre Double" (L.M.D.), and "Short Metre Double" (S.M.D.) and have eight lines per stanza.

Also seen are six-line stanzas; "Common Particular Metre" (C.P.M.), "Long Particular Metre" (L.P.M.) and "Short Particular Metre" (S.P.M.). Besides these forms, there are "Sevens and Sixes," "Tens," "Hallelujah Meter" and many others.

Eastern European and Middle-Eastern music use a variety of strange meters and rhythm forms, but these are usually classified according to drumming patterns and dance forms rather than poetic meter.

3.8 "Courting The Muse"
by Ann Reed

Rhythm, Rhyme & Inspiration

When I began writing, it was a cosmic thing: Inspiration! Wham! Short spurts of time when I felt out of touch with reality, temporarily insane and the result: a song!

Well, Mostly a Song

Songwriting is an art. It is also a craft. The inspiration still strikes, but after that "timeless time," when every word and idea seems to pour out faster than you can write them down, is when the craft becomes important. That is the time to listen critically. Is this saying exactly what I want it to say? Is this how I wanted to say it?

This is also an excellent time to ask this question: Did I get lazy and go for a quick rhyme? Here's an example from the song "Heroes." In the original chorus, the last three lines went like this: "As time goes/ You find you depend/ On your heroes to carry your name." It didn't feel right when I wrote it down, but I kept going because a whole bunch of other good stuff was coming fast and furious. When I went back to take a more critical look, I knew that the last line of the chorus was the culprit and needed to be changed. After all, there I was talking about how heroes or role models are people who light a path. I ended up using a slant rhyme. A slant rhyme is where it sounds like you have a rhyme, but in reality, you don't. The lines ended up like this: "As time goes/ You find you depend/ On your heroes to show you the way." You'll see that the word "way" doesn't exactly rhyme with "flame," but when it is sung, it sounds like a rhyme. The slant rhyme gives the writer more flexibility and a few more choices in what words can be used.

Never leave home without either a small notebook and pen or a microcassette player.

A great love of mine in songwriting is simply feeling the rhythm and the individual "personalities" of words. There are textures to words; some sound hard, some soft, some words fall on our ears very gently and others grate. We all learned about syllables in school. Those syllables are the rhythm of words. When I'm working on a song then, I'm working with two rhythms: The musical rhythm and the word rhythm. In "Heroes," the rhythms of the words were crucial when it came to listing the names of the women at the end of the song. So, I had a double challenge: The names needed to rhyme (or at least sound like it – again, I used the slant rhyme technique), and they needed to have a certain rhythm that varied from time to time. What's interesting about songs where the writer is genuinely in love with words is that it's easy to read the lyrics like a poem.

As for tools of the trade, I've found that simple is best. There's no computer in the world that will turn you into a great songwriter. I do have two practical tips: Never leave home without either a small notebook and pen or a microcassette player (yes, people on the bus do give you strange looks when you're humming into the recorder, but just ignore them). Second, get yourself a rhyming dictionary. Yes there is such an animal, and no, it's not "cheating" any more than a writer using a thesaurus is cheating. They make pocket-sized rhyming dictionaries, and for four or five bucks, it's a good investment.

Writing a song isn't that hard. Writing a *good* song is difficult. Let's face it, we're faced with taking a complex feeling or event, making words rhyme and saying exactly what we want them to say in a short amount of time. Ah, the time issue. In songwriting workshops, I encourage writers to keep their songs at around 3½ to 4 minutes. Why? Well, radio airplay for one. Your song, if recorded, will have a better chance at being played over the airwaves if it's 3 minutes than if it's 5 minutes or more. But the primary reason for keeping it short and to the point is to be certain that you're not boring your audience. I mean, "Hey Jude" is okay, but after the third time through the "na-na-na-nas," I'm ready to move on.

Because songwriting is both an art and a craft, the more you write, the more your skills as a songwriter will develop and grow. So what are you doing reading this? Get busy and go write.

3.9 The Rhythm of Words

"It don't mean a thing if it ain't got that swing."
— DUKE ELLINGTON

The Words Are the Whole Band

Examples of songs in which the words by themselves are evocative of the rhythmic character of the song.:

"Oh, Susanna."
"Blackstrap molasses and the wheat germ bread."
"The Atchison, Topeka and the Santa Fe."
"Hard-hearted Hannah, the vamp of Savannah, G.A."
"Get your kicks on Route sixty-six."
"Good old Rocky Top ... Rocky Top, Tennessee."
"Wake up, little Susie"
"Bye bye love, bye bye happiness."
"What a mouth, what a mouth, what a north and south."
"My Bonnie lies over the ocean."
"East side, West side, all around the town."

"I can't get no satisfaction."
"La cucaracha, la cucaracha."

Spend some time with these examples and with others of your own and determine if the time signatures are 4/4, 6/8 or 3/4 like "My Bonnie Lies Over The Ocean." Try changing to a three-based meter to see if your four-based lyrics still make sense. Another thing to notice in the examples is the use of syncopation or tied notes including rests.

It might take a few minutes to write out the musical notation of some of these, but I think it would give you a good sense of what's involved in doing this kind of writing. Some of the process is unconscious and some is just trial and error, but some of these have survived for hundreds of years intact.

Jump-rope chants and work songs have all explored this territory and time has worn off the rough edges. It's a good thing to work toward this kind of rhythmic magic, and recognizing what the elements are gets you halfway there.

3.10 The Melody of Words

It's true that words do have a melodic component. Some words or combination of words have in them the suggestion of an inherent interval. We've all heard someone calling out a name, perhaps of a child late for dinner, "Har-old," or "Mar-vin" or "Ju-li-a" and heard in these a musical performance.

In songs, this is known as **prosody**. Prosody is the sense that words and music really go together in a way that rings true.

When the singer starts into "Climb Every Mountain," and the orchestra builds on the natural lift of words and melody, the effect can be thrilling.

In their excellent book *If They Ask You, You Can Write a Song*, Al Kasha and Joel Hirschhorn cite as an example of good prosody Elton John and Bernie Taupin's song "Your Song." In the first line of the chorus, "And you can tell everybody ..." the word "every" leaps up in the melody and gives a strong emphasis to the emotional character of the line.

In traditional songs and children's songs there are many examples of prosody and it's easy to see that this effect has contributed to the longevity of the song in the popular culture. Here are a few more examples:

"Ding, Dong, the wicked witch is dead."
"I'm always chasing rainbows"
"My Girl"
"Come to me my melancholy baby"
"You ain't nothin' but a hound dog"

3.11 Syncopation

"Here comes the doctor,
here comes the nurse,
here comes the lady with the alligator purse."

In this playground jump-rope chant we have a good example of the kind of interplay of weak beats and strong beats which give us the syncopation effect. It's possible to recite the chant in "straight" time:

Straight time

But, on all the playgrounds I've ever been on, this "straight" time soon gives way to a more syncopated reading:

Tied note syncopated time

In this example the word "comes" moves up into the eighth note before its normal beat, and ties over through the next eighth note. This is similar to the phrasing of the comic expression, "Here come the judge" originated by "Pigmeat" Markham and popularized by Sammy Davis Jr. on *Rowan & Martin's Laugh-In*.

A similar eighth note emphasis is found in this example from *Oklahoma*:

"Chicks and ducks and geese better scurry,
When I take you out in the surrey."

There is more happening here than just simple staccato eighth notes. It's as if there is an implied triplet in each beat. Count diddledy, diddledy, diddledy, diddledy, etc.

Here is a popular phrase from the big band era. The second line takes up the exact same number of beats as the first line. There is also a real jump to the last phrase.

Little Richard created the Rock standard, "Tutti Frutti" and with it this riff which has a similar syncopation.

a whomp bomp a lu bomp a whomp bomp boom

Drummers use a number of phrases to "describe" in onomatopoetic terms the sound of certain drum figures. "Paradiddle" is the simplest example. To make the sound of a paradiddle, the drummer plays two notes with each stroke while alternating left and right hands.

The "flamadiddle" begins with a "flam" or a grace note with the opposite stick just before the downbeat of the figure. This sounds a little like "k-flamadiddle" only not quite so obvious. The "ratamacue" begins with a slight drum roll. (In the examples below, "R" means right hand, and "L" means left hand.)

Paradiddle

R L R R L R L L

Flamadiddle

ʟR L R R RrL R L L

Ratamacue

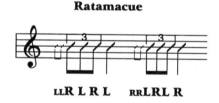

ʟʟR L R L   RrLRL R

Drummers talk about "roughing the beat," "pushing the downbeat," "accenting a beat" and other ways of giving emphasis and expression to musical passages. Often these features are written down on their session charts. It's important when using these ideas to keep the song in perspective; these devices should liven up the song, but never distract from the basic message of the words and music.

Syncopation In Three/Four Time

Three/four or waltz time affords the same opportunities for syncopation and interesting use of accented beats. Again the whole idea is to play off the listener's expectations and keep the rhythmic song fresh.

In Kenny Rogers' enormous hit "Lucille," the word "hungry" in the second line of the chorus is a good example of this type of surprise accent. Count one, two, three, one, two, three,

"Four <u>hun</u>-gry children and the crops in the field."

In singing the song, you might phrase this two different ways. In the first example the syllable "hun" falls on a regular quarter note, the second quarter note in the measure, but is slightly stressed vocally.

In the second example, the same syllable is sung slightly early, in true syncopation and falls on the eighth note before the expected beat and is "tied" over through the normal quarter note.

Lucille: (Example 1)
Words and Music by Roger Bowling and Hal Bynum

With   four   hun gry   chil - dren and a   crop in the   field

Lucille: (Example 2)

With   four hun - gry   chil - dren and a   crop in the field

3.12 Breathing, Pulse, Heartbeat & Stride

Songs can be said to have physical life signs. A sense of breathing, coming to rest, almost like a comma in a sentence, there seems to be a natural phrase length and the phrase lengths at different points in the song seem to complement each other. This is expressed in the urgency of certain parts of the song balanced with the calming of other parts of the song.

Pulse is not always the same thing as tempo. Even when a song has a steady, even rhythm, there may be an overriding sense of subtle emphasis or pulse. Sometimes there is a subliminal quickening or "lift" of pulse, often at the beginning of the chorus, but sometimes at the beginning of the bridge, or when the bridge ends and the next section begins whether it be a chorus, another verse, or some sort of extended ending. Often verses will be rhythmically centered "in the pocket" while the choruses will "get up on top of the beat" to give a very different "feel." Some songs seem to "hit their stride." Some start right out with "stride."

Ragtime flowered as a form for only a little more than ten years at the beginning of this century but it influenced what came after in many ways. Ragtime piano was really a very restrained and precisely noted form, but it engendered the much more raucous and rolling styles that came later. Many of the players of this next era we refer to as "stride" pianists.

W.C. Handy wrote "Memphis Blues" right around the end of the ragtime era and released "St. Louis Blues," probably the best-known jazz tune of all time, in 1914. James P. Johnson recorded "Carolina Shout" in 1921. Jelly Roll Morton created "King Porter Stomp" and "Milenberg Joys" during this period which culminated with the songs of Fats Waller in the thirties. Waller, a student of James P. Johnson, wrote such well-known songs as "Ain't Misbehavin'," "Two Sleepy People" and "Your Feet's Too Big." All of these were favorites around my house and I could hum them before I could talk.

3.13 Back Beat

"It's got a back beat, you can't lose it,"
— CHUCK BERRY, "ROCK 'N' ROLL MUSIC"

Earlier we referred to "boom-chuck" and "boom-ba-chuck-a" as ways of showing the difference in rhythmic emphasis between straight metrical time and what has become known as the "back beat." It's not quite as simple as just dividing four quarter notes in a measure into eight eighth notes. There is truly a different musical sense inherent in the idea of back beat.

One way of thinking of back beat is that it is almost like an echo. It's interesting to note that the whole notion of back beat took a big leap in popularity with the development of tape recording and the discovery of tape echo.

Recording engineers found that by being able to record a sound and play it back after a very slight interval, usually just about an eighth note later, a very distinctive and identifiable effect could be achieved. This sound is so prevalent in the recordings of the fifties that it is often used in the studio today when the producer wants to invoke the nostalgia many people feel for the records of that era.

Les Paul, Elvis Presley, Eddie Cochran, Ricky Nelson, Carl Perkins, and of course, Chuck Berry all made well-known recordings using "tape slap" and all these songs have a strong back beat. The electric guitar seems to be one of the sounds besides the human voice that is flattered by the tape slap effect. So much so, that for years until the advent of digital reverb units, most guitarists carried with them a tape echo unit, and wouldn't be caught on the bandstand without one.

3.14 Polyrhythmic Beats

In the late fifties, Richie Valens recorded a traditional wedding song from Mexico called "La Bamba." It had a very distinctive rhythmic pattern which immediately became very popular and has been re-recorded hundreds of times. The most recent revival of this song was by the group Los Lobos.

There were two things going for this song besides a catchy lyric. One was a very memorable guitar riff used in the introduction and generously throughout the song, and the other was the rhythmic figure which underlay the guitar riff and chugged along through the song.

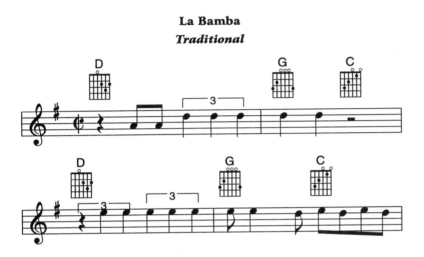

There are many wonderful rhythmic forms to be found in the traditions of Mexico, Latin America, and South America. Among these are the rhumba, the cha cha, the conga, and many folk dances. Over the years there have been times when each of these forms has enjoyed popularity. It is useful to understand the underlying rhythmic elements since these can inspire and improve our songs in many ways.

One of these rhythmic patterns from Mexico is called *huapango*. I believe the name of this rhythm comes from the sound that is made when this rhythm is played on the guitar. Like many others of these rhythmic figures, slapping and strumming are combined to emphasize the notes.

Bo Diddley

Elias McDaniel, known to us as Bo Diddley, established his fame and went on to make a whole career out of one rhythmic pattern. This is the now very familiar pattern of:

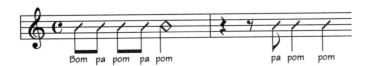

So many of his songs used this device that it is inseparable from our sense of his music. In the original tune, a line of lyric is sung and then the rhythmic pattern is played, then another line of lyric, and another time through the pattern, and so on.

"Bo-Diddley, Bo-Diddley where you been?
(Bom-pa-pom-pa-pom,-pa-pom-pom,)
'Round the world and back again."
(Bom-pa-pom-pa-pom,-pa-pom-pom,)

Willy & the Hand Jive

Johnny Otis is one of the true greats of early rock and roll and is still a fine musician today, though now the full-time pastor of a church in South Central Los Angeles. He had a large touring band, discovered and developed many blues and rhythm and blues artists, among them, Jackie Wilson, Hank Ballard, Big Mama Thornton, and Little Willie John, the writer of "Fever." He wrote many standards including "Harlem Nocturne" and produced some of Little Richards' early recordings.

Otis had his own version of the same rhythmic figure that we identify with Bo Diddley and with it he created a big hit song in the mid-fifties called "Willy and the Hand Jive." By developing a series of hand claps and circular motions rolling one hand over the other, almost like reeling in a coil of rope, Otis created a series of movements which were like a new dance and could be done by dancers. These motions accompanied the song and as the song went through its verses, the motions adapted to tell the story.

In the last verse, "Way out Willy gave 'em all a treat, By doing that hand jive with his feet," needless to say, the dancers would accommodate with hands and feet at the same time.

Dance Rhythms

There is much more to be discovered about the rhythmic aspects of songs and dances. Here is a partial list of the kinds of dances that are associated with the different time signatures:

2/2 Charleston, Pavane.

2/4 Basse Danse, Bergamasca, Black Bottom, Branle, Cha-cha, Galop, Habanera, Hornpipe, Los Matlanchines, Maxixe, Marengue, Moresque, Morris Dance, Paso Doble, Polka, Reel, Rigaudon, Rumba, Samba, Schottische, Shimmy, Tango, Trescone.

3/2 Tordion.

3/4 Allemande, Basse Danse, Bolero, Bourree, Chaconne,
    Courante, Fandango, Galliard, Jig, Jota, Mazurka, Minuet,
    Passapied, Polka-Mazurka, Polonaise, Redowa, Saltarello,
    Saraband, Seguidillas, La Volta, Waltz.

4/4 Barn Dance, Cha-Cha, Fox Trot, Gavotte, Hornpipe, Mambo,
    Morris Dance, Piva, Quadernaria, Rigaudon, Rock Dances,
    Rumba, Running Set, Strathspey, Tango.

6/4 Slow Courante.

6/8 Fandango, Farandole, Furlana, Jig, Tarantella, Two-Step.

9/9 Jig.

12/8 Jig.

Tunes which don't adhere to a regular meter but insert extra notes
or phrases are called "crooked tunes."

3.15 Words & Their Meanings

Words are loaded with meaning. Even more so when you start to
put them together. Words play. There is an effect almost like magne-
tism when words start to work off each other. Sometimes this can
work against your intended meaning, just like magnets which are re-
pelling, and sometimes this can work for you and create a strong pull
on the listener's sensibilities.

Ambiguity

Ambiguity means literally that something can be taken more than
one way. We've all had a good laugh at someone else's expense when
they said what they thought they meant and what they said also meant
something that they would not have said had they known that what
they said also meant that.

I remember one woman who was so exasperated at her young
son who kept putting her off with "just a sec, Mom," that she shouted
out for all the neighbors to hear, "I am sick and tired of secs!"

In songs, we are always grappling with words and their many
unwieldy extra meanings. It seems we always have to be alert for
those errant inferences. If we were trying to write an inspiring line
about being a good influence on our children, we might think to
say, "Give the children a way!", but this would be very readily
seen as a mistake. In the film *Carnal Knowledge,* Candice Bergen
told Jack Nicholson and Art Garfunkel about thinking as a child
in school that she was singing about a little bear when she sang.
"Gladly the cross I'd (eyed) bear."

Even though words often seem to have their mischievous evil twins or even triplets, ambiguity can also be a good friend to the songwriter. There are many times when you are not ready to say that something is one thing or another and you find that saying a third thing that is, in a way, both things is the best thing to do. In my song about Johnny Appleseed, I was pleased to discover that I could say "You really are a friend indeed," and have the benefit of both interpretations, "indeed" and "in deed" working for me, almost as if I had said both things.

This helpful ambiguity is often just a lucky accident, but as you work with words more and more, you may find that these accidents are more likely to occur and embellish your work. This is especially true if you work at it by collecting words with interesting qualities and remembering puns and jokes that use them.

One place where this language of controlled ambiguity can yield real profits is in song titles. This is true in all fields of music but is most obvious on the country charts.

Chart singles and double entendre:

"She's acting single, I'm drinkin' doubles"
"It's Your Call"
"On the Other Hand"

3.16 Title Nobility

A good title can represent the song well to us. Pique our curiosity. At the very least, the title should relate to the song well enough so that we can find the song when we are looking for it. But titles often do so much more. Titles capture our attention with some common wisdom or time-honored phrases.

Where Do Great Titles Come From?

Anything that seems to have an extra something about it makes a good title. If it makes us stop and think or seems ironic or poignant it will pull us into the song. Many of the phrases which make good titles already have that going for them. Some of the phrases take on new meaning within the context of our song. For instance the old saying "Family Tradition" means something very different when Hank Jr. sings about the traits of behaviour he shares with his dad, Hank Sr.

Sayings as song titles:

"As Time Goes By"
"A String of Pearls"
"Behind Closed Doors"
"Big Girls Don't Cry"

"Blue Monday"
"Born Too Late"
"Break It To Me Gently"
"Brown Sugar"
"Chances Are"
"Dime a Dozen"
"Don't Get Around Much Anymore"
"For All We Know"
"For Once In My Life"
"Good Time Charlie"
"Goin' Steady"
"Great Balls of Fire"
"The Great Pretender"
"Heart and Soul"
"In The Mood"
"In The Still Of The Night"
"It Don't Matter To Me"
"It's Only Make Believe"
"Let It Be"
"Livin' In a Fool's Paradise"
"The Man In The Mirror"
"My Girl"
"Return To Sender"
"Smoke Gets In Your Eyes"
"Sweet Nothin's"
"Take The Money and Run"
"Takin' Care Of Business"
"Tell It Like It Is"
"Tell Me Why"
"That'll Be The Day"
"Too Late To Turn Back Now"
"Under My Thumb"
"Walk On By"
"What's New"
"The Wind Beneath My Wings"
"You've Got a Friend"

> *You can start with even the most worn out old saw and with a good idea you can add another dimension to it.*

When does time honored wisdom become cliche? When has it been said just too many times? You can start with even the most worn-out old saw and with a good idea you can add another dimension to it.

Cliches Taken to the Next Step

You can get a lot of new energy out of an old cliche by using it in a way that shows that you know full well what you're saying, and what you are saying by saying it. There are many good examples of folks who took a well-worn slogan and recharged it by giving it a little twist that plays off of our expectations. Here are a few:

"Friends In Low Places"
"One of These Nights"
"She's Got the Rhythm and I Got the Blues"
"I Second That Emotion"
"Cross My Broken Heart"
"I Had Too Much to Dream Last Night"
"Stop In the Name of Love"
"Put Yourself In My Shoes"
"We'll Burn That Bridge When We Come To It"

Puns:

"Cleopatra, Queen of Denial"
"Guitarzan"
"My Sugar Is So Refined"

Words of wisdom:

"Don't Leave Your Sugar Standin' In the Rain"
"You've Got To Stand For Something, Or You'll Fall For Anything"

A Dictionary of Cliches

Even though it would be great to find a list of every expression that has been in popular use, such a list does not really exist. Each of us has back pages of a notebook with possible titles we've come across but it would take a lifetime to compile a list of every catchy phrase even if we just kept track of the ones we hear.

There are, however, several books that come close to being useful lists of cliches and common expressions. One of them is *Partridge's Dictionary of American Slang*. This book is particularly useful when writing story songs and character songs.

There are dictionaries of contemporary usage. The reference section of any library will provide you with many useful books which list all kinds of language listed by every conceivable attribute. Books of quotations are filled with colorful language. The thesaurus is the most common reference book besides the dictionary.

The typical entry in a thesaurus will give you a dozen synonyms for almost any word. An example would be for the word "renovate": my paperback thesaurus gives "repair, mend, fix, remake, revamp, modernize, redecorate, restore, and refurbish." Run each of these quickly through your rhyming dictionary and you have lots of good healthy words and phrases ready to go to work for you.

What's In a Name?

Many wonderful songs have been written with people's names in the title. Sometimes just a name and sometimes a memorable phrase with a name. Here are some of the women's names:

"Amy"
"Barbara Ann"
"Billie Jean"
"Delilah"
"Delta Dawn"
"Dizzy Miss Lizzy"
"The Lonesome Death of Hattie Carroll"
"Lucille"
"Lucy In the Sky With Diamonds"
"Maybelline"
"Norma Jean"
"Polk Salad Annie"
"Rhiannon"
"Sweet Caroline"

And some of the men:

"Bad Bad Leroy Brown"
"Duke of Earl"
"Dumas Walker"
"Hey Joe"
"I'm Henry the Eighth"
"Johnny B. Goode"
"Kawliga"
"Louie, Louie"
"Mr. Bojangles"
"Ode to Billy Joe"
"Running Bear"
"Reuben James"
"Stagger Lee"

What about place names?

"Alabama Waltz"
"The Battle of New Orleans"
"California Dreamin' "
"Chattanooga Choo Choo"
"Dixie"
"Does Fort Worth Ever Cross Your Mind?"
"Georgia"
"Houston"
"Kansas City"

"Key Largo"
"Lodi"
"Luckenbach, Texas"
"Memphis"
"Missouri Waltz"
"Moonlight In Vermont"
"New York, New York"
"Penny Lane"
"Rose of San Antone"
"Tobacco Road"

3.17 Synesthetics

Literally, a mixture of senses, the conscious use of synesthetic images can really lend power to a song. A combining of the language of sight, smell, taste, feel, and hearing can make a moment in the song come to life. This phenomenon may also account for the longevity of some songs which just seem to connect with us at a deep and possibly unconscious level.

In the Van Morrison classic "Brown Eyed Girl," lines like: "Slippin' and slidin' all along the waterfall with you" and "Makin' love in the green grass behind the stadium" carry with them a potent sensuality and stay with us.

Speaking of brown eyes, Crystal Gayle has established a lasting synesthetic image with her song, "Don't It Make My Brown Eyes Blue."

The song, "The Presence," with words by S. MacGregor and music by Archie Fisher, has many beautiful examples of poetic lines that have about them a quality of synesthetic metaphor.

"It was out on the long spring grass, she said
When the night was soft on the hill.
He touched my ear with his voice, she said
And my blood ran sweet and chill."

And in a later verse;

"He never came back to my father's byre,
But on an April night
When the moon sits fat on a scudding cloud
And the stars are quick and white
I have known his clutch like a cloak of fire
His limbs like swords of light."

4.

Songwriting Mechanics
Part 3: Words & Music Together

4.1 Introduction to Songwriting Techniques

Some writers can make the form speak for them. Some songs seem so perfect as to be beyond technique. But, though seemingly wonderful accidents or gifts from beyond may appear in our songs, the writing can be approached in a methodical way. My experience is that the lucky accident tends to come more often in the course of regular writing time, and while it is good to be open to inspiration, you don't have to wait to be inspired.

4.2 "Courting the Muse"
by Lou & Peter Berryman

No Subject Is Too Small

Lynda J. Barry says, "No subject is too small." Maybe it's these new bifocals, but I agree. Our songs often fixate on details, so when it comes to discussing songwriting itself, it doesn't surprise me that we find ourselves being drawn to the details of that, too. So for now we leave the loftier considerations of creativity up in the loft. Here is a condensed, Heloise-style list of a few of the conventions and inventions we use in our own writing.

For a Muzak protest song, instead of writing "Muzak Stinks," write "Whatdjasay Joe?," about conversation in Muzakland, or an imitation of how rap will sound when Muzaked. These angular approaches are called "devices." While cruising for subjects, cruise for devices, too. Often they entail having the song say more about the narrator than about the ostensible subject. "How Young The Cops" could be about the singer's aging, which is never mentioned directly. The device, often a song's most interesting aspect, can be lyrical, musical or both.

For subject and device inspiration, check writings with song-length ideas, like poems, reviews, letters, router instructions, classified ads, graffiti, comics, obituaries, and prescriptions. Eavesdrop. Paraphrase or parody an existing song. Write a special interest song, like a march, anthem, holiday song, or jingle. Try a list song. Steal ideas from paintings and photographs. Write a song around one word like "folderol." Think small: feature the postmark and paper cut. Write about contemporary things (silicon caulk, modems) even though they may feel "unsongy" at first; you have our permission. If stuck for a chorus or verse idea, look for something appropriate in your old half-finished songs.

To warm up, write three pages of nonsense, until words are popping like popcorn. Song ideas can come out of wordplay. If you don't have a melody yet, use a working melody: write new lyrics to "Jingle Bells," then rewrite the melody; this keeps your meter consistent. Try writing in a nonspecific gender, even lusty love songs: this doubles the size of your empathic audience and prevents sexism. Experiment with different rhyme schemes, meters, and stanza patterns. Play with the tenses and voices: "One goes to the doctor" is more ominous than "I went to the doctor."

Words should tumble out easily, particularly in a fast song. Keep a low s-count. Watch words joined with the same sound, like "half-fast." Beware of bunched-up consonants, as in "packed clay." Street usage has good flow; "Djeverava" for "did you ever have a."

Avoid diffident words like "just" as in "I just want your love"; they weaken your point. Make every word count: "She went over to the store and got a newspaper" and "Jean hitched north to Don's Bait and stole a Wall Street Journal" both have thirteen syllables. If you don't have one, don't write for a Southern or other accent (unless it's as a device). Use repetition, as in "Irene Goodnight." If a song needs perspective, try adding a bridge.

> **To warm up, write three pages of nonsense, until words are popping like popcorn.**

Write with a crummy instrument or no instrument; a fancy guitar can make bad writing sound good. A tape recorder is handy for trying out rounds and two part songs with your live self as second voice; use it in the car for ideas. Have a rhyming dictionary, thesaurus, encyclopedia, atlas, and other reference books, within reach. Display an alphabet so you can eyeball it while looking for rhymes: aab, bab, cab, dab...

Every verse should have its own raison d'etre.

Use product names, people names, place names: if Sally Rogers would have written "Lovely Wife," instead of "Lovely Agnes," and had said "We'll cross over the lake again" instead of "We'll cross over Lake Michigan," the song would have lost its wonderful verisimilitude.

If you need to use an awkward rhyme, try to put the forced rhyme first: "I'm mad as fudge, my horse won't budge" sounds less forced than "My horse won't budge, I'm mad as fudge." If you're stuck, try place names and proper names.

If you're sailing along, keep going until it's done and edit later or risk losing momentum. If you think your lyrics may be cloying, imagine some creep singing them; if you can stand that, they're okay. When a subject is exhausted but the song is too short, add to the beginning instead of the end.

Develop the melody before, or at least along with, the chords. For plaintive melodies, don't use the tonic much; hang around the fifth. For grounding melodies, return to the tonic often, as in "Amazing Grace." Use a single melody line as a base and develop it by inversion, raising or lowering it, or putting it in a different chord, instead of joining lots of totally different melodies. Listen for the melodies of conversation. Find the natural time signature of your subject before writing the melody: Antimacassar Embroidery sounds like a waltz. When writing the melody before the lyrics, test it using gibberish.

Save everything. Work after you want to quit; that's when good stuff happens.

Finally, use only those suggestions that work for you. As a matter of fact, one device can be the breaking of a writing rule. "Mairsy Doats" is a good song *because* it defies the rule that words should be understandable.

Some songs need lots of technical analysis and twiddling, while others (whoopee songs) almost write themselves. When you analyze a whoopee song, often it has automatically conformed to the conventions you've applied painstakingly to difficult songs. Neither is intrinsically better, and a whoopee song often comes after a grueling session with a difficult song, without which you would end up with neither.

Keep grueling. As we say in the flatlands, no plain, no grain.

> "Every morning between nine and twelve I go to my room and sit before a piece of paper. Many times I just sit for three hours with no ideas coming to me. But I know one thing, if an idea does come between nine and twelve, I am there ready for it."
> — FLANNERY O'CONNOR

4.3 Getting Down to the Writing

> "Prose writing is architecture not interior decoration."
> — ERNEST HEMINGWAY

Doing What Songwriters Do

1. Write often. If you can, try to write every day ... even for a few minutes. Don't just wait for inspiration. Morning time is good for many people because it seems that there is a clarity as well as an abundance of energy available. Some people prefer late at night when there is unbroken quiet time and a chance to reflect on the days events.

    I work up to a draft of a full song, taking some of the writing time to work on details of lyrics or melody but then, if only for reference the next time I get to work, aiming to get one whole version of the song down on a cassette before I quit.

2. Many writers will tell you that ritual is important – that special blue pen, a certain kind of paper, or a certain coffee cup. Some start with the coffee, and some reward themselves with a cup of tea or even a snack. Some wear a lucky shirt or slippers or arrange the objects on their desks in a certain way. It seems that it is the comfortable reassurance of predictable order that helps concentration.

3. You are more likely to make time for the writing if you are facing a deadline, or if a collaborator is expecting you to do your part. It's hard for a writer to "stay on the case" because there is more to the writing than simple perseverance. But as songs are important to us, we find ways to bring them along even though the process doesn't seem suited to an assembly line.

4. Allow yourself an occasional escape or digression while still sustaining the tenuous process of songwriting. For me, walking is the best way to resolve the ambivalence of working on the song while not working on it. For others it may be driving or housecleaning but all writers have their ways of getting out of their own way.

"'Fool,' said my muse to me, 'look in thy heart and write!'"
— Sir Philip Sidney

5. Songwriters often experience blocks. Sometimes the writing seems to be held up in traffic and sometimes it just runs out of gas. This may be the minds way of telling us to stop ringing the doorbell and leave a note and go on. Getting back into the flow may just be a matter of taking up a different section of the song or recopying what we've done before, or getting up and reciting the words as the character in a play.

6. Songwriting is often a matter of successive approximations. The first draft may be just a dummy construction of a certain rhythmic beat, and a bunch of nonsense syllables leading to a tentative setting of the "hook" phrase. Or, if no title or "hook" are yet a part of the song, it may be that a few lines of poetry or a few notes of melody represent the song while its embryo is forming.

    Tom Campbell used to sit in the back yard under his favorite tree and sing indistinct syllables while he played the chords to a new song until the sounds formed into recognizable words. It's good to employ a combination of these activities to make progress on a song.

7. It's also good to cultivate the ability to step out of and back into the song. Hearing the song as others will hear it may require you to do some selective forgetting. Here again taking a break after getting a draft down on the cassette may be a good idea. You can come back to it with fresh ears.

8. Have faith. Good writing is generative. That is, it leads to good writing. Think, and jot down the ideas as they form, but let them keep coming before you force them to fit into a master plan. It may well be that the best idea or the special title or unique thought is just ahead of you.

> *"How do I know what I think until I see what I say?"*
> — E.M. FORSTER

9. There is a recursive aspect to writing. Going back over what you have done is helpful to recenter your thoughts. It may be very difficult to get back to that moment of inspiration but you may be able to explore it in retrospect. This will help you to decide which are the really relevant parts of what you have done and give you enough "raw" materials to make some choices.

10. Let the song have the opportunity to be fully realized over a series of encounters. Most songwriters expect to rewrite and are happy to show the song at any stage of its development to get some perspective on it. Don't feel you have to answer to every comment that is made. Sometimes those comments simply say more about the listener's own ideas about songs than real objective criticism. By being willing to let the song live as many lives as a cat, we will eventually come to the balance of things that really make the song live.

    My friend Bill Bergquist mentioned to me that it is not unusual for him to do fifteen drafts of a book. He asked if that was true for songs as well, and I realized that I may play and sing a song hundreds of times in the course of working on it, and in the hours I'm not working on the song I also think of ways to improve it.

> *"I start my work by asking a question and then trying to answer it."*
> — MARY SETTLE

It's good to listen to good songs ... and to sing the ones you really like, too. Not for ideas so much – and not to borrow or copy – but just to remember what songs are. Just to get the taste in your mouth. Listen to the best; it's more inspiring. Don't worry about being intimidated, look ahead.

4.4 Think, Then Write

*"My working habits are simple: long periods of thinking,
short periods of writing."*
— ERNEST HEMINGWAY

It may seem from this that only important thoughts or finished thoughts should be written down. Let the writing be guided by the thought and let it take the time that thought takes. Let the editor inside you have a shot at it later. For now just let it flow. Many writing teachers and workshops encourage timed sessions of five or ten minutes. This can be a good way to create a body of background for a song that will give you something to edit.

This back and forth from the writer to the editor can be a very productive dialogue, as long as nobody insists on keeping the ball. Another way of expressing this process is as if you were taking one step and then another. A little bit of progress in the melody, a little better setting of a phrase, a little more idea of who the characters are and what has happened to them, and a little clearer sense of what the song will ultimately sound like.

*"Get it down. Take chances. It may be bad, but it's the only way
you can do anything really good."*
— WILLIAM FAULKNER

"Write On! Don't Think, Just Write."

*"The only way to find out who you are as a writer is to let 'er rip
and write on!"*

*"Writing is just a man alone in the room with the English language,
trying to make it come out right. The important thing is that your
work be something no one else could do."*
— JOHN BERRYMAN

4.5 Get Some Exercise

Timed Writing Exercises

Many writers begin with a timed writing exercise. It's a good way to get the words flowing. Don't try to write actual song lines, but if a good line should come to you, that's fine. Most people use this opportunity to write "around" the song. Write about what the song is about, and let that give way to some examples of dialogue or sayings that fit. Just getting down the page may give you the opportunity to observe something that "you just can't see from here."

Many times you will "write yourself around the corner." You will end up in a different song than you started in. Many times the last line of the song will become the basis for a whole new song, or the song will take place long after the events which are originally the subject of the song have happened. Deciding what goes with what is partly a process that the editor will sort out and partly something that comes to you in unexplainable ways during this fast and loose prewriting.

"Every thought is a feat of association. All thought is a feat of association: having what's in front of you bring up something in your mind that you almost didn't know you knew. Putting this and that together. That Click."
— ROBERT FROST

Some Tricks with Paper & Pen

Many writers keep a small notebook with them to jot down ideas. Some use a portable cassette recorder in the car, but even a folded piece of paper in your wallet will serve for a week's worth of random thoughts and will relieve you of the need to think about remembering them. A glance at these notes will enable you to keep the songwriting process going even during the odd moments of waiting to get your teeth cleaned or for the light to change.

"I keep a small sheaf of three-by-five cards in my billfold. If I think of a good sentence, I'll write it down. It won't be an idea ... what I put down is an actual line of intended text."
— JOSEPH HELLER

Do It Today

Perhaps the best writing exercise of all is just allowing time for the writing. I know the song will progress if I just give it the time. Slow and steady is much more productive in the long run that the hurry up and get it done.

5.

Your Own Worst Critic,
(& Best)

"Real criticism begins in the capacity to grieve because that is the most visceral announcement that things are not right."
— WALTER BRUEGGEMANN

5.1 Give Yourself the Benefit of the Doubt

We can be awfully rough on ourselves at times, and writing is one of those activities we have a hard time giving ourselves a chance to do. We want to see something right now, and it had better be good.

I have learned to be a little more charitable to myself in hopes of keeping it all going so that I have something to criticize. I say things like, "I know it's good. I may not know how good it is, and I may never know, but I know it's good and I can build on it." I also know that my best writing is ahead of me and that's where I'm going.

It's good to get feedback from people who have dealt with the same problems and have found ways to explain and help you to see the potential in your work. Even in the worst case, all any of us is asking for is the chance to see how we can improve what we do. I've heard that some poets would struggle and search for a word for weeks. Gene Shay reminded me of a placque that hangs in Mark Twain's boyhood home in Hannibal, Missouri. It says, "The difference between the right word and the almost right word is like the difference between lightning and a lightning bug!"

"I've been in writing workshops where we have worked on a bad poem, criticizing it for twenty minutes. That's ridiculous. It's a waste of time. You can have confidence that the writer of that poem will write other poems ... (you can say) 'There's some good stuff here, but it just doesn't make it.' And go on. It's a good process to be willing to just let go."
— NATALIE GOLDBERG, (FROM *WRITING DOWN THE BONES*)

Usually there is some good in any thought or line. Try to get back to the moment when the thought occurred to you. Try to feel what it was that was going on and let the thought come through again or give a little thought to what it was that attracted you to an idea in the first place. Sometimes by stating something as a question or by putting it in someone else's mouth as a line of dialogue you can expand on its meaning and find another aspect of the idea.

Sometimes things just come out spontaneously and strike us as strong language. It can take some time to find the most effective setting or figure out how the line relates to the rest of a song. In collaboration, a writing partner can just react subjectively to a line or two and take the song in a whole new direction. Often someone else can hear things in a song idea to which we are too close to have a fresh idea. There is no reason, at any point in its development, that a writer can't hear the song as if for the first time, but this is a trick that may take awhile to learn.

"If only one line of the poem has energy, then cut the rest out and leave only that line."
— William Carlos Williams

5.2 Second Verse, Same As the First

The second verse problem is always there. You've written a great first verse, led us into the chorus, the chorus lifts beautifully, and comes to a perfect resolution, then what? You've got to go back – not to square one, but where?

One way I like to envision this problem is as if we were going up the mountain again, but this time from a different side. There are different considerations in this verse, it takes on a different area of experience. If we come up with the right approach, we may find when we get to the place from where we can all see the top of the mountain this time, that we will be pleasantly surprised to find that the chorus has taken on another meaning which takes the first time chorus to a new level of profundity or universality.

5.3 Are You Hearing What Isn't There?

You can fool yourself as you sort out subsequent drafts of a song. Have you kept track of all the thoughts that lead up to this point, did you say that or did you just assume it was understood ... did that idea get left out of the verse with the previous draft?

Popular among classical composers was what is called *word painting*. This was the practice of placing notes on the page in such a way as to create forms and symbols. For instance, if the choir was to sing a line referring to Christ on the cross, the notes might intersect between the parts to actually create a cross on the page of music. This could not be seen by anyone not looking at the music and was not heard in any way that it could be recognized by the listener but was just written in as a gesture by the composer.

Names, as has been mentioned earlier, were often spelled out in musical notes. Bach's name was often written into musical scores (with the "h" represented as an "a," the note above "g").

As songwriters we have to concern ourselves with what is heard and how its effect on the listener can be better understood. We may have some personal reason for placing some element in the song which only the initiated will understand, but most of the time it's difficult enough just to balance the notes and the words to the satisfaction of the audience.

You Mean It's Not Done?

With experience comes the ability to better understand what is lacking in a song or what level of the song might benefit from additional work. As we listen to hundreds of songs we begin to have a sense of what territory a song is claiming, what emotional language the song is speaking, and how it might succeed in its chosen mission in terms of what songs have done before.

It's always possible to do what has never been done before, but even this possibility seems to be subject to the dynamics of human perceptions and musical and verbal expectations. This work of reconciling originality and convention, inspiration and structure, is the constant concern of the professional songwriter.

"There are, it seems, two Muses: the Muse of Inspiration, who gives us inarticulate visions and desires, and the Muse of Realization, who returns again and again to say, 'It is yet more difficult than you thought.' This is the muse of form.

"... It may be, then, that form serves us best when it works as an obstruction to baffle us and deflect our intended course. It may be that when we no longer know what to do we have come to our real work and that when we no longer know which way to go we have begun our real journey. The mind that is not baffled is not employed. The impeded stream is the one that sings."
— WENDELL BERRY

Is form the cornerstone of good writing, or is it the millstone? Isn't it true that the more we work with these things the easier it is to just see them as suggestions and sense the new and original things that may work within the form?

Songwriting and The Creative Process

"Grammar is to a writer what anatomy is to a sculptor, or the scales to a musician. You may loath it, it may bore you, but nothing will replace it, and once mastered it will support you like a rock."
— B.J. CHUTE

5.4 The Stack of Plates Theory

If you can think of the song as many songs existing at the same time like a stack of plates that can be unstacked and restacked, you can develop the ability to examine each layer for its own values and to more effectively understand the interaction of the different layers. Some of the layers or plates can be described as follows. Can you see how some of these layers interact? Use these ideas to analyze the best songs you know.

The Melodic Song

Do-re-mi. Can you whistle the tune? Does it sound too familiar? If you heard a Muzak arrangement of it on an elevator would it have its own recognizable identity?

The Harmonic Song

Major or minor, diminished or augmented chords or intervals. Is there a sense of resolution? Do the song's harmonic elements seem to be well integrated and memorable?

It's always possible to do what has never been done before ...

The Rhythmic Song

Dum-diddly-dum-dum, dum-dum! Can you dance, walk, or dream along with the song? Does it have its own clock and is it rhythmically interesting or even enchanting? Does the language chafe and grate or does it resonate?

The Rhyme Scheme of the Song

ABAB, AABB, AABC-DDEC, etc. Are the rhymes true rhymes? Are there other forms of alliteration? Are the rhymes natural and conversational? Do your choices honor the listener?

The Thoughtful Song

The treatment of strong lines and ideas. Are there original thoughts? Are there thoughtful lines? Are they presented in a conversational and singable way?

The Structural Song

Verse, chorus, bridge, refrain, intro, outro, fade, tempo changes, instrumental breaks and riffs. Does the structure seem fresh, appropriate and musical?

The Story of the Song

Does the song begin somewhere and go somewhere? Does the second verse merely restate the first verse? Is there a sense of having made progress in the course of the song?

Central Concept

Usually the title, or "bottom line." The essential element or concept that brought the song about. Is it valid? Is the idea worthy of a song and is it handled well?

"Hooks"

Musical or lyrical devices that "hook" the listener. Some of these devices can be very subliminal. Are they effective? Are they used smoothly and tastefully?

The Geography of the Song

The soft meadows, the rugged peaks, the romantic hills. The hard climb, the rapid slide, the sense of journey, the sense of coming home.

The Mood Song

Is there a quality of nonverbal, synesthetic expression to the song? Have we worked it too long, or not long enough? Have we lost the first sense?

The Character Song

Who are the characters in the song? Are the characters balanced, consistent and interesting? Can the listener empathize? Is the language "in" character?

The Speaker

Who is speaking? Is he or she intensely involved, dispassionate, ironic, undergoing a process of learning as the song unfolds, humorous, wistful, singing to someone in particular? Do we believe we know this person? Is it me?

5.5 The Principles of Rewriting by Rick Beresford

Lyric Rewriting

Just a few brief comments about writing in general and the "first write." I treat myself with kindness. I try to consider myself a great songwriter at all times. Even when I'm down, I'm a master songwriter who is down. This really makes a difference in my results.

Try writing in one phrase or sentence what the song is really about.

I encounter my craft with great intensity, knowing there is no other way to make progress. This may be the single most important bit of knowledge I've learned in the study of songwriting. I test my limits every day, honor my curiosity, listen to my wild mind, nurture my sense of humor, and have no fear of mistakes. I know that great results may come only after many failed attempts. In short, I explore the possibilities.

Because no two creative moments are the same, when an idea comes to me, I *overwrite* until my creativity is exhausted. I often get my best ideas at the end of these sessions. After this wild and lengthy first write I use the following six principles to hone my song into the pocket, keeping in mind that rewriting can be creative and fun and that the results are well worth the effort. Much thanks to Bob Gibson, the first director of the Kerrville Songwriting School for his brilliant teachings, many of which are incorporated in this chapter.

Headlining

At the top left hand corner of the title page, I try writing in one phrase or sentence what the song is really about. I'm talking about the emotional message, the old-fashioned emotion or truism. As Charles John Quarto once told me, to give an example, "'Send in the Clowns' is not about the circus." The emotional message could read, "the reality of breaking up is very painful." That is the headline. I sometimes start the headline by simply stating, "what I really mean to say is ... ." Any side issues or plots need to be edited out and moved to another page called "New Ideas and Lines" where they can be expanded on at another time.

Does the song have an interesting angle – a "new" way of expressing this old-fashioned emotion? I can start to write a song without an angle but I can't finish a song without a good angle. A great line is fine as far as it goes, but a great angle can be expanded into an interesting plot with a logical conclusion.

Detailing

Detail is that little hint of color here and there using my personal history that gives my song its style and signature. One of my favorite writers doesn't start writing a song until he can see a clear "painting" of his song, the setting, time, characters and their actions. He also "sees" the characters' feelings and questions, knows their dialogue, their inner dialogue, the reasons and consequences that his heroes know or have missed. This gives his songs import, dynamics and color, interest, impact, and immediacy. I try to make sure all my songs have this balance of physical and emotional color. As in "headlining," I check to make sure all my details support the emotional message.

I'm always on the alert for "conceits" – those beautifully written, poetic lines that I really love but which, regrettably, do not fit the song. These seemingly pretty lines can dilute the headline. I relegate these poetic rogues to my "New Ideas and Lines" page.

Viewpoint

I make sure the viewpoint of my song is clear. I ask myself: Who is talking? Is the song a narrative or is it someone thinking to himself, reflecting? If a narrative lyric switches to a reflective inner dialogue, does it make sense right away? An example: "Love is the passion. Love is the key. I woke up this morning at quarter 'til three." The first two lines are thinking, but the last one is narrative. It will be a challenge to make this song work because the changing of viewpoints can confuse the listener.

I also check all pronouns, and make sure they don't confuse the listener or detract from the headline. I sometimes switch viewpoints of the characters, for example, you to I, or I to he, to see which is most effective.

I also check the good light factor. I keep in mind that artists, including myself, wish to be seen as nothing less than fantastic in the eyes of an audience. For angry, downgrading, or hopeless songs, placing the song in the third person sets the singer apart from the plot as an observer, thus protecting the artist's good image while enabling him or her to tackle difficult issues.

I also watch for the fine line between sympathy and pity. It's a powerful statement for a man to say he's sorry or a fool for love. It makes him seem more human. But for the same man to say, "I was never good enough for you" takes him out of the good light.

Attitude

I check to make sure both my headline and my details are believable. Less than realistic plots and characters will lose an audience. However, I never let the truth get in the way of a good story. Are my characters and plot reflecting the feelings of the day? I remember what Hugh Prestwood once told me: "Stay hip." I'm careful not to use outdated slang unless it suits the song. I listen to the radio to get a reading on the topics of the moment. For writing commercial songs, I take notes on the do's and don'ts of individual artists. Do they like to sing about relationships? Drinking? Traveling? Zen aerobics?

I check my songs to be sure that my poetry is conversational, that the subjects and the verbs are in their clearest form. If my topic is heavy, I remember that even subtle humor can lighten the song and help drive the message home. If a song can either be positive or negative, I try the positive, the hopeful, first.

Form

For me, there are really only two types of songs: chorus songs and non-chorus songs. They all must have: 1) a setup, 2) a build that leads to 3) a payoff. I look at my lyric to see that the plot is in the proper order. I'm not afraid to reverse the third and first verse, for example, if I feel the third verse is a stronger setup. Ralph Murphy taught me that if my first verse says it all and I feel I cannot write a second verse, instead, to write a verse prior to and leading up to the first verse.

Another easy technique for coming up with that elusive third verse is changing tense. If the song has been in the present tense, how were things yesterday, last month, how will they be tomorrow?

I like most of my songs to have three noticeably different musical sections. This means: verse, chorus, lift, bridge. Even strong intros can be considered separate musical parts.

> *For me, there are really only two types of songs: chorus songs and non-chorus songs.*

Alliteration

The use of similar sounds, either vowels or consonants (like "long lost lover"), is another way of using repetition to bring listeners closer. I am aware of alliteration in rewriting but try not to overuse it.

I check for cram writing, and overspacing, making sure that my meter is satisfying throughout the song. I know the use of fracturing, giving more than one musical note to a single syllable, can help. There is always a way to make a song scan correctly. I never give up until the song is easy to sing.

For lyrics that are hard to rhyme, I use four tricks:

1. Soft rhyme such as "love" and "enough." Because of the surprise they can bring to a lyric.

2. The AAAB rhyme, three lines which rhyme followed by a fourth line which does not. For example, "I know that 'til this day, I've never

found a way, To really come to say, I love you." Now, I don't have to rhyme "I love you," I simply repeat "I love you" at the end of the next section.

3. Burying a difficult ending rhyme in the middle of a longer phrase. I know how hard it is to rhyme "love." So instead of ending my rhyme, "We have love" I could end it with "We have love everyday. Now I'm dealing with a much easier rhyme to match, "ay" instead of "uv."

4. Don't rhyme at all. This usually only works for the first two lines of a four line rhyme pattern. "I'll be there ... Everyday ... You'll know why ... I always cry ..."

I check repetition. Do I have enough? Is it properly placed? I know I can take a hackneyed line like "I love you" and by repeating it three times can convince the listener that it's a powerful lyric.

I also look at the lyric's use of figurative and literal language. Figurative language means metaphors, similes and puns. Literal language means real descriptions of characters, objects and events. If my song is written metaphorically (for instance "Love Finds Its Way Without a Road"), I am careful not to introduce literal language unless it makes complete sense right away. Songs are "flash art." Everything must be understood, make sense, lyrically and melodically, the instant it's heard.

I check the balance of detail and "grand statement." I know that the most powerful points of the song are usually the beginning and end of the verse and the beginning and end of the chorus. In chorus songs the big statement is in the chorus, the detail in the verses. In non-chorus songs, for example, "Somewhere Over the Rainbow" or "Blowing in the Wind," the big statement which is usually the hook and title is at the beginning and/or the end of each section, except maybe the bridge if there is one. So, placement is important. I use a bridge only toward the end of the song because the bridge is used to tie the song together and that kind of information is too revealing for the beginning of the tune.

In summary, I try to keep in mind the balance of all the above aspects in lyric writing. I remember that songs have compression: they say what needs to be said only – no side issues. Yet, they breathe: have a feeling of space and rhythm. I also check the balance between repetition and surprise. I call it familiar surprise. I feel strongly that most songs need surprise. However, those surprises should be understood and enjoyed immediately. No time to go back and ponder in songwriting.

Is there an unexpected note, rhyme, rhythm change, chord change, twist of cliché, repeat, pause, stop, note held, or shift in the meaning of

Songwriting and The Creative Process

the hook? All these surprises when used carefully can catapult a song into the hallowed halls of greatness. When rewriting, remember to explore the possibilities and to enjoy the process.

> *"I have never thought of myself as a good writer. Anyone who wants reassurance of that should read one of my first drafts. But I am one of the world's great rewriters. I find that three or four readings are required to comb out the cliches, line up pronouns with their antecedents, and insure agreement in number between subjects and verbs. It is, however, this hard work that produces a style."*
> — JAMES A. MICHENER

5.6 "Courting the Muse" by Nancy White

I used to divide my songs into two categories, the "real songs" and the commissioned songs. Real songs were the inspired ones about love (oh woe) and relationships. The commissioned songs were mainly the topical songs I write for a national radio show in Canada called *Sunday Morning*. For years I thought the real songs had more value, although most people seemed to enjoy the topical ones more.

Eventually, I realized they're all just songs, and the writing process is pretty much the same for them all. (Write a verse. Go to the fridge. Write two lines. Phone a sociologist. Back to the piano, squeeze out a bit more. Check fridge again.) The tight deadlines of the radio show put more pressure on me, of course, but it isn't really that different from the pressure I put on myself.

Well, I'm lying. With a *Sunday Morning* song, if I don't finish it, I don't get paid, and the breathless nation is devastated that weekend. With inspired songs, who cares? Only me.

"Daughters of Feminists" was an inspired song. I wrote it when my first daughter was about 3. A young baby-sitter had described her to me as being "really girly," which shocked me a bit, but it was true. On Halloween, she had to be a fairy, an angel, a princess. She went for a couple of years refusing to wear pants. This is fine, but in a Northern clime, skirts and dresses mean tights for half the year, and tights are always too something. Short, long, itchy, yucky. Mornings we fought and scrounged for clean tights. Pink was the color of choice. She was not too flexible. Cute, though (to paraphrase Utah Phillips).

"Daughters of Feminists" is a simple song, but it wasn't simple to write. I boxed myself in with the first line: "Daughters of feminists like to wear pink and white short frilly dresses, they speak of successes with boys, it annoys their mom." Dresses and successes, boys and annoys were internal rhymes, so I had to find other internal rhymes for the next line, which is why the next line is a bit clumsy. English is a terrible language to write in.

I can't remember much more about writing "Daughters," except that when I got together with my piano player, Bob Johnston, to rehearse it, he made it better. Put in a couple of modulations and added the counterpoint line "daughters of feminists just want to play with their toys." When we recorded it, we got our own daughters to sing that line. Actually Bob (whose musical *Theda Bara and the Frontier Rabbi* is being produced off-Broadway this winter – check it out!) arranged the song so that I can no longer play it. It's so embarrassing. But then, embarrassment is pretty much your constant companion when you have children.

I promised myself not to babble in this article, which is about songwriting, right?

Interviewers always ask songwriters how they write. I usually tell them I write on the piano and use a rhyming dictionary, or I stare at a flame and my hand just starts to move. Then I change the subject.

Actually, I am not a songwriter. I used to think I was. Then a couple of months ago, I got to hear a talk by Stephen Sondheim.

Now I feel like a total hillbilly hack. I bet Stephen doesn't even have to go get a snack when he finishes a verse. But I do subscribe to some of his rules, especially the one about approximate rhyme. I really hate it and try to avoid it. I once lost a chance to write a jingle for someone by pointing out that gum and fun don't rhyme. Yet some of the writers I love most use approximate rhyme with abandon. Take a look at "Closing Time" by Leonard Cohen. If you're a poet, it's okay. But there's something in the brain that goes "ahhh" at the sound of a perfect rhyme, and I think we have a moral obligation to provide the "ahhh" if possible. I hope that doesn't sound too pompous, but I am pedantic about this. Also about parodies, which I consider to be straight-ahead theft. I know. The folk process and all that, but I stand firm.

For me, the hardest part of songwriting is clearing the deck.

Sorry, I blacked out for a while. Where was I? Oh yes, songwriting.

For me, the hardest part of songwriting is clearing the deck. When you free-lance, and especially when you have kids, there's always a mountain of other stuff to do, and working at home is a curse. Some people I know can write music in one room knowing there are noodles on the floor in the room next door – not me.

Then there's career management. Every performance has its own red tape. Phone calls. Rehearsals to organize. Reports to the performing rights organizations. And always things to be mailed. Like many performers, I sell tapes through the mail, and it is so labour-intensive, it's almost not worth it. In Canada, postage varies from region to region. A sale made in your own province includes sales tax; there's also a national tax called the goods and services tax (GST) that's making us old and bitter before our time. But I don't have the volume to hire someone to help, and it's too complicated to turn over to the children.

Consequently, writing a song is about the last thing I find time to do. Fortunately, I write fast, so I'm considered wildly prolific.

Some of the best advice I've read about songwriting was in Peter and Lou Berryman's contribution to a previous "Coutring the Muse" column in *Sing Out!*. It was wonderful, and practical, and I recommend it, and if I had time, I'd take it! I've also heard it's helpful to study the lyrics of Cole Porter. I'm going to do that too. And learn to play my banjo properly. And find the surface of my desk.

Getting back to "Daughters of Feminists" – it's turned out to be a song many people identify with. They tell me so. And happily, one woman told me what a psychologist friend had said about this tendency of daughters of progressive parents to be ultrafeminine. Little girls who do this have identified so strongly with their mothers that they want to look as female as possible. Even if Mom lives in jeans, they've still seen the silhouette on the washroom door. Isn't that nice?

The daughter who inspired my song is almost 8 years old now, and these days she dresses in pants and sweatshirts almost exclusively. But her 4½-year-old sister WILL NOT wear pants. Not even shorts in summertime. The saga continues.

5.7 Coming to Terms with Your Internal Editor

There is a voice within each of us that is ready to say, "oh yeah?", "what do you think you're doin'?" or "what's so good about that?", or "who's gonna listen to that?" Sometimes you find yourself looking over your own shoulder. You may be beating yourself up over something which can be a fullfilling and enjoyable process of discovery if only you can give yourself to it.

At these times it may seem that psychotherapy is in order and it may be, but it is always OK. to devote a few minutes to a song and anything you do with that time is up to you. Hopefully you won't have to win a Grammy before you can justify your songwriting to yourself. You'll just have to give yourself the benefit of the doubt and believe in what you are doing and the work will justify itself.

"In order to take control of our lives and accomplish something of lasting value, sooner or later we need to learn to believe, ... we simply need to believe in the power that's within us, and use it. When we do that, and stop imitating others and competing against them, things begin to work for us."
— BENJAMIN HOFF

5.8 Advice to a Young Poet In the Wings (HA!) by Butch Hancock

i'm tellin' ya kid ... it ain't in the glass ... not in the glass of the bottle ... not even after you've seen gawd's awmighty face scowlin' back at you in neon replicas an reflections on the tiny rim of the mouth of that bottle – and it's not ... not in the glass you pour the contents of the bottle into ... as if there's somethin' civil or moral or spiritual or humane or even proper about doin' that ... like it will dilute the fluid of its duty ... which it won't ... it's just another layer you put between what you're drinkin' an what you're trying to drink ... an it ain't in the dance ... tho' you're wise, if not innocently so, beyond your ears to get your ass out there ... with the slinkiest or the fattest ... or the slowest or the fastest or the firmest or the flabbiest ... or the floppiest or the flattest ... or the craziest or the classiest ... or the cleanest or the clammiest ... SHE-DEVIL-GAWD-ANGEL-WHORE-QUEEN-EARTH-MOTHER-VIR-GIN ... you can possibly find ... and get your moves down tight ... and loose ... an everywhere in between ... cause you're for sure gonna need em when you least want em ... an if you're lucky ... you're gonna want em when you most need em ... no ... it ain't in the dance ... tho that's one of the places you can get as close to it without gettin there as it is possible to get ... and it *is* one of the requisites ... sort of puts you in the general vicinity ... it's not there ... you can't even see it from there ... but sometimes you can actually see its shadow from there ... and ... it ain't in your words ... your songs ... tho you'll soon think it is – cause it'll come whizzin past you ... come whizzin' right thru you when you're writin your best or when you're singin your best ... it'll come an you'll think it came right FROM you ... right outta your own hands or outta your very own throat – it'll feel that good ... but it's long gone like that turkey thru the corn, boy ... long before you even get the twitch of reaction to its been-an-gone-ness ... to its dust in your mouth ... to its long distance rumblings over the horizon ... so don't lie to yourself over *that* one ... it could cost you ... YEARS!!! but don't stop writin or singin either ... get it?

and ... it ain't in the wisecracks ... and the fun ... and the jokes ... and the fronts ya put up ... and the fronts ya put up with ... and it ain't in the laffin ... and it ain't in the cryin ... and it ain't in the laffin just to *keep* from cryin ... and you'll find out too ... it ain't even in the cruel soul-savin' cryin you do – that cryin that is the cryin that keeps you from laffin ...

IT ... for lack of a shorter word ... slips right thru the wisecracks in the walls we build an goes on its merry way ... not even wonderin or carin if we follow ... IT does not wait and ... **it ain't the wind** ... tho it's close – it's close to breath ... tho' it ain't there too ... but you'll think it is when you breathe her breath in your lungs ... and she, yours in hers

and ... i could go on ... and i will ... but that's none of your bizness or anybody else's just yet ... just i'll add ... *YOU'LL GO ON TOO* ... and you'll look under every rock an leaf ... you'll lift every dress an every eyebrow ... you'll look into layers and beyond layers upon layers of this-ness an that-ness an thus-ness an be eternally satisfied and bothered ... disappointed an fulfilled ... and each an every step of the way ... just remember:

DON'T GET ANY SMARTER THAN YOU'RE WILLING TO BE DUMB

if space is curved, so is form in any form ... we don't even see thru a glass darkly ... we see thru minds distorted ... even face to face the best we see of truth is that it too is a mask ...

TRUTH IS A MASK MADE OF LIES

just remember: *EVERY SO OFTEN* ... you must somehow remove it ... so you can put a new one on ... because humans in all their many roles of helpless-ness ... do have a charming little quality ... a continuing small opportunity ... in fact ... and ABILITY to do this thing: to remove the mask that quickly replaces the one they remove

TRUTH IS A MASK MADE OF LIES ... when you wear it out you *will* replace it ... this is your blessing and your curse.

5.9 Self & Self-consciousness

"Virtually every spiritual tradition distinguishes the self-clinging ego from the deeper, creative Self: little self as opposed to big Self. The big Self is transpersonal, beyond any separated individuality, the common ground we all share."
— STEPHEN NACHMANOVITCH

Who's watching?

As hard as it is, it's so important to hear all the voices of our inner wisdom clearly no matter how faintly they may speak to us. So it is important to keep the chorus of wise crackers to a minimum. Don't just take anybody's word for the big things and certainly be cognicent of the built in critics we all carry around with us.

"Inspiration may be a form of superconsciousness, or perhaps of sub-consciousness – I wouldn't know. But I am sure that it is the antithesis of self-consciousness."
— AARON COPLAND

With others, too. Be aware of the difference between the editor and the censor. Be open to the information in what is said, but always be aware that the process and the path are your own.

When we think of our work finding success in the marketplace, that thought can magnify these inhibitions and uncertainties. It's important to establish a strong sense of the value of our writing, the finished product and the process and make sure that we don't sacrifice one for the other.

It helps to be aware that many people in the music business are in the emperor's new clothing business. If they had a healthy regard for the quality and content of songs they would do more of that kind of work and encourage it in others. Just as in the old saying, "You can't cheat an honest man," make sure you are not making the worst of a hard bargain with soft sell. Money may be the least accurate measure of the worth of your writing.

5.10 Writer's Block

The sense of feeling at an impasse or feeling that you are "dry" or somehow unable to come up with a thought is probably just a subjective impression of the moment having no basis in fact. Blocks have nothing to do with your talent or songwriting ability. All writers experience blocks. It's more likely that blocking has something to do with expectations and the desire to be in control of a process which is more complex than you may wish to believe. The impasse may just be the beginning of a new direction and a requisite part of the greater work.

Four Tested Block Busters

For me the best block-breaker is time. I derive a great benefit from just knowing that there is the freedom to experiment with a direction of thought that, if not as succesful as I would like, has not really cost me anything but a little time. It makes "inspiration" that much easier. Like a three-year-old up to his elbows in fingerpaints I can indulge myself in the luxury of the enjoyment of ideas or fantasies, or toy with melodic fragments with little pressure to be brilliant.

The Buddhists talk about the issue of "self-justification" and the need to be able to distance oneself from the imagined critical voices of others in order to be truly present. The songwriter must be willing to provide himself with at least some time for the completely unattached immersion into the creative moment.

Walking is recommended at every stage of the songwriting process. If you are stuck, change your scenery, change your level of physical exertion, just getting up and going for a walk can give you a whole new sense of what you are doing. You don't have to concentrate on the song throughout your whole walking time, just come back to it once in awhile.

Look at what you already have in a new way. Maybe it's the beginning of a song and maybe it's the end. Maybe it happened before the real song begins. Does the idea still inspire you? Is it enough of an idea or is it not quite enough? There are many ways to expand on an idea. Most of them have to do with setting up some activity during which new ideas can present themselves.

Write a letter, write an outline, write an itemized bill.

Go back to the beginning. Tell the story with your hands. What are the colors of things in the song? Is there an unseen irony lurking in the song? Pretend that you had to shout to be heard and had to convey the idea of the song in only a few words. Think of two notes that best represent the song. Change the gender of the characters. Sing the words in reverse order.

Imagine a situation where someone is telling you the story and then tell how you felt about the whole thing. Do a five- or ten-minute timed writing version of the story or character description or other aspect of the song. This is especially helpful if you suspect that one area of the song may still be unexplored.

If you write with a word processor, try this suggestion from a novelist in California. Turn off the screen of your monitor. That's right, write blind. There is something about the feedback of the printed word in front of you that may at times form an attachment or a fixation which is removed when we turn off the monitor. This seems to apply to prose more than to songwriting, but it may be a way to free up our creative energy when we write what the song is about before we write it.

Sometimes progress can be made by acting out the characters in the song.

Yes, Cluster

Clustering is a very useful technique although it has been the subject of ridicule among some writers. Clustering amounts to simply writing down the central thought and in a circle around it writing down every thought that the central thought suggests to you.

If the title of your song is "Down By the River," your cluster might include: water, fog, rain, sunlight, sunlight on the water, glistening, rushing, waterfall, mud, muddy water, gurgling, sliding by, boats, steamboats, horizon, flow, to the sea, cool, clear, etc.

Each of these words or phrases can be the center of its own cluster and in this way you can create a substantial amount of ideas and images with which to develop the song.

Psychodrama and Dress Up

(Just kidding about the dress up part.)

Sometimes progress can be made by acting out the characters in the song. What has happened to them? What would they say about it? In theatrical tradition of Stanislavsky and "The Method," the job of the actor is to get centered in the character. From this place, the actor is able to speak "in character" and saying what the character would say in the way he would say it will give you some realistic dialogue.

I always need to get to the place in the song where I can hear this character come through to me to get a feel for the language and the point of view of the song. Take your time, give yourself a chance to be here now as yourself as well.

Most of all just write. Take the pressure off, give yourself lots of pages of stuff to draw from. Let the editor in you assemble the song out of tons of fresh raw materials. The more the better. Trust that out of a lot of ideas some will fall into place in a way that you can't be expected to know about now and the song will grow and strengthen as you just do your work.

> *"Talent is a question of quantity. Talent does not write one page: it writes three hundred."*
> — JULES RENARD

5.11 "Courting the Muse" by Bill Staines

My Song, My Child or "Lord, Won't Someone Just Send Me A First Line!"

I have long been aware that, for me, music is the voice with which I can best express my deepest and truest feelings. It can be one of the most powerful and wonderful forces that we experience as we make our way through life. It is within us all. It is around us all. It touches us and takes hold of our hearts. It leads us to laughter and softens our tears. As a songwriter, reaching someone with one of your own songs is one of life's great rewards, and for those times I will forever be grateful.

So where does a song come from? I think perhaps in the beginning it is a little bit of magic. Some would call it "the muse" or a gift from some other place. But I think it makes its way into being as a concept, an idea – or, if you will, a zygote – something to be built upon. The creation of this concept is not something that can be taught, but must simply be recognized. Therein lies the writer's ultimate talent.

I have to be by myself – alone in my home or staying at somebody else's place while they're at work. Then the process can begin. I stand about eight inches from a wall (the acoustics are better that way) and begin to bombard the wall with guitar chords, lyrical phrases, verbs, nouns and sounds, some of which are not even in any particular language. If I have been inspired by a person, place or experience, the lyrics will tend to have a direction to them and that will make things easier. At any rate, if I happen to be lucky, before long some combination of those ingredients triggers something inside me that says "There it is! There's that idea. There's my road to travel with the song. There's the magic."

Think of some of the great and lasting concepts for the songs that we all know: "If I had a hammer ... a bell ..." dozens of verses could have been written to Pete and Lee's song. Before the concept there was nothing, then there was a path to travel. That's where the songwriting craft begins – the reason for the song, the rhymes. For me, it's important to make the song as universal as possible. We are all human beings, we all have the same basic feelings about living, dying, home, love and work. It is the sense of that human spirit that, to me, makes a song universal and lasting. (I've heard so many songs lately that really don't have anything to say.)

A song, like a child, needs to be nurtured. A song is meant to be sung, and if it's not, it will die without ever having lived. If you are happy with your song, don't ever be ashamed to sing it in front of others. If it's a strong song, with something to say, it will survive, grow and develop its own relationships. These relationships will have nothing to do with you as a writer. Just as a child grows, so grows a song, meeting new friends, going places, finding its way out into the world and standing on its own. Though a song legally belongs to the writer (providing you haven't relinquished the rights to it), the essence of a good and lasting song eventually becomes part of the greater world of music to be enjoyed by all who will listen.

Occasionally, someone will ask me how I feel about another artist's recording of one of my songs. It's a great feeling to reach someone enough to have them record one of your songs. If the true essence of the piece is not changed, an artist's new interpretation of the song strengthens it. It's nice when it's sung or played in tune, but how each artist or listener relates to a song is a unique thing and is simply another stage in the song's growth.

A good and lasting song really has no life span. The first time someone hears a song, it may as well have been written yesterday – even if it was written 10 years earlier. A writer should never lose faith in a song that truly has something to say. Eventually it will be heard and, like a child, it will leave you for a life of its own.

6.

Inspiration & Perspiration
The Painter Free of His Palette –
The Writer Clear of His Words

As we work with the materials of songwriting the hope is that a facility will come to us so that we can just let the music flow. All writers talk about the magic of those moments when ideas seem to come "through us" as if from another place. The more we work the more likely this will be the case but there will always be those slower and more tentative times.

6.1 Go With the Flow: "Automatic Writing"

In timed writing exercises and at some other times when we have this flow going it seems to be more a matter of believing in the idea that is at hand and letting it have its say than in evaluating it and criticizing it as a final draft. It is important to allow this flow to continue even if we have to "lighten up" as we would if we found our table saw binding up as it cut through a thick piece of wood.

The Grape, the Weed & the Work

Writers and lovers noticed a long time ago that a little of the fermented grape freed up the tongue and the mind to do some of their most effective persuasion. Assuming there was enough to go around, it probably meant that the one being persuaded was a little more receptive as well. Here we have a clue to some of the problems encountered when we rely on a little of the drink or smoke or whatever artificial aid have we to help us produce the work.

When we are under the influence of any substance, be it champagne or catnip, we may "feel" like the magic is happening but it may not be happening for anybody else. Within reason this is OK if it sustains our interest and efforts long enough to produce enough good work so that our editor self can make some sense out of it all later. Given the nature of most of these "helpers," the effect tends to set up a need to get back into the "groove" and this process eventually takes its toll not only on our time and energy but on our perspective as well.

There is a certain kind of work that is not taking place and can't take place until we are "normal" long enough to really sort things out. Residual effects of some substances can postpone awareness far longer than the momentary illusion of awareness that they produce. For the sake of the people around you and the best potential of your own work, you will find as most mature writers have (those who have survived) that it is better to be on top of your form than to be "under" the influence of anything but your own best judgement.

Dionysus & Apollo – Creative Chaos Versus Order & Calm

The ancient Greeks believed that creativity was a struggle between the forces of chaos (the Dionysian) and the forces striving to bring order to chaos (The Apollonian). It is true that in times of upheaval there is much food for creative thought. There is also a lot of upheaval. My sense of it is that there is plenty of struggle in the world and that by being a willing witness to the reality of all struggle, more than enough material for creative work can be found.

By consciously providing quality images and thoughts for the mind to work on and learn from we have the ability to make more fertile the unconscious process of our art. Some of this may require real problem solving, and at times may require that we relinquish our detachment and get involved in some very real issues. There will always be the time for reflection and to make order out of what in reality is pretty chaotic.

"Consciously or unconsciously, all writers employ the dream, even when they're not surrealists. The waking mind, you see, is the least serviceable in the arts. In the process of writing one is struggling to bring out what is unknown to himself. To put down what one is conscious of means nothing, really, gets one nowhere."
— HENRY MILLER

6.2 Creative Listening

We live in a time when there is so much good music. Anyone interested in writing for a commercial market can find a dozen such marketplaces right on the radio dial. In addition to being inspired by what we hear, we can also pick up some less welcome messages. You can get the impression that songs don't always have to be written to a very high standard. Or you can get the idea that some of the "borrowing" that goes on is no big deal, or that the best way to write a "hit" is to simply rehash what was a hit last month.

It's worthwhile to take a hand in your own musical education just as you would nurture the musical development of a child. Be careful what you hear. Seek out the best. Remember why you got interested in songs in the first place. Find more of the real essential "good stuff" even if it means opening up to some new kinds of music. If you want to write a country single then spend some time studying the songs that currently occupy the charts, but don't be limited by the narrow scope of some of the songs you hear.

Is anybody out there? Is there anybody that wants to hear what I want to hear? If you are grooming your own writing for the folks high on the charts then it makes sense to study the protective coloration and trappings and history of those artists, but you should always maintain your own center.

It may be that you will find some aspect of your chosen radio band intolerable. It may be too sexist or too racist or too fundamentalist or a hundred more subtle "ists" but it's not that you are called upon to compromise your own values. It is really more a matter of finding a way to speak to the universal understanding in all of us through your chosen medium.

6.3 An Interview with Charles John Quarto

What can you tell us about the songs that you write?

Charles John: When you have a wide range of objects being called by the same noun, "song," it's like people in the bar talking about love. One of them is feeling something that in contrast to what two others are talking about is absolutely gigantic, and the other two are simply talking about attraction.

I would say initially that the type of song that I'm talking about is a song that has depth in it. That would include songs that have what you might call poetic elaboration and songs that have some magical quality in some instances much bigger than the seeming ingredients of the song. Personally, I don't find the second category to be as rampant as radio often does.

Having said that, what I'm interested in doing is making a sincere impression on myself. So that I would enjoy the finished product regardless of whether or not it had my name attached to it. What we're talking about is an attitude that is more interested in supplying wonder than just cranking out something that may be someone's next single. Whatever "single" means. When did a single stop being a song? I'm not sure, but I'm very happy when it is a song.

Sometimes I literally get a feeling that I'm about to write something. And I go and honor it. My system is a lot like radar when it comes to the idea that I'm about to turn a blank page into something interesting. There's a reliability there that has always been there for me and so it's not so much a question of how do I work as opposed to when do I sit down. I sit down when I have that feeling.

I also have what I would call a very healthy sense of guilt, small "g." What that does for an artist is like saying to yourself, "Hmm, I'm going to bed now, have I earned my rest?" Without carrying a hammer over my head, I like to have a good relationship between work and rest. Generally I find that if I have written something during the day, which is often the case, I just feel a little bit easier about going to sleep. It's a good guilt.

I do my very best to say interesting things interestingly, and I do my very best to establish a personal relationship with each new song that I'm working on. In the same way that you just happen to meet somebody that you have a good sense about, and you get to know them. It's the same thing with starting a song. You've got to let it tell you where it's going. I find that it's worthwhile to poke around like Mr. Chan early in the film and find out what isn't going to be necessary.

Is there a sense of having to grow or having to learn more in order to bring that song to completion?

Charles John: It seems as if I work very quickly. I don't get caught up a lot in spending months on something. It's just that in some instances, something isn't ready to become a song yet. We've all had those times where we've come up with a couplet and it really doesn't seem to go anyplace even though it's very good. And then maybe years later, we're working on something and all of a sudden those lines pop up, almost like a human computer and we go, "Oh, of course, that's the bridge." It's like stashing something in the bottom of a knapsack and three of four days later up on the mountain you reach for it, you just know it's there.

What do you hope for in a song?

Charles John: For me, I like to think of people who might be like me, and what their sense of universal vitamin is. What is it that sees them through. When music first started to come into my life in the form of records, I had a little 45 player that my mom and dad had gotten me for a birthday. It was just a tiny little thing. And I was purchasing some of the Elvis Presley records and the Drifters, and the Coasters and the thing that amazed me the most was the power of ballads in my personal life, my evidently huge range and depth of emotion and an undeniable feeling that music supported completely. When music was there it was as if to say there is a language here, a language that you understand in a part of you that doesn't seem to be spoken to in other dialects.

And so, what I hope for as a writer is that there are people like me or even unlike me who are capable of those kinds of emotional and spiritual relationships with themselves and I'm hoping to either stir the sweet coals of an experience for them or to be one of those people they can rely on by continually supplying that kind of work. And maybe even something greater as I come to find out what that is. I don't think it's dissimilar to the metaphorical concept of a lighthouse: It may never know how much good it's done, it just has a sense of what its job is.

So, you feel confident that if you are just open to the truest expression of your own feelings that the product of that will be heard and understood by a wide range of people with different regional and philosophical backgrounds?

Charles John: I would simply say, I have always had that trust. Now for individuals who are not quite sure what songs are yet, you're going to learn what songs are by writing them. Not necessarily studying what others have written, although that may help you here and there get a sense of what can be done. I would also say that I don't think of form first, I don't think of radio first. Sometimes I'm writing a song and it strikes me that this is a song that gets on the radio, for some reason or other, and often that's the case, but the thing that's important is that I feel like I'm taking dictation, some of it from myself.

Activity in one area of creativity pays off in others.

Does money complicate things? The idea that songs may earn money or that you may even need to honor someone else's expectation of how you write or what you write because there's money involved?

Charles John: I would say, in all sincerity, that if your music publishing circumstances have you writing for a company, you have to take a deep look at what is expected of you and what you are actually doing. If you can create a company for yourself, or find one that simply is interested in what you're already doing, then that's not an issue. There is a lot of money to be made if you happen write songs that become singles, and possibly not a lot of money if you don't.

As to whether that inspires you, disturbs you or whatever, that's a personal thing. For me, I see the law of prosperity in a growing way. And so, the idea that my songs can earn money, and they are earning money, is basically me getting paid for being myself and also me getting paid for everything else I do. The songs are beginning to pay me for the work that I did for years without thought of payment. I'm so glad that it's happened for a number of reasons, but at the same time, if you can keep your head in your writing, I believe the money takes care of itself if you have a good attitude. It's not why I write. At the same time, I'm open to receiving, I've grown as a soul, I feel comfortable with it, and if for some reason I get too much, I can think of lots of people who'd welcome it. The same way that I was assisted by people who were doing well financially as I was coming up through the ranks.

Songwriting and The Creative Process

I don't see it as a problem, but I do think it's important to know what a writer is, and when you get your own personal definition of what a writer is then you can go about having a relationship with the world of money. If you don't have your definition worked out as to what a writer is, you may end up writing anything. It's like hearing one of your favorite songs in a commercial. Usually it's disturbing.

If a writer or a hopeful writer will be honest with what they really love or what really gets to them, if you have a song ... it's like some of these jingles from commercials you hear so many times that you really can't stand to hear it any more. But a really good song, you may not want to listen to it again right now but it's going to maintain its magic if you pick it up a year later.

If you're fussy in a good way, chances are someone else is going to be grateful. If you don't know that much yet, the only way you're going to find out is by paying loving attention to what writing is. And the best way to learn what good writing is – is to write and grow until your writing grows. And then you begin to see, and then you begin to develop something called a style. People might hear a song of yours one night, and even though you weren't singing it, they had a feeling that it was one of yours.

In summary, it's just like saying, "Charles John Quarto writes a certain kind of work as a poet, as a writer, as a songwriter. He writes with people who have a certain kind of magical ability and are very nice to be around. That's the kind of work he does." Not that I'm the only person who writes that way, but that I'm one of the people who write that way. Not to take myself so pompously like a guest on a talk show, that I think my way is the high way, at the same time to be willingly sincere about how a good writer is the only critic he'll ever need.

> *"Writing well is at the same time perceiving well, thinking well, and saying well."*
> — BUFFON

6.4 The Good Stuff

Activity in one area of creativity pays off in others. Many painters talk about listening to music while they paint. It may be that music is a helpful distraction. It's not so important for the painter to "pay attention" while creating a painting. Since painting is a nonverbal form of expression it may be that songs are very compatible and even help the process along.

Many songs have been inspired by painters and paintings. But there's another level on which paintings can help the writer to integrate emotional, nonverbal expressions and the process of producing good work.

There is something very satisfying and uplifting about the values of a great painting. It's no coincidence that words like harmony, rhythm, and tone are used to describe qualities of paintings as well as songs. Some of the ways in which paintings are experienced are very close to the ways we make emotional sense out of songs.

Watching a painter work can be helpful to a songwriter. What comes first, what next? How does he or she arrive at a balance? How much experimentation, how busy, how obvious or obscure, etc.?

Painters and songwriters share many of the essentials of their respective crafts. There is the need to "compose." This is a word we have heard so often that it may be good to take a moment to step back and see what we mean by it. What do we expect to happen as we compose? When do we know we have composed?

So many of the writers in these pages have spoken of a feeling that accompanies a new idea. Just as Archimedes was moved to shout "Eureka!" at the moment he realized that the water he displaced as he got into the bathtub was the clue to the principle of specific gravity, in songwriting our own breakthroughs also produce an exciting "aha" response. When we have one of these events, a special insight or a solution to a problem that has been hanging us up at some point in the development of a song, it often comes in a moment of transition of some kind.

A man named John Steele spoke once on radio station KPFK in Los Angeles and mentioned several concepts of thought that he had developed. He talked about "cross-state retention" the ability to remember in one state of mind the work that was done or the processes that took place while in another state of mind. This may make the mind seem like a patchwork like a map of the U.S., but I think it's obvious that we do experience these "states" of mind.

Many people talk of "dreaming" songs and some say it is a good idea to have a pad and pen by the bed so as to be able to write down ideas that occur in sleep or in the twilight transition period between sleep and waking. John Steele also talked about "double remembering," remembering to remember and "double forgetting," forgetting that something has been forgotten. He felt that this last is something that can happen to a whole culture.

Getting to the market without our shopping list, we may have a realization of the different state of mind we were in when we stood in the kitchen and thought about what we would need and wrote the list in the first place. Sometimes we can "imagine" ourselves back in the kitchen and "see" ourselves writing down each item. A hypnotist could probably help us in this process, and hypnotists have helped many people to experience other states of mind inaccessible to them for one reason or another.

Cross-state retention is a handy idea. If we can accept the fact that we need not be too concerned about moving from one state of mind to another, then it follows that in the interest of creative work, we would want to immerse ourselves as deeply as we can in that one time and mind-state when we are doing our creative work. One way to provide for this is to give some structure to our lives in general so we know that the time is there for us. And, when we are in that time, we can relax, knowing that there will be more time so we need to do no more with the present than to be here now and let this be the only moment that concerns us.

It's important that, if possible, nothing intrude to interrupt this time and process. This may require making a deal with loved ones so that they will honor this wish for structure. A quiet place is important also, so that you can freely explore ideas and make sounds and try out language and dialogue without hearing what it must sound like to someone else. At least not until you are ready to have someone else hear it. I like to know that I can go with whatever emotional idea may be finding expression even if that means crying, or moaning, or laughing like a maniac, whatever is supportive of the process of moving ideas from the deepest and best place within to the page and the tape.

This process may take several approximations and the more free we are to let this process be more "real," the closer each version will be to the desired result. We know from so many works and talks about creative visualization that the mind is the place where the work is done. It is only to support this activity, if we can call it an activity, that we try to provide a place and a time.

Walking is one thing we can do that seems completely compatible with this process. We have all had great ideas when we are driving, but we can't stop and think about things for a minute when the lives of others around us may depend on what we do. Walking seems to be the perfect thing. It has a natural cadence, although this doesn't seem to have to be that same cadence as the song we are thinking about. We are free to listen to the symphony orchestra in our minds and the infinite resources of melody and harmony which come through to us in a pretty realistic performance.

There is always a point in working on a song where, for me, the appropriate thing is to get up from the pages I've been working on and without talking to anyone else, or doing anything else, I go for a walk. I let the elements of the song occupy my mind and I just let them sing to me. I may focus in on one verse or one particular part of the song, and I may even sing out loud, but I let the song fill up the whole space of my time.

6.5 Time Waits for No Man

"If it wasn't for time, we'd have to do everything all at once."
— ART THIEME

Your Own Pace

When you're not running to catch up, or wishing time would pass more quickly, but you're in the moment, you've escaped the clock. There is time, time enough for the writing we are capable of. If there is anxiety about the time we have left to us or about how fast others seem to be progressing or anything else that may impose a framework on time, none of it has anything to do with doing creative work.

The Faster I Go the Behinder I Get!

In workshops, I'm fond of saying that if it took you 20 years to write "Gentle On My Mind," you still would have earned at least $100,000 a year. The idea is not to try to get in step with the industry and its voracious appetite for songs, but to get into our own rhythm of creative productivity. That appetite for new songs will be there when we feel our songs are ready to be heard. The idea *is* to do the kind of writing that honors the time spent. If we can remove the artificial speediness of the so called "success" orientation, we can really do something worthwhile.

Songwriters are notoriously bad letter writers. I know for me the reason is that when I have that kind of quality time and suitable concentration, I'd rather be writing songs. Actually, I feel bound to write songs. I feel guilty, because it's pleasurable, but I feel compelled to write. So, perhaps the songs are my letters and hopefully, will convey my thoughts.

Nancy White has written that it is hard for her to write when there are noodles on the floor of the living room. I want to write even if the living room is on fire. But I know other things must be done, so I try make the best use of the time that I can get for the writing. This time is what I chose to think of as "real time."

There is a famous old saying that to the tight-rope walker only the time on the wire is real, all other time is waiting.

6.6 Synchronicity

In Tune & In Time

Time is the commodity of the songwriter on several levels. An interpretation of time is created by the notes and the spaces between them. It's a measure of the listener's attention span and the songwriter's window of communication. In those moments when we perceive something profoundly relevant to our lives, time may seem to stand still while the whole of our awareness is focused.

As we interact with time and our sense of it, we can sometimes seem to occupy it more fully. It may seem that we manipulate it. When we speak of feeling the earth move or seeing our lives pass before us in an instant, we have shifted the normal perception of time considerably. Just as the shortstop seems to defy the boundaries of time by reaching out for a line drive in an almost unbelievable jab at the ball and miraculously comes up with it, we may discover that we can do things musically with time that we had not thought possible.

My feeling is that the very best source of time reference for any issue more complicated than a simple metronome is the human body. The heartbeat is a faithful indicator of a wide range of the tempos of dance and romance. The muscles and limbs of the body are really the primary instruments at the root of dance and movement music. Much of our perception of music takes place in the proprioceptors – those tiny sensors present in the connective tissue of the body. It is the chorus of proprioceptors that gives the true physical-musical meaning to a snap of the fingers. Without these sensations it would be just a sound to be heard by the ears.

The keys and hammers of the piano, the strings of the guitar and the violin, and the heads of the drums all have these time-linked properties. When the tension of the guitar string gives it a "bounce" that resonates in a pleasing way with the "thump" of the kick drum and the "thrum" of the string bass there is a perceptual physical joy in their synergy. So in this aspect, music becomes not so much a calculated intellectual pursuit of mathematically pleasing relationships of notes on a page, but a dance.

6.7 "Courting the Muse" by Suzzy Roche

I do have a few thoughts about writing. First, everybody does it *their way*. I know a bunch of incredible writers – some people are given the gift. Some have no trouble claiming the right to write. I know a guy who thinks he's a genius. I go about my business and hope ... the hardest part for me is giving myself permission. I suspect there are a pile of us out there, for one reason or another – maybe somebody laughed at us once, maybe we're too intimidated by someone else's song, maybe we're afraid of what will come out. There are a million reasons why. One thing I learned about myself is that I gotta put in the time.

Do I know how to write a song? I know how to sit there and listen for ... for what? The moment I give up? That's a good place for me to begin.

But first I read. With a cup of coffee, I'm almost still asleep. I have two or three books going at once. I love novels – and anything psychological that makes me feel hopeful. I enjoy reading for sure, but I also find that other writers inspire me. I can sometimes trace a song to a book, even though the author would never know. And reading clears my mind. So, maybe by then I'm ready to scribble a page into a notebook that I keep. That's just me babbling – better burn it before I die.

After that, I'm usually itching to pick up the guitar. I invite myself to hum and strum – or get a drum beat going – turn on the keyboard and four-track, get a nice reverb on the microphone so I like my voice, and snuggle up under the headphones because they make me feel safe and I can hear even my softest voices there. If I sit for a spell and nothing comes, I'll play an already-written song or pull out a half-done one. I'll search for a chord I like. Maybe I'll play two chords for half an hour. I wanna go real slow.

If something comes, I tape it. I think I lost some songs by killing them before they were really born. Now I immediately tape the little buggers and leave them alone. Many times the heart of the song is in that very first tape. Once in a blue moon a song will write itself in 10 minutes. But if I like what I have and can't finish it, I'll play with it as if it were a doll. I'll try on a keyboard part or a bass line, add a harmony, make it feel special – let it imagine how great it could be! – and leave it for the day.

If I have a track on tape, I can the sing the words I've got and then whatever pops into my head. Sometimes those turn out to be just right. Or I hop onto my going-nowhere exercycle and listen over and over till the tune gets into me – hangs out in the back of my brain throughout the day like a broken heart or a true-love kiss. It's amazing how a line I wished for can beam in on the way to the post office later that day, or week, or ... year.

I like to work with different chords, too. I tend to use simple chords at first, but often they will change when I put a bass part or a keyboard part against them. I am "self-taught" – a musical scavenger. I've taken lessons here and there – which is *so* great. I wish I could study more. I was too scattered when I was younger, and now I grab my lessons like a thief. As a result, my approach to music is unorthodox (this is what I've been told). I might never be an accomplished musician, but I probably know a lot more than I think I do. Working in The Roches for so many years, I've learned bucketfuls of harmony and music. My songs tend to be simpler than my sisters', although just as idiosyncratic. That can be a blessing in disguise. I shy away from judging – "good" and "bad" had to get kicked out of my vocabulary. I try to get what I like, that's all. Leave the judging to others. There are plenty of people who are great at that. However, if you're trying to be a pop star on the radio, pay no attention to me!

Some other things that help me – assignments. Write a song in a certain key, for example. Let the key change in the middle of the verse. Or make a list of titles off the top of my head. Write a song about an object in the room. Pick some words I love and use them. Describe someone in as much detail as possible. Be mean, really mean! Be a lover. Listen to a record. Ask a question. Pick three chords I've never used. This may seem silly or superficial, but it often leads me somewhere. It's a game and it can be fun: "Queen for a day, I wrote a poem!" or "Put down the guitar and get the hell out of the house!"

Oh, one more thing. Once a song is written I sing it a million times. It makes it real and helps it live. I've been writing one thing or another since I was a little kid, mostly just to rock myself – to hear myself. The world is a noisy place. Sometimes I get drowned out.

I've written for money and I've written for free – for TV shows, commercials, movies, albums, album covers, press kits and for my heart and soul. The only real thing I know about writing is that if I don't write anything, then I don't write anything.

7.

Psychology

"I am not fond of the word psychological. There is no such thing as the psychological. Let us say that one can improve the biography of the person."
— JEAN-PAUL SARTRE

7.1 The "Divine Madness"

It may have been in response to the "scientific revolution" of the late 1800s, but much artistic work began to take issue with the ever more prevalent idea that a person was no more than a complicated machine. Many authors from Henry James to Dostoyevsky sought to characterize the working of the human mind and raised new questions about thought and creativity.

Many of these writers explored the mind not in terms of logic and determinism, but in terms of magic and myth, even insanity. Much of the writing of this century could be characterized as a movement of "The Wild Mind," the "Theater of the Absurd," and "Impressionism" and "Fantasy."

Writers for centuries have noticed that dreams and fables spoke in a language that defied logic and had about it a powerful component of non-verbal truth.

Sigmund Freud and Carl Jung made great strides in formulating an organized approach to these issues and have influenced creative people in all fields. They, too, have focused on dreams and on myth as repositories of deep truths.

Freud concentrated on the personality structures of the brain. He talked about the *id*, the *ego*, the *superego*, and many other personality features and processes. His names for these are the ones we use today.

Carl Jung worked closely with Freud for a time, but then broke with him and expanded upon Freud's work and took the field much further into the areas of dream analysis and the interpretation of symbols and mythology. Jung has become a father figure for artists of all types because of his work in relating the processes of the mind and the meaning

Songwriting and The Creative Process

of symbols and myth. It is from the work of Carl Jung that we have the *anima*, the concept of the feminine aspect in each of us, man or woman, and the *animus*, the corresponding masculine aspect in each of us.

Jung also took an early interest in meditation and the teachings of oriental philosophers, especially Lao Tsu, and is largely responsible for the modern acceptance of these concepts by the established psychological community.

Jung suggested that the *psyche* consists of three interacting systems: the *conscious*, the *personal unconscious*, and the *collective unconscious*. His idea of the ego was that it comprised the conscious perceptions, memory, thoughts and feelings, and the person's interaction with the environment.

The personal unconscious is a vast reservoir of the person's feelings, reactions, wishes and impulses which were once conscious but have been forgotten or repressed. These may brought to consciousness in therapy, hypnosis, or through dreams, stories and art.

The collective unconscious is beyond the conscious awareness of the individual. It is the inherited racial, family and distant animal past represented by *archetypes:* universal symbols and mythological imaginative structures. This is where we encounter the composite *persona*, anima, animus and the *shadow*. As the **self** strives to integrate all these levels of consciousness this process is known as *individuation*.

> *"He looked at his own soul with a telescope. What seemed all irregular, he saw and shewed to be beautiful constellations; and he added to the consciousness hidden worlds within worlds."*
> — COLERIDGE, "NOTEBOOKS"

7.2 The Psychology of Creativity

> *"Creativity is the encounter of the intensively conscious human being with his or her world."*
> — ROLLO MAY

Rollo May is a Jungian psychotherapist who has written many books on the relationship of emotional and artistic ideas and their bearing on the quality of human life. The two books I recommend most often and most strongly are *Love and Will* and *The Courage To Create*.

In *The Courage To Create*, May says, "We are called upon to do something new, to confront a no man's land, to push into a forest where there are no well-worn paths and from which no one has returned to guide us. This is what the existentialists call the anxiety of nothingness. To live into the future means to leap into the unknown, and this requires a degree of courage for which there is no immediate precedent and which few people realize."

In speaking of physical courage, May points out that there is a different sort of strength required for the doing of creative work. Not for the creative impulse to run rampant in violence or to assert its ego over others, but for the cultivation of sensitivity and acuity. This, he says, will mean the development of the capacity to listen with the body, to nurture a holistic view of mind and body, not to deny the body as profane or incapable of enlightenment as has been taught in the past.

In a discussion of moral courage, he mentions the courage of Aleksandr Solzhenitsyn who in his books protested the Soviet bureaucracy's inhumane treatment of men and women political prisoners. Solzhenitsyn wrote at the risk of suffering the same fate himself. He is quoted as saying, "I would gladly give my life if it would advance the cause of truth."

May also writes about social courage. "It is the courage to relate to other human beings, the capacity to risk one's self in the hope of achieving meaningful intimacy."

In a chapter on creative courage, May talks about the need to come to an acceptance of all aspects of life, even the sad and the frightening. To embrace it totally and still be able to reach for the transcendent truth in our creative work.

He writes, "But the essence of being human is that in the brief moment we exist on this spinning planet, we can love some persons and some things, in spite of the fact that time and death will ultimately claim us all. ... By the creative act, however, we are able to reach beyond our own death. This is why creativity is so important and why we need to confront the problem of the relationship between creativity and death."

Ecstasy

According to May, Greek drama evolved out of the Dionysian revels. In this peak of creativity was achieved a union of form and passion with order and vitality. Ecstasy is the technical term for the process in which this union occurs.

We have come to think of ecstasy as a sensual release or hysteria, a thrill. But the origin of the word is the Greek "ex-stasis," literally, "to stand out from." To transcend the split between the subject and object, which is the perpetual dichotomy in most human activity. Ecstasy is the proper term for the intensity of consciousness that occurs in the creative act bringing intellectual, volitional, and emotional functions into play together.

Elegance - In Song As It Is In Quantum Physics

We've heard it said that the hardest thing is to write simply. It is easier to get very complicated in trying to express an emotion or an issue of a song, but the one simple phrase that really "nails it" may elude us.

In workshops, I've used the example of the old game of trying to balance the salt shaker on a few grains of salt. I'm sure most of us have seen it done or tried it ourselves. You sprinkle a few grains of salt onto the table, brush then into a small pile and place the salt shaker on its edge. The grains of salt will help you keep the salt shaker on edge once the balance point has been found. Then you gently blow away the loose grains of salt and because only two or three grains are actually holding the salt shaker, it appears to be magically standing on edge with no help from anything at all.

In songs, too, we need to find that perfect balance point and "blow away" the extra stuff, the stuff that is not contributing to the essential meaning of the song. By working and reworking we can distill the song down to its essence. By ridding the song of excess baggage we give it room to be, room to stretch out and fill the space in a more satisfying way. Early drafts can be wordy and clumsy as we work toward the indispensable elements of the song. We still have to come up with good lines but without them we wouldn't have a song anyway.

Insight & Hindsight

According to Lao Tsu, insight is a manifestation of the spirit. Insight is that wonderful (and wonder is the word) thing that happens when from somewhere deep in the unconscious mind a thought springs forth that is surprisingly relevant and seems to be true in some poetic and magical way. We speak of a particularly perceptive observation as being very insightful.

By ridding the song of excess baggage we give it room to be ...

Those who have written about insight suggest that it tends to come after some intense work on a difficult problem. It seems to be accompanied by a sudden vividness of the senses. Insight may occur in a moment of transition between working and relaxing or in that vulnerable time between waking and sleeping.

Insights seem to break in on us. They seem to break through our rational thoughts and business. This breakthrough is often accompanied by an "aha" as we "get it." As magical as this all seems, most songwriters are very used to having these moments of insight and really expect to have this kind of help from the unconscious mind.

It may be that as in "let the force be with you," having the right spirit in songwriting and trusting in the help you receive from all the voices within is connected to how close to the truth you are writing. Psychologists talk about "cognitive dissonance." This has to do with the idea that if we hear something we don't want to hear, something that goes against our sense of ourselves or our sense of the way things are, we experience the feeling that this new information could not be true. That it just doesn't "jibe" with what we know is the real way that things are.

If in our writing we are able to characterize the world in a way that rings true to the listener, then we have fostered what we could call a "cognitive resonance" with the listener. The writers who seem best able to say what is true for most of us don't seem to be kidding themselves. They seem to have an integrated or "individuated" vision of the world and be able to convey that in a song.

When a song is written out of a factual incident or from the memory of a real place, certain details may just naturally find their way into the song which give it an authenticity which would be hard to create out of the imagination. It is this kind of verisimilitude which we admire in the writing of good songs even though many of them are "made up."

Often in a song we will get a sense of knowing a character who doesn't even get to speak in the song at all. We can tell a lot about this character just by the way he or she is spoken to by the singer of the song. It can be almost as if we were "listening in." Writing songs that sustain the believability of character and situation requires paying attention to these kinds of details.

I remember seeing a news story about a young man who had won a national amateur hole-in-one contest and won a prize of 1 million dollars. As the camera moved in close he was talking on the phone to his grandmother, giving her the amazing news. After a pause he was heard to say, "Yes, Grandma, I'm still in school." I'm sure that without hearing the other side of the conversation, we all know a great deal about that young man's grandmother.

7.3 The "Right" Side of the Brain

One of the key discoveries of research on the human brain was the revelation of the dual nature of human thinking – verbal, analytic, thinking mainly located in the left hemisphere, and visual, perceptual thinking mainly located in the right hemisphere of the brain. Much of this is the original discovery of psychologist Roger W. Sperry who published his studies in 1968 and was awarded the Nobel prize for his work in 1981.

The two hemispheres of the human brain are very much alike in physical structure but have become specialized in terms of their activity. The left side of the brain is connected through the nervous system to the right side of the body, and the right side of the brain is connected to the left side of the body. Verbal skills are centered in a small area of the brain at the back of the left hemisphere in most people. That is in 98 percent of all right-handed people and two-thirds of all left-handed people.

Left-handedness or right-handedness is one of the most apparent effects of the hemispherical asymmetry of the brain. Until recent times left-handed children were discouraged from using their left hands and an attempt was made to force them to learn to write with their right hands.

Left-handed people today still encounter some of this righties prejudice in ordinary objects like scissors and handles, which tend to favor the right-handed. Words like "sinister" which is Latin for "left," and "dexter" or dexterous and dexterity, for the "right hand." The french word "gauche" which means "awkward," and "left-handed compliment" are examples of the kind of superstitious onus which has been the burden of left-handed people.

A list of famous left-handed people would include; Julius Caesar, Benjamin Franklin, Albert Einstein, Paul McCartney, Lewis Carroll, Charlie Chaplin, W.C. Fields, and Ringo Starr.

The *left brain*, which controls the function of the right side of the body, is associated with the kind of thinking that involves analysis, counting, step-by-step procedures, numbers, sequential and symbolic thinking. Logic is the province of the left brain. We retreat to the left brain when we are told to "be rational." It is the linear, methodical, objective brain.

The *right brain* has a different way of functioning. It can "see" imaginary things, recognize faces, recall images, understand metaphors, and solve jigsaw puzzles by relating shapes and wholes. Insight, intuition, and the "aha" breakthroughs of creative thought are associated with the activity of the right hemisphere of the brain. Right-handers find it more difficult to do mirror writing than do left-handers.

Since the left side of the body is controlled by the right half of the brain, many people have spoken of doing certain tasks, writing or painting with the left hand in order to encourage right brain participation. In our society the left brain seems to dominate and also tends to impose its "time" priority on most activities so it becomes necessary to help the right brain to have its say in creative matters.

Scientists have studied what it is that determines which hemisphere may "claim" certain tasks and have concluded that the brain makes a choice as to which side is more suited based on time, how quickly something might be accomplished, and on which hemisphere has the greatest degree of concern or empathy with the task.

When looking for a certain reference in a book, the right brain may visualize the shape of the blocks of paragraphs on a certain page and may even guide our eye to the shape of the phrase we are looking for, but at some point, the left brain will interpose to decide if the word accurately and logically answers the description of the information we seek.

It is possible with practice to identify the exact point at which this shift from the dominance of one hemisphere of the brain to the other is made and to recognize the little inaudible "click" that accompanies this transition. One way to encourage the activity of either hemisphere is by attempting a task that is unsuited to the particular traits of the other hemisphere.

Many authors have put into practice the ideas on right and left brain research begun by Sperry. The best know and most widely used book in this field is undoubtedly *Drawing On the Right Side of the Brain* by Betty Edwards. Much of the information in this chapter is from this amazing book. The book is actually a course on drawing taught in the context of a personal exploration of left brain and right brain activity.

According to Dr. Edwards, drawing is largely a right brain function. She writes, "As I have explained, to draw a perceived form we want the left mode mainly 'off' and the right mode 'on,' a combination that produces a slightly altered subjective state in which the right hemisphere 'leads.' The characteristics of this subjective state are those that artists speak of: a sense of close 'connection' with the work, a sense of timelessness, difficulty in using words or understanding spoken words, a feeling of confidence and a lack of anxiety, a sense of close attention to shapes and spaces and forms *that remain nameless.*"

In the book, she gives a series of exercises to help the student to experience the shift from left to right brain. Several of these are based on figure-ground problems, the kinds of things that have been thought of as optical illusions.

We've all seen the paintings that are two things at the same time, depending on how we "see" them. The face of Lincoln that seems to leap out of five or six solid blocks of color. The young woman sitting at the mirror which becomes a skull is another example of a design which enables us to experience this shift of perception. There are also the drawings of vases which are also seen as profiles of two people facing each other.

The parallels between graphic artists and songwriters are numerous, but it may be a little more difficult to pin down this left brain/right brain shift in songwriting. Again, the imagination is the place where the activities of the two hemispheres of the brain seem to sort each other out and promote the flow of good writing.

By listening and learning, we give ourselves the resources by which we create. A part of our songwriting work is to put into practice the things we have learned about how our minds can be better expected to accomplish these tasks.

7.4 Meditation - Visitors to the Alpha State

Did you hear about the Zen master who said to the hot dog vender,
"Make me one with everything"?

When we talk about the muse and the thoughtful, trance-like state of "musing," we are looking at thought in a new way. In recent years there has been an ever increasing emphasis on the study of thought and how to take a more active role in the processes associated with the mind.

Athletes, actors, scientists, dancers, poets, and salesmen have all discovered the issues of awareness and meditation. We hear about inner tennis, inner golf, releasing your powers of mind, and many other applications of "mind" science. But there is an important distinction to be made between the "productive" uses of the mind and meditation.

The place to begin with this exploration is in a comfortable chair. You don't need to master the lotus position or even the half lotus, although you may wish to eventually. All that is necessary is to be erect and comfortable so that your mind can be alert, not sleepy, and not distracted by cramps or aches.

There are several basic techniques that are taught, but each has the purpose of promoting the same practice of mindfulness. The one I will suggest is a form of following the breath. This is the most common practice.

Every athlete knows the importance of maintaining his or her "cool," and the importance of breathing in keeping calm. Every trained paramedic knows techniques for controlling panic and shock in cases of injury and trauma and many of these techniques involve breathing deeply or counting the breath.

Counting the breath is the basic practice of meditation. We are not working with athletic performance or trauma or shock, but we are interested in calming the mind and allaying fear and anxiety in whatever form they may be present.

If we imagine there is a gate keeper watching our breath as it comes in and goes out, like a lighthouse keeper at the mouth of a harbor keeping track of the tide, we simply focus our awareness on the fact of our breathing. Counting is one way to do this but it is not so important to keep a count as it is to be sure that our conscious awareness is focused on this one task.

This alone is a calming mental activity and keeps our mind from being drawn into the many anxious conflicts which may claim the stage of our awareness. This is the beginning of the process of meditation. By continuing to breathe in a calm and regular way, and only being aware of the flow of our breath in and out, we begin to experience a deeper, more open state of consciousness. And it is to this place we will return in regular practice to explore the processes of the mind.

Daydreaming is different. While it may be pleasurable to be carried away in a fantasy, and may even seem like a message from beyond, and may serve as a wonderful inspiration, this is not what we are doing in meditation. When we find ourselves drifting into the dream state, we recognize this and chose to return to the open, empty, unattached atmosphere of following our breath, just being aware of that.

In some meditation practice we may meditate on some object, like a tree, or a painting, or a symbolic representation such as a mandala, but even in this practice we begin by following the breath. Some have talked about visualizing the flame of a candle; the wind may disturb the flame, but it is always there.

What we are attempting to do is distance ourselves for a time each day from distraction and let the busy little voices inside, often called the "monkey chatter," fall away and leave us to have a quiet communion with the moods and subtleties of our deeper understanding.

We are seeking, if seeking is the word, to be present in a wider, more balanced reality where a diversity of "shoes and ships and sealing wax, and cabbages and kings" can all be perceived in the full perfection of their textures and fragrances without one overshadowing the other.

This is a place where all thought is just that, thought. No voice is disturbing or worrisome in the greater sense. All ideas are free to bubble up uncensored from the unconscious and the thinker is not compelled to become anxious or emotionally compromised in any way.

It may be the only time when some of these more difficult thoughts can find expression. It's not important to act on any of these thoughts at this time. This time is for a process which is not the servant of any issue or priority. There will be time later to come to a determination of what it all means and how we are to take action on our new understanding, but for now, let all thoughts have the same weight.

In Plato's allegory of the cave, one idea is that the thinker sits as if deep inside a cave and thoughts are no more than the shadows of passers-by. There is no need to be drawn out of this detachment in order to answer the implications that may be the baggage of each thought that makes its appearance. It's simply true that each person has the right to chose which of these thoughts will guide him or her and which in the light of consideration will have merit.

When we explore all the things which may be impediments to creative thought, we come up with what have been called in various cultures and schools of meditation the "hindrances." Usually listed as four or five "hindrances," these generally include desire or desire of the senses, anger, sloth or torpor, anxiety or agitation or other manifestations of fear, and doubt.

These hindrances are the issues that lay claim to the free activity of the mind and "attach" its process. Each has its own timetable and priorities and imposes a certain urgency on our thinking. Much as a mother must respond to the crying of a child or a pot overflowing on the stove or the ringing of the doorbell, these fears, desires and concerns may keep our minds occupied or at least "on call."

Of course, there are many real things that must be taken care of in each of our lives and it's not a question of dropping out of the world in order to have beautiful thoughts. But you will find that if the fire insurance has been paid, and the garage door is closed, and that letter from your aunt has been dutifully answered, there is a time and a place when and where it is appropriate to seek a new understanding of awareness and the working of our minds.

Here we may be aware, though, of a certain confusion or even guilt. Each of us has some idea of the "purpose" of our existence and the nature of our duty to others. We also live in a world which is in recent times a cacophony of suggestions about who we are, what we need, and what we should do. As we begin to sort things out, we start to see that there are choices to be made. Inaction may come to be a hindrance in itself. It soon becomes apparent that to have the best experience of this meditative process, we must respond to the new understanding that comes to us and act, or risk ambivalence and confusion.

In other words, once begun, enlightenment involves taking action. But hopefully a fairer, more enlightened action. As we begin to understand that there is work to be done, we must do it. If a question raises thoughts which are unwelcome to us, then that is precisely the question we must ask and be open to its true answer. If we have something we are not proud of, we must ask what can be done, and progress may depend on doing what we can.

This is why almost every religious and psychological discipline has in it an aspect of service to others. This is not to be resented or resisted, just let it carry the authority of any other thought. Eventually, this sitting practice becomes comfortable, although comfort is not the purpose of it. Soon we see it as a therapeutic time, and we will not want to be without this time. And in this time, we will do the work of fostering our own growth.

"I may not ever know you, nor may I know what you do, but I do know this about you – unless you choose a life of love and service, you will never be happy."
— ALBERT SCHWEITZER

There is, however, another benefit, and that is as we proceed with this sort of practice we find that we are able to maintain our perspective even at times which used to cause us to be agitated. Traffic, chores, spills, setbacks can all be seen in perspective of the greater journey and can be dealt with and may actually afford us time for creative thought.

This issue of service and work has another side to it too. Did you ever notice that dogs seem to their happiest when they are retrieving some object, a Frisbee, a ball, even a stone? Did you ever have the thought that really what they are doing is working. Dogs love to work. There is a level of joy and animation at those times which makes a great impression on us humans. We are a lot like that. Walking, driving, mowing the lawn, washing the dishes all seem to promote a state of mind which is creative. Some of the best ideas occur at these times.

Here we encounter an important distinction between meditation and the "active dreaming" of writing. As we have said, meditation is the freedom from the attachment to thought. This freedom from sequential, captivating thought is basic to meditation. In writing, we allow ourselves to hear the characters speak, and to hear and respond to each other. We allow our emotions to show us what they mean and feel and we respond, often from a very deep place. Through meditation we can develop the detachment which can provide for the free and fearless immersion of our emotional understanding in the creative process.

It is at these times that we can say what we understand deeply without hurting ourselves or others with the pain that was never really there at all, but was only the fear of pain. We can achieve a life and quality of work closer to our ideal of transcendence. We can disengage our lives and our work from the meaningless adherence to the "myth of separateness" and truly live as if we were all the same, which, of course, we are.

When they asked the Buddha if he was an angel or a god, he said, "No, I'm awake."

7.5 Attending

We often hear stories about the young Mozart, who could remember intricate pieces of music and play them perfectly upon only one hearing. Aside from the issue of special qualities of genius, this seems to be largely a matter of conscious attention and focus. The more we understand about something the easier it becomes to hear what we just heard or suspend a complex thought in the air until we have enough of a grasp of it to write it down.

Sometimes the best way to think of something is not to think about thinking of it at all. Sometimes it's best to forget all about it and remind yourself to ask yourself about it later after your unconscious mind has had a chance to "think" about it.

A little experiment may serve to demonstrate that you can program your mind to come up with the idea you need. You can make a strong suggestion that at a certain point you can expect a new idea or the solution to a problem. Frame the question as clearly as you can and make it clear to your subconscious that after a certain time, or after walking a certain distance and perhaps arriving at a certain place, there will be an idea there which is relevant and promising.

Sometimes the best way to think of something is not to think about thinking of it at all.

Again, walking is very useful in this practice. I used to go for walks at the ocean and there was a rock jetty that went a couple of hundred yards out into the ocean. The rocks were large and had large gaps between them so it took considerable concentration to get from one rock to the next and took about fifteen minutes to get out to the end. I used to go out there often and would sit and write with my clipboard. The sound of the waves seemed to be helpful and I could mutter and shout all I wanted without worrying about being overheard.

I don't know when I began the practice, but one day it occurred to me to try an experiment. I would make a suggestion to myself, not necessarily out loud, although that may be helpful, that I would have a new idea or some new insight about the song I was working on when

I got out to the end of the jetty. Sometimes this would work better than other times but it was always worth trying. Second verses are often a problem, as has been mentioned elsewhere in this book. I would "ask" for a new idea for a second verse, and usually there would be something there for me.

Now this is something we do in the normal course of problem solving in many pursuits, but we are not always willing to give our unconscious mind the time to work on complex problems and we don't always pay attention to what might be there for us. In this dialogue, there is a chance to hear what our own helpful voices have to say to us. Our perception of time is very illusory. I'm sure we would all be willing to spend hours to make long lists of words if we believed that doing this work would provide us with a good line. It's surprising how hard it is to just let ourselves hear the line that is already there for us in our own subconscious mind.

Many writers on writing have created exercises by which we can work with this dialogue of the mind. The power of suggestion and self-hypnosis are available to us in many forms. If we are speaking of literal or technical writing, then the effort is to make sure that the writing is accurate and well-organized. But songwriting and poetry may require a different sort of writing. This writing seems to exist in several dimensions at once. It is not only literal, it is metaphorical and may have about it an aura, or a spirit. Some of these attributes are difficult to pin down, but good people have been working at it for a long time.

7.6 Poetry

We've held off discussing poetry until insight, cognition, symbolic language and a few other things could be discussed. That's because poetry is much more that just words that rhyme. It has depth. Poetry has the power to express things that cannot be said in any other way.

"It is difficult to get the news from poems; yet men die miserably every day for lack of what is found there."
— WILLIAM CARLOS WILLIAMS

Robert Bly has written one of the poems that I always think of when I recount a time in my own life when I needed to hear just what this poem had to say. "Far out at sea are white caps answering questions no man has asked." At a time when the poet was leaving one chapter of his life behind, he wondered what the future held and how he would fare. He says: "Even though I do not march to the sound of golden trumpets, I must march." And as he stares out to the horizon deeply pondering the meaning of his insecurity about this, he realizes: "And the waves give up their answer as they fall into themselves."

In his book, *American Poetry – Wildness and Domesticity*, Bly makes several observations on the awakening of poetic thought taking place in our time. "... The problem of poetry now is to find ways to go into still more intense states of consciousness. Its daily helpers in this will be discipline and solitude. Its intellectual helpers will be writers like Thoreau, Marcuse, Norman Brown, Akhmatova, and Vallejo. It will have to imagine a new start in the inner life of the West, for the way we are following is a disaster."

In his introduction to the work of the Russian poet Yevgeny Yevtushenko, George Reavey writes: "There is something about the poet and his poetic utterance that has a terrifying effect on some Russians, and especially on the Authorities, be they Tzarist or Soviet. It is as though poetry were an irrational force which must be bridled and subjugated and even destroyed."

7.7 Setting Poems to Music

Based on metrical considerations alone it's easy to find a well-known melody to fit most poems of regular meter. A couple of examples may serve to point out that there are obviously other considerations. Mary Bryan reminded me that Poe's "The Raven" could be set to "Deck the Halls." *"Once upon a midnight dreary, Fa la la la la, la la la la."*

And Robert Frost's "Stopping By Woods" works well with the melody to "Hernando's Hideaway." *"Whose woods these are, I think I know."*

In "Bone By Bone," Gary Krist tells of the woman who claimed that any poem by Emily Dickinson can be sung to the tune of "The Yellow Rose of Texas." Try: *"Hope is the thing with feathers / That perches in the soul ..."* or *"Success is counted sweetest / By those who ne'er succeed."*

There is nothing really wrong with this approach except that these very familiar melodies interject another element into the mood and message of the poems and turn the combination into a joke. Try staying on the same note and reciting each poem to the example song and they don't really sound that bad.

The part of the problem that remains is that the rhythm of the well-known melody doesn't conform to the "rhythmic meaning" of the poem, since it was written to another set of words which have a rhythmic understanding of their own. Or, if the melody was written first, which is the case in so many of the familiar traditional songs, it was certainly written without reference to the poem we have chosen.

In any case, we are talking about compatibility and support, a synergy of words and music which gives strength and unity to the work. This synergy is arrived at through a number of considerations, but for me the starting point has always been reciting the poem out loud. As you speak the words of the poem you begin to be aware of a rhythmic characteristic. If the poem is suitable for singing, it will have its own natural tempo, and will allow for places to breathe.

In speaking the poem aloud it will be easy to see if the language of the poem is conversational and natural enough to be sung. If the poem uses difficult language, this will limit its possibilities as a song. Anything can be set to music, but it is rare to find a poem that has solved all the kinds of problems the songwriter deals with before ending up with a complete lyric. It's more likely that a favorite poem will represent a departure from your usual type of song.

It is worthwhile to consider some of the differences between a poem and a song. A poem can be read several times, from top to bottom and from bottom to top. You can stop and reread a line if its meaning is not clear or if you are considering its relationship to the other lines of the poem. With a song, you must rely on the songwriter to emphasize the line, to set it in such a way that its meaning is clear or to repeat a line when it is helpful to do so.

A poem has its own pace and that pace can change with the complexity of the ideas. A song would have a hard time justifying any tempo change at all. In a song, the songwriter has the help of the music to create and sustain emotional atmosphere. The poet must create that atmosphere with words alone. Poets have found ways to say things and things to say that can be of great help to the songwriter. Time spent with a good poet is always a good idea and if that yields a song, that's fine too.

One other possibility is that you will find a poem in another language and you can translate it or work from an existing translation. This gives you the opportunity to restructure the rhyme scheme and carefully chose the words which for you best express your understanding of the poem. Just as in any other collaborative work, you must make sure you abide by copyright where it exists. You may need permission to publish your treatment of someone else's work.

There are many examples of successful settings. Several of the poems of William Butler Yeats, "Song of the Wandering Angus" and "Innisfree;" "The Bells" by Edgar Allan Poe; "Captain My Captain," the poem by Walt Whitman; "The Highwayman;" "Winkin', Blinkin' and Nod;" many of the poems of the Australian poet, Henry Lawson, and the poems of Robert W. Service.

Peter Bellamy was a British ballad singer and collector and was at one time president of the Rudyard Kipling Society in England. He set many of Kipling's poems to music including "The Smugglers" and "Philadelphia."

7.8 Disappearance – Getting Out of Our Own Way

I remember hearing about a six-year-old, the son of a friend, who went into the hospital for surgery. The next day he described his experience. "I remember the doctor putting something over my face and then I disappeared."

"For art to appear, we have to disappear. This may sound strange, but in fact it is a common experience. The elementary case, for most people, is when our eye or ear is "caught" by something ... Mind and sense are arrested for a moment, fully in the experience. Nothing else exists. "When we 'disappear' in this way, everything around us becomes a surprise, new and fresh. Self and environment unite. Attention and intention fuse. We see things just as we and they are ..."
— STEPHEN NACHMANOVITCH

Many writers on the subject of the creative process have thought about this question of identity and our attachment to thinking of ourselves in a certain way. We know how much difficulty we can create for ourselves by being attached to being thought of by others in a particular way this kind of attachment can also be a great hindrance to creative thought.

We have all had the experience of being lost in thought, in a trance, some would say. This trance-like state can be entered into at will and to a certain extent we all cultivate our rituals of concentration. It might be helpful to hear some of the things that others have said on this subject.

One of my favorite thoughts along this line is the statement of Gertrude Stein's that "I am I for my little dog knows me." It is true that animals have a way of being aware that is very revealing.

At one point I had three dogs and I used to love to get down on the floor and wrestle and growl and snort with them. One time when I was having this fun dialogue and trying to keep all of them responding and laughing, I realized that each dog had an uncanny awareness of whether he or she was the focus of my undivided attention or just one of the "others." When the dog felt that "personal" connection, he or she would be enthralled, almost embarrassed. But, upon sensing that one of the other dogs was having that connection, he or she would begin to compete to get back on that special "wavelength."

7.9 "For My Little Dog Knows Me"

Gertrude Stein & Her Theories of Creative Process

Primarily a poet, Gertrude Stein was an American who lived in Paris with her friend, Alice B. Toklas, of whom she wrote her famous *Autobiography*. She was at the center of an active group of artists and writers. She was a friend of many of the impressionist painters and had a stormy relationship with Picasso, who painted her well known portrait. She often had gatherings of poets, painters and others of the arts scene of the Paris of her day. Hemingway, Sartre, Simone de Beauvoir and others convened to talk about writing, painting and creativity in general.

Many people considered her to be an expert on art because she owned the work of many of the best painters of her time long before they were recognized by the public. Her iconoclastic explanation for this was simply to say, "I like to look at them."

Gertrude Stein rejected the popular cliche that you should write what you know. She said, "Writing is writing what you do not yet know. Writing what you already know is not writing, that's typing." She made the distinction between this kind of "primary" or "original" writing and what she called "secondary writing."

She did a lot of what people call "original thinking." She thought and wrote a great deal about the nature of consciousness and the creative process. In a series of lectures delivered at Harvard University in 1936 she posed the famous question, "What is a masterpiece and why there are so few of them." The following is quoted from these lectures.

"The minute your memory functions while you are doing anything it may be very popular but actually it is dull. And that is what a master-piece is not, it may be unwelcome but it is never dull.
"And so then why are there so few of them. There are so few of them because mostly people live in identity and memory that is when they think. They know they are they because their little dog knows them, and so they are not an entity but an identity ...
"...Think about how you create if you do create you do not remember yourself as you do create. And yet time and identity is what you tell about as you create only while you create they do not exist. That is really what it is."

The flow of her thoughts is often difficult to follow, but always provocative. She might have said something like "It is that that that concerns me." It's enough to drive your spelling checker crazy, but she means what she says and what she says is often insightful.

Anyone who has had a dog or a cat will connect with her idea, that one way of being aware of being is to be aware of the way in which "my little dog knows me." Presenting the issue in this way creates the possibility of a realization about the nature of being and consciousness.

If our idea of being is attached to identity, what would it be like to simply "be." If this seems a little new "New Age" for you, think about how you might benefit as a writer by being able to recognize what attachments or assumptions may be framing your creative thought without your being aware of them. The word for this kind of ground plane is "ontology."

If we'd never heard anything but a polka, we might think that we'd created every kind of song there is if we had written polkas about everything from fresh fruit to fire engines. One trip to the local jukebox would be quite a revelation.

"We write about what we don't know about what we know."
— GRACE PALEY

8.
Mythology & Tradition

8.1 The Hero With a Thousand Faces

One place to look for those elements of dreamscape and the symbolism of the unconscious is in the stories and creative work of the past. The older and therefore less tainted by sophistication and "audience" conscious editing, the better. These primal works are known to us as "myths," and the strong universal characters as "archetypes."

In *Finnegan's Wake*, James Joyce talks of the "monomyth," the universal saga of the heroic journey. The universal hero is everyman, you and me. The mythical journey has been a subject of every folklore that has ever existed.

One man who made a life's work of the analysis of these themes in the folklore and mythology of the world was Joseph Campbell. In his introduction to *The Hero With a Thousand Faces*, Campbell writes: "There are of course differences between the numerous mythologies and religions of mankind, but this is a book about the similarities; and once these are understood the differences will be found to be much less great than is popularly (and politically) supposed. My hope is that a comparative elucidation may contribute to the perhaps not-quite-desperate cause of those forces that are working in the present world for unification, not in the name of some ecclesiastical or political empire, but in the sense of human mutual understanding. As we are told in the Vedas: 'Truth is one, the sages speak of it by many names.'"

In their book, *King, Warrior, Magician, Lover*, Robert Moore and Douglas Gillette have built on the work of Joseph Campbell and Carl Jung to explore man's history in myth and to postulate four archetypal aspects of a man's character. Moore and Gillette suggest that the fully mature and self-actualized man is a balance of the attributes of these four archetypes and that a man must claim the strengths of each of them.

This book admittedly deals with these ideas only as they apply to men, but I'm sure similar work dealing with women's issues can be found. One wonderful book along these lines is *The Chalice and the Blade* by Riane Eisler. Another is *Women Who Run With the Wolves* by Clarissa Pinkola Estes.

The Hero obviously has traits to be desired and, in the context of this work, is seen as the peak of development of the Boy psychology. The Hero helps the boy to assert himself in the world and to break with his mother. But the Hero is immature and must be brought into balance by the calm authority of the King, the aggressive might of the Warrior, the discerning eye of the Magician and the playful passion of the Lover. Moore and Gillette write: "[The Hero is] the archetype that characterizes the best in the adolescent stage of development. Yet it is immature, and when it is carried over into adulthood as the governing archetype, it blocks men from full maturity. If we think about the Hero as the Grandstander, or the Bully, this negative aspect becomes clearer."

The death of the hero is the "death" of boyhood or the boy psychology. The "end" of the Hero in myth and religious teaching is usually a transformation into a god or legendary status. The authors site Jesus' resurrection and ascension, Oedipus' final disappearance in a flash of light at Colonus, and Elijah's ascent into the sky in a fiery chariot. Contemporary examples of this archetypal legend might be James Dean and John Kennedy.

When the Hero has made his journey and the young man returns having slain the dragons and faced the demons he has grown into full stature in each the four archetypal aspects.

" ... *The lover keeps the other masculine energies humane, loving, and related to each other and to the real life situation of human beings struggling in a difficult world. The King, the Warrior, and the Magician, as we've suggested, harmonize pretty well with each other. They do so because, without the Lover, they are all essentially detached from life. They need the Lover to energize them, to humanize them, and to give them their ultimate purpose – love. They need the Lover to keep them from becoming sadistic.*

"*The Lover needs them as well. The Lover without boundaries, in his chaos of feeling and sensuality, needs the King to define limits for him, to give him structure, to order his chaos so that it can be channeled creatively. Without limits, the Lover energy turns negative and destructive. The Lover needs the Warrior in order to be able to act decisively, in order to detach, with the clean cut of the sword, from the web of immobilizing sensuality.*

"*The Lover needs the Warrior to destroy the Golden Temple, which keeps him fixated. And the Lover needs the Magician to help him back off from the ensnaring effect of his emotions, in order to reflect, to get a more objective perspective on things, to disconnect – enough at least to see the big picture and to experience the reality beneath the seeming.*"

8.2 "Courting the Muse" by Jack Hardy

Before You Sing / Before You Write

These days it seems that every person who turns 13 is issued a guitar as a rite of passage. What started out as the great equalizer, the Colt .45 of the sixties, which first allowed the nerds to outgun the jocks and win the hearts of the ladies, has now become so commonplace as to scarcely cause a pang of guilt in the yuppies when they come home from their six-figure life sentence and take down their herringbone D-28 from the wall. What has also become commonplace is songwriting. And, as with many other things that caught on in the sixties, from marijuana to baseball, it has made a rather quick jump from the mystical to the recreational. It has gone from a socially conscious, self-less ritual that existed outside the economic system to either a "me first, look at me, aren't I great" way to make money or a pipe dream hobby. Songs that were sung to anyone who would listen are now only sung either in huge stadiums or in front of the mirror.

Songwriting should be sacred. It should exist outside of the economic system, outside of the ego, outside of time in that timeless, nameless tradition that far predates the written word. But even the tradition has been corrupted. Corrupted by the academics who somehow think that songs are artifacts to be dug up, dated, catalogued, dissected, authenticated, criticized, and then generally ignored. And they're so condescending. "Aren't they adorable, the little natives, with their primitive baskets and their cute little songs." So where does that leave us, the remnants, the survivors, the writers of songs, the true poets. For what the academics forget is that at some point somebody wrote these songs.

The true songwriter today must be a wild man in terms of Robert Bly's *Iron John,* or in the terms of Moore and Gillette, he must be a king, warrior, magician, and lover, and all at the same time. If you want to be politically correct you can substitute your own politically correct language here by changing he into she, king into queen, Lawrence of Arabia into Joan of Arc, but later on you're going to have to change goddess into god and you're not going to like it. I prefer to write from a male perspective as I believe it is honest, and I do it without apologies. I also think it is possible to put the concepts "sensitive" and "singer" and "songwriter" together without creating the gestalt of "wimp."

The songwriter must be a king in his definitive actions, in his benevolence, and his concern for his people. But he must *live* like a warrior: an austere life of self-deprivation, of long hours serving a higher cause. He must be a magician, adept in the initiated knowledge of the Earth, its shapes and its signs. He must be a lover, whispering secret thoughts into the ears of all the ladies, and he must be a wild man actively working to initiate others, seducing them away from their bourgeois complacency.

The songwriter must seek knowledge, absorb it, commit it to memory. He must work long hours actively invoking the muse, hunting her. He must give in to his instincts, trust in the magic. He must passionately enchant all humanity as though it were the most beautiful woman in the world, no matter what cities he burns. Songwriting should be sacred, but not the songwriter. The songwriter should create his own ritual. His tabernacle should be language. He should absorb language and wear it as a sensuous robe. The sounds of the words are sacred. The sounds control the subconscious mind. He should not tie his work to his ego. He should not fear his own mortality, as all authorship fades with time and only the song is immortal.

This is where the bourgeois backlash begins. Chorus: "But you have to earn a living." "Surely deep down inside you must want to write a hit song." "You're just filled with sour grapes." To which you reply: "Render unto Caesar what is Caesar's and render unto the goddess what is the goddess'," knowing full well that what is the goddess' is far more interesting that what is Caesar's. Consider the word "tongue."

You see, the battle lines were drawn long ago. In the time of King Arthur the lines were drawn between the bards and the gleemen. The bards, being the inheritors of the true poetic tradition, were thrown out on the road to live in abject poverty while the gleemen, the official court bards who were the "entertainers" laid false claim to the poetic tradition and wedded it with the written word, although they did make a lot more money with it. A counterattack was started by Clarence Mangan, W.B. Yeats, Robert Graves, and only a handful of others who took out their Celtic (s)words and singlehandedly saved us from iambic pentameter. There's nothing wrong with being a gleeman, I just don't concern myself with them. They all end up in Las Vegas anyway, and I couldn't wish a worse fate on anyone.

But for all my masculine talk, "Before You Sing" (published in Sing Out! with this article) was written from the perspective of the goddess. The goddess warns: Before you sing, be aware that what you sing, you write, as we each interpret a song differently. Unless of course we are imitating, which is the sincerest form of irrelevance (although a necessary building block in learning).

The goddess also warns: Before you write, beware that what you write, you sing. A song only can exist insofar as someone listens to it. Do not write for yourself. Songwriting is not a form of self-expression or masturbation; it is a form of communication and intercourse.

You are now the singer. But as the singer you are a metaphor for society. Songwriting is metaphor. It is allegory. It is not rhetoric or simile, it is not *like* anything. As the singer, you will be confronted by the goddess your entire life. The *virgin* says you have not dealt with love in its purest sense. The *mother* says you have not dealt with the miracle of family in its purest sense. The *crone* says you have not dealt with your mortality in any sense. Unless you grapple with all three of these constantly, she says, still you will not know her.

"Before You Sing" was written for my play *The Blue Garden*, first performed at Sullivan County Community College under much controversy in March of '91. The play, set in Arthurian England, concerns the battles between peace and war, feminine and masculine, pagan and Christian, bards and gleemen, initiation and ignorance, and enlightenment and intellect. The song is the prologue of the play where a dying Lancelot appears on a field of dead knights, about to launch into a heroic aria, but is thrice silenced by the three phases of goddess. This all seemed to threaten people in the patriotic frenzy of Desert Storm. The goddess works in wondrous ways.

8.3 Honoring What Has Gone Before

The Letter From Chief Seattle

Chief (Stealth) Seattle's letter was his reply to the request by Governor Stevens on behalf of the U.S. government for the purchase of 2 million acres of tribal land in 1854. It was delivered as an oration and copied down and perhaps embellished in translation from the original Duwamish. The land comprised the region where a great city now ironically bears the chief's name.

The chief had converted to Catholicism in the 1830s and knew enough about the dealings of native peoples with the American government to know he could not really refuse the "offer." Instead, his letter gives a few words of wisdom to a race of people he felt could use the advice. In the letter we have a very eloquent description of the spiritual quality of life as practiced by the native American people.

The Letter

How can you buy or sell the sky, the warmth of the land? The idea is strange to us. If we do not own the freshness of the air and the sparkle of the water, how can you buy them?

Every part of this earth is sacred to my people. Every shining pine needle, every sandy shore, every mist in the dark woods, every clearing and humming insect is holy in the memory and experience of my people. The sap which courses through the trees carries the memories of the red man.

The white men's dead forget the country of their birth when they go to walk among the stars. Our dead never forget this beautiful earth for it is the mother of the red man.

We are part of the earth and it is part of us. The perfumed flowers are our sisters; the deer, the horse, the great eagle, these are our brothers. The rocky crests, the juices in the meadows, the bony heat of the pony, and man – all belong to the same family.

So, when the Great Chief in Washington sends word that he wishes to buy our land, he asks much of us. The Great Chief sends word he will reserve us a place so that we can live comfortably to ourselves. He will be our father and we will be his children.

So we will consider your offer to buy the land. But it will not be easy, for this land is sacred to us. This shining water that moves in the streams and rivers is not just water but the blood of our ancestors. If we sell you the land, you must remember that it is sacred, and you must teach your children that it is sacred and that each ghostly reflection in the clear water of the lakes tells of events and memories in the life of my people. The water's murmur is the voice of my father's father.

The rivers are our brothers, they quench our thirst. The rivers carry our canoes, and feed our children. If we sell you the land, you must remember, and teach your children, that the rivers are our brothers and yours and you must henceforth give the rivers the kindness you would give any brother.

We know that the white man does not understand our ways. One portion of land is the same to him as the next, for he is a stranger who comes in the night and takes from the land whatever he needs. The earth is not his brother, but his enemy, and when he has conquered it, he moves on. He leaves his father's grave behind, and he does not care. He kidnaps the earth from his children, and he does not care. His father's grave and his children's birthright are forgotten. He treats his mother, the earth, and his brother, the sky, as things to be bought, plundered, sold like sheep or bright beads. His appetite will devour the earth and leave behind only a desert.

I do not know. Our ways are different from your ways. The sight of your cities pains the eyes of the red man. There is no quiet place in the white man's cities. No place to hear the unfurling of the leaves in spring or the rustle of the insects wings. The clatter only seems to insult the ears. And what is there to life if a man cannot hear the lonely cry of the whippoorwill or the arguments of the frogs around the pond at night? I am a red man and do not understand. The Indian prefers the soft sound of the wind darting over the face of a pond and the smell of the wind itself, cleansed by a midday rain, or scented with piñon pine.

The air is precious to the red man for all things share the same breath, the beast, the tree, the man, they all share the same breath. The white man does not seem to notice the air he breathes. Like a man dying for many days he is numb to the stench. But if we sell you our land, you must remember that the air is precious to us, that the air shares its spirit with all the life it supports.

The wind that gave our grandfather his first breath also receives his last sigh. And if we sell you our land, you must keep it apart and sacred as a place where even the white man can go to taste the wind that is sweetened by the meadow's flowers.

You must teach your children that the ground beneath their feet is the ashes of our grandfathers. So that they will respect the land, tell your children that the earth is rich with the lives of our kin. Teach your children that the earth is our mother. Whatever befalls the earth befalls the sons of the earth. If men spit upon the ground, they spit upon themselves.

This we know: the earth does not belong to man; man belongs to the earth. All things are connected. We may be brothers after all. We shall see. One thing we know which the white man may one day discover: our God is the same God.

You may think now that you own Him as you may wish to own our land; but you cannot. He is the God of man, and His compassion is equal for the red man and the white. This earth is precious to Him, and to harm the earth is to heap contempt on its creator. The whites too shall pass: perhaps sooner than all other tribes. Contaminate your bed and you will one night suffocate in your own waste.

But in your perishing you will shine brightly fired by the strength of the God who brought you to this land and for some special purpose gave you dominion over this land and over the red man.

That destiny is a mystery to us, for we do not understand when the buffalo are all slaughtered, the wild horses are tame, the secret corners of the forest heavy with the scent of many men and the view of the ripe hills blotted by talking wires.

Where is the thicket? Gone. Where is the eagle? Gone. The end of living and the beginning of survival.

The treaty was signed at Point Elliot in January 1855. Seattle was adamant that the new settlement should not be named after him since he believed that in death his spirit would be disturbed each time his name was spoken.

The Houkumele

My friend Liko Martin talks about the tradition of the Houkumele, the songwriter of the Hawaiian tribal culture. In a ceremonial role, the Houkumele works in a medium of ancient mythology and values, expressed in musical performance. These song-performances translate contemporary issues and developments of tribal law into a musically and emotionally grounded oral tradition.

Liko describes Hawaiian music as symbolized by the three sides of a triangle. In order to be experienced in a meaningful and memorable way, a song must have a rhythmic dimension, a harmonic dimension, and a lyric or melodic dimension. The rhythmic song is felt in the drum, the guitar, and the dance; the harmonic song, in the sense of dissonance (tension), and consonance (resolution) in the chordal makeup of the song; and the melodic song is represented by the voice or birdsong whether or not there are any words.

9.

Stops Along the Dial

9.1 Radio Formats & Demographics

Marshall McCluhan has written extensively about the explosion of the media and its effect on our lives. He observed that the product of the television industry is not plays and shows and news and entertainment. The product that is created by television is an audience. This product is sold to the advertiser and so the "work" that is done by television is to deliver the viewer to the advertiser who pays well for the service.

How does it feel to be a commodity? Does this come as a revelation to you as it did to me? I always thought I was paying for the shows by buying the sponsors products but this put things in a whole new light.

How are we to participate in this marketplace? How should we think about the work we create and submit to this voracious monster? Is it reasonable to proceed in the possibly misguided belief that we all are participating in a universal tribal culture and our art has the dignity of being a rejoinder to other sincere and loving creative work? Or are we just forced to buy what is offered and will not be allowed to participate until we can figure out a better way to sell the sponsors' products to our unwitting neighbors? Perhaps both things are true.

"Hegemonic corporate forces encourage constant changes in artists, sounds, and products, perpetually fostering dissatisfaction subverting conventional meanings of desire and pleasure until we 'can't be satisfied.' Consumer mythologies of style and fashion condense fulfillment of our desires into the act of buying that which is 'new,' now. Clearly, such change seldom includes any significant disruption of the day-to-day, 'natural' acceptance of the 'given' order of things – of received 'reality.' Since meaningful change can be a serious threat to corporate control, superficial change – through the subversion of satisfaction – has been institutionalized. And every repackaged sound or product is pronounced new and 'revolutionary.'"

— NEAL ULLESTAD, *ROCKIN' THE BOAT*

9.2 Adult & Contemporary

Writing for Your Peers

Working for pay, even a lot of pay, is still just a job if it doesn't somehow connect with your dreams. The dream of coming through those speakers on the juke box or being up there on that stage is close to the hearts of many songwriters. For many of us it's that chance to speak to our peers, to be a part of a sacred dialogue, a validation. The process seems to begin with getting caught up in an emotional attachment to the music around us. On one level this can be analyzed and observed dispassionately but on the levels that count, we just have to give ourselves to the music and grow in it.

Looking back we can enumerate all the big events of the music of our generation and the generations before us. So many of the strong young voices of our time are tragically no longer heard but there are glorious songs that live on. It seems that to have a legitimate hope of writing a song which speaks to our generation we need to simply center ourselves in the best songs that we know and write from there.

> *Working for pay ... is still just a job if it doesn't somehow connect with your dreams.*

The shifting margins of radio formats may make this process of centering a little more complicated. These shifts of demographic tectonics are generated more by ratings and market share than by trends in the music. As one generation's music makes way for another's we may find that the writing we do relates better to a new place on the dial.

In an interview with Graham Nash we talked about the songwriters who come to mind when we think of writing for one's own generation. His voice and ideas were so pervasive throughout a time and struggle that seemed to involve us all. The songs "Teach Your Children," "Please Come to Chicago," "Our House" and other works by Graham Nash have come to represent an era of our lives.

Graham's response was, "Well you don't start out intending to have that happen, you just speak about what you see and say what you believe and if the song survives, it's just one of those fortunate things. 'Our House' was really just written as a note to Joanie.

"Songwriting has been a way of working with the problems of life. I've saved thousands in psychiatrists' fees and probably couldn't have survived without the writing. A good song has to come from someplace and has to be the real thing. All the synthesizers and electronic effects in the world can't make a song work if the human spirit isn't there."

Writing for your contemporaries seems to be a matter of writing for a community which really exists even though the structure of markets and media may impose on it a lens that ignores some great work while elevating some mediocre work to prominence. After a while the songs are the only evidence of all that struggle and the passage of time tends to sort out the good from the not so good. A good song is its own reward.

9.3 Cowboy Country

It's Not "Cowboy & Western" Anymore

Gail I. Gardner was born in the 1890s and was a real cowboy. He lived to be 95 years old and always remembered his cowboys days as the happiest of his life. Warren E. Miller wrote, "In 1917, [Gardner] wrote 'Sierry Petes,' also know as 'Tying Knots in the Devil's Tail,' which became a cowboy folksong immediately, and is still the most widely sung and recited cowboy poem among working cowboys. He wrote many other classic songs as well, among them 'The Dude Wrangler,' and 'The Moonshine Steer.'"

"Sierry Petes" was a real tall tale about some drunken cowboys who lassoed the devil and trimmed his horns and tied knots in his tale in a rugged mountain region know as the "Sierry Petes." Even in 1917 there was already a thriving tradition of cowboy songs and poems. An earlier song which is still popular today among cowboys is "Little Joe The Wrangler," written in 1898 by Jack Thorp, a rancher and collector of cowboy songs.

"The Strawberry Roan," originally titled, "The Outlaw Bronco" was written by a rodeo promoter named Curley Fletcher in 1915. It is also a kind of a tall tale about an unrideable bronc. "Whoopee-Ti-Yi-Yo," a real work song, goes back to the 1880s. Like most cowboy songs written before the singing cowboy era, it portrays the cowboy's life as hard, dangerous work, hardly edible food, and lonely hours of herding cattle. Later songs tended to romanticize the cowboy life as carefree and picturesque. Current country songs have taken this transformation a step further to emphasize the rugged independence and the gun-toting machismo of the outlaw West.

As popular music began to embrace the myth of the cowboy, songs became more musically sophisticated and the romance aspect played a larger part. "When the Work's All Done This Fall" was a poem written by cowboy poet D.J. O'Malley in the 1890s. Recorded as a song in 1925 by Carl T. Sprague, the record sold 90,000 copies and generated some interest in the commercial possibilities of cowboy music. Jimmie Rodgers recorded his song "When the Cactus Is In Bloom" in 1931 and also lent commercial energy to cowboy songs.

A new image of the cowboy began to emerge with songs like "I Want To Be a Cowboy's Sweetheart" by Patsy Montana, the first million-selling country song by a female singer, in 1935. The Sons of the Pioneers were formed in 1934 and released "Hold That Critter Down" written by Bob Nolan in 1937. They had a very smooth vocal blend and went on to have many hit records including "Cool Water" and "Tumbling Tumbleweed." Gene Autry was an established "singing cowboy" in films and on record when he wrote "Back In the Saddle Again" with Ray Whitley, also a successful singing cowboy, in 1939.

The band formed by Bob Wills, a traditional Texas fiddler, and Milton Brown developed a unique blending of regional and big-band musical influences and created a new form of dance music which is known as "western swing." Their many hit records include "You're From Texas," "Rose of San Antone," and "Faded Love." Woody Guthrie and his cousin Jack Guthrie had a big hit in 1945 with a song called "Oklahoma Hills." This song and the early work of Hank Williams began to suggest a new direction in country music but the cowboy songs have made their reappearance year after year.

With the advent of television and the many cowboy-oriented shows interest in cowboy songs was renewed. Roy Rogers and Dale Evans adopted Dale's song "Happy Trails" as their theme in 1952. Marty Robbins connected with a whole new generation with his gunfighter ballads and the song, "El Paso." The "Outlaw" image has worked for Willie Nelson and Waylon Jennings and the myth of the cowboy will probably be with us forever.

Today, the songs that wear the big hats are likely to be in the more sophisticated and socialized boy-next-door, mainstream country style that we have come to identify with the "hat" acts of today. Randy Travis, Garth Brooks, John Anderson, Travis Tritt, and Clint Black are a far holler from the busted up, saddle-sore, dust-eatin' buckeroos of a hundred years ago.

Out in the "high lonesome" stretches of New Mexico and Texas and even in Bakersfield there are a handful of songwriters steeped in the traditions of the cowboy but educated in contemporary thought. These "Zen" or "cosmic" cowboys have explored another side of the myth and their work confronts the existential dilemma. Many of them vegetarians, these guys are not committed to the beef industry, but to an admiration of the cowboy's self-relliance and spiritual strength.

9.4 The Blues Ain't Nothin' But a Good Man Feelin' Bad

The slave ships brought men and women in chains from the west coast of Africa. With them came many of the elements of musical expression which have become the blues, gospel music, rhythm and blues and rock and roll. Primarily an oral tradition, the singing of the African slaves served to perpetuate what they could of their cultures, and as their music intermingled with the European traditions of music it changed both.

One of the most obvious of these attributes is the bending of some of the notes of the scale to create "blue notes." Some of the notes are lowered to give the mournful sound of notes "in the cracks" or falling in between notes of the more rigid European scales.

Another of the traits of the early slave music is repetition. One form of this is found in "call and response" songs. In work songs, the leader would shout out a line and the other workers would repeat the same phrase or sometimes a variation of that phrase. These songs were very rhythmic and they coordinated work tasks of lifting or hoeing, and later swinging hammers in coal mines, railroad tunnels and on prison chain gangs.

Instruments were very scarce. The banjo is descended from an African gourd instrument and there were other simple stringed instruments, and much later, guitar, but drums were forbidden by slave owners because of their potential for fomenting and even coordinating an uprising. The primary musical and rhythmic instrument was the body. Many forms of clapping, dancing, even "hambone" are examples of this practice. One ex-slave called the polyrhythmic body music "patting juba." It consisted of "striking the right shoulder with one hand, the left with the other – all the while keeping time with the feet and singing."

Another example of the call and response in music of the African-American tradition is found in church meetings. In the practice often called "deaconing," a church elder will "line out" a hymn and the congregation will follow and repeat each line of text. Interspersed with other vocal sounds and "Amens" and hand claps, this music is still alive and exciting today in churches all across the country.

It is this music which has become the blues. This is the first music that the great bluesmen heard, and this music today is the source of the musical heart of the blues, rhythm and blues and rock and roll. It is the first music of many of the greatest singers and recording artists of our time.

Legendary bluesman Big Bill Broonzy started as a preacher and then went on to record more than 200 songs from 1925 to 1952. He acknowledged this connection between gospel and the blues. He said, "The blues won't die because spirituals won't die. Blues (is) a steal from spirituals. And rock is a steal from the blues. ... Blues singers start out singing spirituals."

In the blues we have a subtle shift from singing about the human condition in terms of a life to be left behind as we make our way to glory in the hereafter, to singing about the condition of one's life to one's neighbor, in simple personal terms. The blues is the way we talk to each other not necessarily the way we would talk to the "Lord."

Many rural Southern blacks migrated to the cities of the North at the turn of this century and especially after World War I. Chicago was the destination for many of these migrants. They left behind the plague of the boll weevil that ravaged the Mississippi Delta in 1915 and 1916, starvation, and terrible racial discrimination and were drawn to the industrialized cities where they could take up jobs in the steel mills and stockyards. This was especially true as the war cut off European immigration.

The Defender was a widely read, black-owned newspaper published in Chicago which encouraged Southern sharecroppers to migrate to the

North. Some of the musicians who made their way to the city during this time were Tampa Red, Roosevelt Sykes, John Lee "Sonny Boy" Williamson (the first Sonny Boy), Peetie Wheatstraw, Ollie Shepard, Blind Boy Fuller, Washboard Sam, Little Brother Montgomery, Blind Lemon Jefferson, Memphis Minnie, and Rosetta Howard.

At first the music of these artists was the straight country blues but as the influences of the city and the travels of other musicians affected their music, many moved into a more rhythmically sophisticated style. One major influence was the boogie-woogie, rolling bass piano style associated with Louis Jordan's jump blues band. Many of these artists released records on the Bluebird Label, and theirs was referred to as the "Bluebird Beat."

The early Delta bluesmen such as Charley Patton, and Eddie "Son" House influenced the next generation which included Willie Brown and Robert Johnson. These influences extended to McKinley "Muddy Waters" Morganfield, Willie Dixon, Elmore James, John Lee Hooker, Chester "Howlin' Wolf" Burnett, Elias "Bo Diddley" McDaniel, "Little Walter" Jacobs, Rice "Sonny Boy Williamson II" Miller, and Riley "BB" King. From here rock and roll is only a stone's throw.

All of these pioneers began in church and describe their early musical training as gospel music and spirituals. But as they moved into the burgeoning world of recording and performing for blues audiences their music took on a much more secular character. A quick survey of the titles of some of their songs will give some idea of this transition.

From "Pony Blues" to "Pea Vine Blues" to "Preachin' the Blues," "Dust My Broom," "Ramblin' On My Mind," "Sweet Home Chicago," "Hoochie Coochie Man," "Sittin' On Top of the World," "I'm a Man," "I Can't Be Satisfied," "Louisiana Blues," "Long Distance Call," "Rollin' and Tumblin'," "Killing Ground," "She Loves Me," "Rolling Stone," "Smokestack Lightning," "I'm Ready," and "I've Got My Mojo Working."

Rhythm & Blues & Soul Music

R&B giants like Little Richard, the Isley Brothers, James Brown, Jackie Wilson, Curtis Knight, B.B. King and Albert King found their acceptance as the emerging music industry began to embrace this music. David P. Szatmary wrote, "The term *soul* had been used by African Americans during the fifties to suggest a black identity. In a vague sense, it defined the essence of being black in America. Bebop musicians had soul." In 1957 hornman Lou Donaldson recorded "Swing and Soul"; the next year saxophone great John Coltrane released "Soultrane"; trombonist Benny Green cut "Soul Stirring"(1958) and "Hornful of Soul"(1959); trumpeter Blue Mitchell played "Blue Soul"(1959); and saxophonist Johnny Griffin led a "Big Soul-Band" (1960). When bop gave way to hard bop during the early sixties, Eldridge Cleaver noted in "Soul on

Ice" that many referred to the sound as "soul music." James Brown ("Papa's Got a Brand New Bag"), Ray Charles, The Genius of Soul, ("What'd I Say?" and "Hit the Road, Jack"), Wilson Pickett ("In the Midnight Hour" and "Mustang Sally"), Otis Redding ("Sittin' On the Dock of the Bay"), Sam Moore and Dave Prater ("Hold On, I'm Comin'"), Aretha Franklin ("Respect") and Percy Sledge ("When a Man Loves a Woman") all found their audiences there.

9.5 Doo-Wop, Hip Hop & Rap

Following World War II, as the recording process became more accessible to black artists and records began to play a greater part in the lives of urban whites and blacks, the sound of the music began to take a new turn. Spontaneous vocal sessions by young urban groups of kids in school or on the streets created a blended and romantic sound that began to reach an enormous new audience of young people.

In 1948 the Orioles recorded a major hit record, "It's Too Soon To Know," which broke with the established vocal styles of the Ink Spots and the Mills Brothers. Then came other early records by the Ravens, the Five Keys, the Crows and the Harp-Tones. These groups, although more in the secular, night club arena, still owed a lot to the gospel process which would later produce Sam Cooke, Otis Redding, Aretha Franklin and other pop giants.

"Earth Angel" by the Penguins is perhaps the most famous of all songs of the era of young love and transcended all barriers. The background vocal "oh-woe-woes" and the slow triplet piano accompaniment established a sound that was to be imitated and built upon by the Moonglows, the Platters, the Flamingos, the Channels the Clovers, the Dells and the Heartbeats.

The Five Satins recorded "In The Still Of The Night" in a church basement in New Haven in 1956. This record brought the doo-wop phrase "shoo doo'din shoo-bee-doo" to the radio and fostered many more groups of young romantic crooners and small independent labels.

The Moonglows' "Sincerely" featured the phrase "Ooh, oo-wee-wooh, vooit vooit." Prominent in the Flamingos version of "I Only Have Eyes For You" was the phrase "Doo-bop sh-bop." The Marcels sang "Bomp-ba ba bomp, ba bomp ba bomp bomp, ba-ba bomp ba-ba bomp, da-dang da-dang dang, da ding-a-dong ding" in their hit version of the standard "Blue Moon." And, the Silhouettes had the nation singing "Yip-yip-yip-yip-yip-yip-yip-yip-mum-mum-mum-mum-mum-mum – Get a Job."

Groups like the Capris, the Cadillacs, Frankie Lymon and the Teenagers, the Monotones, continued the doo-wop lineage which eventually included The Dell Vikings, Dion and the Belmonts, The Four Seasons, and even Diana Ross and Michael Jackson. The creation of the Motown establishment in the sixties and the disco disestablishment of the seventies eclipsed the doo-wop sound except for occasional nostalgia revivals.

Hip-hop is the successor to the street-wise and spontaneous music of the fifties with one obvious difference. The streets seem to be a lot meaner and the subject matter of the songs is a love which is found on very different terms from the innocent and ethereal tones of its forebears. Hip-hop and its irreverent cousin rap are vehicles for the outspoken expression of the issues of a people who feel their disenfranchisement and refuse to endure it in silence. The blues was sad, Rap is mad.

Nas, a 20-year-old rapper from a Queens, N.Y., housing project raps a song called "N.Y. State of Mind." The song lists an arsenal of weapons and portrays the pervasive violence of the city today and its effect on youth. At one point the song says: "It's like the game ain't the same / Younger niggers pullin' the triggers / Bringing fame to they name."

In the form, melodic turns are not there to lend emotional underscore to the lyric ideas. The words must really stand on their own and answer the urgency of the rhythm track. This allows for some range of emotional expression but tends to lean toward the angry and the rebellious. Just as the blues was the true medium of the poor rural black, rap is the voice of the young urban artist. If it isn't pretty, that's because it's true.

The language of the form is also the raw language of the culture. If it seems raw to a listener with an MOR (middle of the road) perspective it doesn't sound so strange to the young people whose lives it represents.

"These words (expletives) are just the way we talk. It's a black thing. If somebody picks up the phone and hears us talking and it disturbs them, just put down the phone!"
— Ice T

9.6 Rock & Roll Will Never Die

The appearance of the first rock and roll creations of the early fifties horrified most people who had a stake in the music of the previous generation. It seemed to open the door to all the frightening things of the world: sexuality, rebellion, racial mixing and the breakdown of conformity and the status quo. This turned out to be all too true. But just as the ancient Greeks had characterized the forces of creation in terms of Eros and Thanatos, with the rising up and the tearing down of one order and the establishment of another, rock and roll changed everything forever.

What has replaced the old music is different, not really better, and not really so different in terms of its musical principles, but a new order to replace the old. Young energetic producers challenge the old intransigent star system and become the system themselves, often for the benefit of the oil companies or multinational corporations which "help" them to reach a larger market. But the new voices and their creative energy spring eternal like blades of grass through the cracks in the concrete. What really seems to be different is that change, rebellion and iconoclasm seem to be a part of everything since "Hound Dog," and there's no going back now.

9.7 Video

I Want Mine on T.V.

The early expansion of videos into 24-hour household exposure on MTV, VH-1 and The Nashville Network has changed things for the songwriter. Record companies have discovered that videos are a great way to market their artists and have committed large resources to video production. With all the hype, it remains to be seen if music videos are truly a new art form or just commercials for the songs. There are some very talented filmmakers involved in the young medium and generally the entertainment values are there, but it does raise some new questions for the songwriter.

Songs are now chosen to be recorded as much for their video possibilities as for any other aspect of their merit as songs. Many are not really songs at all but vehicles for a fashion show, or a series of poses. Many are so committed to the visual marketplace that they don't seem to mind that they don't hold up as songs on the radio. And yet, the same things that make a song a good song are true of songs for the visual medium and in the long will run will prove their worth. Just as in the case of the 5-year-old who said, "I like radio, because the pictures are better," it's still true that the imagination is the place where songs live. If this experience is enhanced by the video, allthe better, better still if the song is really there to be enhanced.

Songs are now chosen to be recorded as much for their video possibilities as for any other aspect of their merit as songs.

9.8 Writing for the Movies by Tom Bocci

Songwriting for the Silver Screen

Have you ever watched a motion picture that was photographed through the lens of a fine artist's eye, directed from the heart with cinematic sensitivity, acted by fully realized characters who ran the gamut of emotions in their performances, and punctuated with realistic sound effects; but noticeably lacking in one primary area of production?

This scenario has occurred many times for me both as a songwriter and music supervisor after viewing a "rough assemblage" of a film in progress. My reaction is always the same. Without *music* a motion picture lacks the impact of an important compatible partner. One can only imagine living in the year 1927 after *seeing* and *hearing* Al Jolson's image and voice in perfect synchronization sing "Toot, Toot, Tootsie!" in the big screen version of *The Jazz Singer*.

From that moment on, songwriters everywhere realized this new and magnificent medium would provide them with endless possibilities for the blend of song and picture. This potential was not overlooked by the songwriting legends of the "Golden Age" such as Irving Berlin, Cole Porter, Jerome Kern, and the Gershwins, who all produced standards while writing for the silver screen.

Today a motion picture by its very nature is a complicated art form integrating a variety of talents that require a strong adhesive to bind the individual parts together and trigger emotions felt by the senses beyond the visual. But that is also the main reason film and music complement each other so perfectly like a string of pearls whose overall beauty is dependent on the exquisite quality of each individual gem. This ongoing partnership has turned into a celebrated legacy which continues to prosper and nurture both sides in the process.

As we approach their upcoming centennial celebration, it is apparent that movies have taken an astounding leap forward in advanced technology. However, it is still the creative talents of the composer and songwriter that remain the key in helping to translate the director's vision musically. Unlike writing a song for inclusion on an album or with a particular artist in mind, the major part of the songwriter's task here is to serve the picture first. This makes the contribution of an original song a significant ingredient in the mix, by adding its excitement, energy, poignancy, tension or nostalgia while furthering the communication of the director's intent toward the audience.

This brings us to the two distinct challenges songwriters face when crafting a song for a movie. First, if the sequence has not yet been filmed, you must rely on a combination of the script's descriptive detail and the ability of the producer or music supervisor to convey the director's vision.

At this point the songwriter must become an architectural detective by asking many specific questions to help determine the musical blueprint for designing the song. "Will the tempo accentuate or be in counterpoint to the action?" "If there is dialogue, should I avoid 'fighting it' with lyrics by modifying a normal verse-chorus-bridge construction with instrumental release sections?" "Do you have a particular musical style in mind for the song?"

"Is there a 'temp track' that reflects the kind of sound you're hearing?" This last question could be very helpful but may also open a Pandora's Music Box. "Temp Tracks" were nicknamed for a good reason. They can be familiar or sometimes even obscure songs that serve as temporary guides until your original contributions replace them. The best advice in this situation comes from a paraphrase attributed to Davy Crockett, himself the subject of a hit song from a movie. "Be sure you're right (about what the 'powers that be' want), then go ahead."

Second and more frequently, a songwriter is brought in during post-production, once the movie has entered the "first cut" stage. This meeting follows a group screening involving the director, producer, composer and music supervisor, as well as the film and music editors gathered to "spot" various scenes of the film to determine where the score will be placed, and where "source music" (songs) will be most effective. At this point the timings for each cue are also calculated and individual assignments given. Now the ultimate role of the song can range from *heroic* (a main or end title song), to *supportive* (strengthening a key scene with emotional impact).

Sometimes the right approach can serve *both* functions while creating an indelible synthesis of screen image and song that cannot be separated in one's memory. Like a word association game, certain movies provide classic examples, such as: "As Time Goes By" from *Casablanca*; "Moon River," from *Breakfast At Tiffany's*; "High Noon (Do Not Forsake Me)" from *High Noon*; "Up Where We Belong" from *An Officer and a Gentleman* and "I Will Always Love You" from *The Bodyguard*.

This last title carries with it a wonderful exercise in song recycling. It was a well-known Dolly Parton country song until being newly arranged and re-recorded for the movie by Whitney Houston. Then it reappeared as a multiplatinum hit that not only furthered the action on the screen, but helped build up considerable box-office receipts. So please don't ever downplay the work you may have already done. You probably have existing lyrics, melodies, or even songs that could be called upon to custom fit a future film assignment after a bit of rewrite and polish. Use this unique opportunity for adaptation and build upon it as a foundation for a more rewarding outcome.

You might ask, "When will my opportunity come along?" There's no way of really knowing; but when it does, it will be the cumulative result of efforts you have already made, talents you have nurtured over many years, and the good fortune to be in the right place at the right time. So whether your journey there has just begun or you're hoping to make a return visit, remember the world of the silver screen is made of very precious metal which will always respond well to the vibrations made by heartfelt music.

10.

Fadin' In, Fadin' Out

10.1 All Songs Are Political

"Culture can seem like a substitute for politics, a way of posing only imaginary solutions to real problems, but under other circumstances, culture can become a rehearsal for politics, trying out values and beliefs permissible in art but forbidden in social life. Most often, however, culture exists as a form of politics, as a means of reshaping individual and collective practice for specified interests ..."
— GEORGE LIPSITZ

What Are the Issues?

"Rock's leftist bias arose from its origins as a music by outsiders – by blacks in a white society, by rural whites in a rapidly urbanizing economy, by regional performers in a pop-music industry dominated by New York, by youth lashing out against the settled assumptions of pre-rock pop-music professionals.
"That bias was solidified by the 1960s with its plethora of causes and concerns ... Rock music was the anthem of that change – racial with the civil-rights movement, and also social, sexual, and political."
— JOHN ROCKWELL, THE NEW YORK TIMES

Speaking Out of Turn

Coming out of a culture with an oral and musical tradition and living through a time of upheaval and the struggle for freedom and human dignity, young musicians in the middle of this century found themselves in an explosion of radio and record opportunities. There had always been issues but there was now the chance to be heard.

Access vs. Content

Small, independent music producers have been able to reach a larger and larger audience with their work, and that work has been able to carry an ever larger amount of their own thoughts and beliefs. at the same time, the giant, connected marketing entities, the corporate music and mediaestablishment have seen fit to take some of this work in hand and promote and distribute it on a worldwide scale. This has created superstars out of a handful of talented people, people who were willing to be the standard bearers of the values promoted by their corporate benefactors.

Anyone who has espoused a view which is troublesome or too radical, has had to make it on his or her own. Amazingly, this too is also possible in our time. The difference seems to be only in the numbers of listeners that can be reached by the artist who holds out for independence. It's not that the mega-stars can't say some pretty outrageous things. Billy Idol can stand naked to the waist in full color video brandishing a broadsword and snarl, "Nice day for a white wedding." or almost any other epithet but my guess is that he couldn't get away with saying anything truly relevant.

It may be that there is a trade-off between the things that contribute to the access that an artist may gain through the stringent application of "entertainment value" and the things that contribute to the content of work that is worth doing. In other words, to be free to say anything worth saying you may have to do it on your own nickel. Many of us are to a certain extent refugees from the music industry and some have learned enough to survive and produce good art. There will always be the belief in the possibility of a true global tribal culture which is not filtered through the corporate sieve, but at this point it is still something to work toward.

10.2 Interview with Len Chandler

Len, I know that you must have a lot of interesting things to share with us about your experience as a writer for the Credibility Gap. How did that come about?

Len: Lou Irwin was the producer of the *Credibility Gap* radio segments for radio KRLA in Los Angeles. I met him in 1966 through my friend Cliff Vaughs, whom I met through the civil rights movement in Mississippi in the summer of '64. At the time I met Lou Irwin he was doing a documentary for CBS on a voter registration drive in Lowndes County, Alabama. Cliff had told him that I was a good writer and how rapidly I could write since I had written a lot of songs overnight for a demonstration that was going to be held the next day and that type of thing.

In Alabama we would meet in a motel room and Lou would describe to me film footage that he had already shot. He would say, "All right, here is a tent city and these are the workers who have been forced off their land because they had registered to vote." So he would describe in detail what the visual image would be and what a lot of the dialogue was saying. And then he would tell me, "So I need a minute-and-thirty-five-second song to go into this place."

So I would go and sit in the bathroom and write because they would be talking in the other room, and then I would write and I would come out and record on his Nagra tape recorder what I had just written. And so we did that ... I think I might have written seven or eight songs for that documentary like that. He won some kind of awards for the documentary and was very impressed by that work and the rapidity with which it was accomplished so when he became the news director of KRLA radio he decided that he was going to use a format similar to *That Was the Week that Was* and that he would use several topical kind of comics who would write sketches and do funny bits on what happened in the news that day.

So, Lou brought me to California in early 1968. We would create three original ten-minute shows a day at 9, and at 12 noon and at 3 p.m. Each of those shows would be repeated three times so it was around the clock, we were on every three hours.

Were there times when you found it difficult to do the writing in that short a time?

Len: When we first started I would be really nervous all the time because I'm wondering where the next song is going to come from. But after about six months, I would get up at maybe 5:30 and make the drive to Pasadena to go to work and I would clip the microphone of my tape recorder to my shirt and turn on the radio. I would hear a story that might interest me and I would just tape the facts. So then I could hand that to the writer for the news lead because all the songs had to start with a news story to set up what was happening.

Sometimes you have a melody in your mind and all the ideas fall into place and you have the song pretty easily, but sometimes you started to get desperate. Let us say that I got my 9 o'clock song and then it was 11 o'clock and I hadn't found a topic for the 12 o'clock song yet. If I haven't found a topic by 11:30 then I'm really nervous. Sometimes you would have to sing the song in whatever form you had it. They would just take it down like it is because we were just out of time. And it would not be the best performance when you just wrote it and are trying to read it off a sheet that's taped to a microphone.

One of the devices that I started to employ to write really fast when I didn't have a melody in my mind would be to use somebody else's melody. What I would do is use the melody as a dummy for the words I was writing, I would be ripping off form, not melody, and nothing else. Let's say that whatever the words were I had decided ... the form that I was going to use was; "You are the da da, da da da" [sings the melody to "You Are the Sunshine of My Life"]. So then I would write my lyric to that and then I would change the melody and I would change the chord structure and I would change the rhythm pattern and Stevie wouldn't even know it had come from that.

But what I have done is just allowed myself a framework so I'm not just drifting all over the place. And I would do that when I needed to and I've written a whole bunch of different songs on known melodies. And I changed everything and so, I even forgot what they were.

There were a lot of things happening in those days. Are there any events that you remember as being particularly momentous?

Len: Well, the show had been on for only two or three days and the first major thing that happened was that Bobby Kennedy was assassinated. I was home watching the news in the morning because every morning you had to be in the studio by 9 o'clock – with a song. And in those early days I was sometimes kind of hysterical trying to find subjects for songs reading the papers and listening to the news. So when I saw on the news that Bobby Kennedy had been shot I just took my typewriter and all my instruments, my oboe and English horn, and my two guitars and my autoharp and my little toy piano and moved into the studio. I went to the studio and just took a sleeping bag with me and we didn't leave for a week.

"... to write really fast [without] a melody in mind ... use somebody else's melody."

That first song, "Circle Dance," was really powerful. When people heard it, they were astounded. They said, "Well, that just happened today, how could that be?" It said, "Bobby stood smiling, the image of triumph, his fingers flashed "V" as he stepped from the stand, pushing through crowds of his youthful admirers, with smiles and waves and the shaking of hands ..." But the hook of the song was "circle dance" – where will it end and when? And there were other songs, too. Let's see, I've got my guitar here – "From a lineage of courage to a legacy of pain, long lines line the long, long tracks of another lonesome train."

I've wanted to ask you, looking back on it now, do you feel as if that kind of work and those kinds of songs really do have an impact?

Len: Well, we would get all kinds of response. We would get mail that said that we should be taken off the air because it would be danger-ous to be driving and listening because they almost had a wreck be-cause they were laughing so loud. I mean, uh ... we did all kinds of parody and sometimes the left would be as mad at us as the right because we would be satirizing silly stuff that everybody was doing. I would be writing funny stuff and sometimes it would be "hits you in the heart" stuff, and ...

Did you feel that people who were listening were looking for something that would reassure them?

Len: I guess the function of a songwriter is to always go to the very essence of it ... the essence of the story and find what the hook is, what the unifying element is ... Sometimes I would take two or three stories and wonder if something was going on. Sometimes it might be funny ... but I think that the function of art is to try to make sense of our existence, and to find that unifying thread and to maybe show a little glimpse of humanity someplace.

Why Speak Out? Why Risk?

As a songwriter you can really make a difference. This has been demonstrated time and again. But there is someone else who is listeningand that person has a greater stake in the content of your work. That person is the you, the writer.

"You can hold yourself back from the sufferings of the world, this is something you are free to do and is in accord with your nature, but perhaps precisely this holding back is the only suffering that you might be able to avoid."
— FRANZ KAFKA

What Is There to Speak Out About?

Just a little breeze out of the sky,
The leaves pat their hands as the breeze blows by.
Just a little breeze with some smoke in its eye,
What have they done to the rain?
— MALVINA REYNOLDS

10.3 The Women's Movement & Music

It is only very recently that women have been able to participate in the music industry in a way that did not limit their expression to the few roles that men have created for them. A few talented women artists, encouraged by a small but supportive community of strongly feminist record buyers and concert goers, were able to forge an active mini music industry on the West Coast. They were seeking to provide a medium for the expression of their own ideas and also to support other women who wanted to work in music as singers, writers, engineers, producers and agents.

Early recordings were "Angry Athis" by Maxine Feldman, Goffin and King's "Lady" by Meg Christian, "If It Weren't For the Music" and "Sweet Woman" by Cris Williamson. Sweet Honey in the Rock recorded "B'lieve I'll Run On ... See What the End's Gonna Be."

All of these were successful within the women's music community, but these artists had not yet gained acceptance in the mainstream, for a variety of reasons. The mainstream may not have been ready for them, but they were not ready to compromise the values they lived by and so worked to make their own music community more successful. Ronnie Gilbert, Margie Adams, Holly Near, Linda Tillary, Ferron, Hunter Davis, Nancy Vogl, Betsy Rose, Phranc, Melissa Etheridge, and 2 Nice Girls have all had a presence in the emerging women's music movement.

Alix Dobkin wrote in the liner notes to her album "Lavender Jane Loves Women": "For a dozen years I tried to 'make it' in the music business – as a solo artist, demo artist, in groups, as a songwriter, a commercial writer and even in coffeehouse management. So many times I came so close, and felt great frustration and disappointment. Always there was this rough element of mine – an abrasive edge – an imperfection. Record and publishing executives, independent producers, managers, agents, PR men and assorted hustlers could never quite polish me into a neat commercial package. Lucky for me."

> " ... to detail the relationship between the 1970's and 1980's phenomena of women's music and the new wave of women performers who've become popular in the late '80s and '90s: Tracy Chapman, Michelle Shocked, k.d. lang and others. Do these performers represent the cooptation of women's music by major labels that now realize the buying power of feminist and lesbian audiences (for example, Michelle Shocked's Texas Campfire Tapes, an album originally recorded on a Sony Walkman, sold 30,000 copies to the women's community in England)? Are the more 'androgynous' artists (we don't say 'lesbian' on major labels) now acceptable to fans who have tired of the stereotyped male fantasies of female pop singers, or is this another quickly passing trend in the music business?
> — CYNTHIA M. LONT, ROCKIN' THE BOAT

Michelle Shocked's *Texas Campfire Tapes* was recorded in the campgrounds at the Kerrville Folk Festival and brought a lot of attention to the festival as well as to the songwriting community of Texas.

Suzanne Vega's song "Luka" created a breakthrough for women's issues in the mainstream media. A song about physical abuse, it connected with a substrata of American experience and fostered an interest in "serious" songs. At least it served to lend impetus to those who would like to see the music industry be more responsive to "real" human (and especially women's) issues.

In any case a handful of talented and dedicated women have made a workable sub-genre where little existed before. These women seemed to be doing what they did for the right reasons and their efforts benefit all who come after.

"There I am, hacking with my machete, making my way through the jungle and I look behind me and Tracy's striding down the path. Part of me is a bit jealous of that success. And in my rational mind I say, Cris, this is why you did it."
— Cris Williamson, in an interview

10.4 "Courting the Muse" by Ani DiFranco

On Writing Women's Music

I often read in reviews, previews, programs, and articles that I am a "feminist songwriter" or that I write "women's music." Since men tend to own newspapers, dominate the media, define the culture, write the history, run the government, and generally rule the world, I'm inclined to think I should give their portrayal of me some consideration. And I have.

After careful consideration I have come to the conclusion that you can't believe everything that you read. Or, as Chuck D. would say, "You can't truss it."

For example, the notion that I write women's music is sorta silly when you consider that women make up 53% of the world's population. If I am speaking from the majority of human experience, doesn't that mean that I write music, and men write "men's music"?

The label "women's music" only makes sense from a patriarchal frame of reference which positions men on the inside and women on the fringes. The problem that I have with the labels used by the media to describe my music is not usually with the words themselves but the perspective from which they stem. This perspective reduces me to anger and portrays my music as somehow specialized or extreme rather than as a legitimate voice speaking to and of the human condition. It ghetto-izes my music and marginalizes my experience. Most of the words I read are true, and yet they perpetuate a big ol' lie. The lie is that my life is unusual and/or one-dimensional.

In fact, I am three-dimensional. I love women and womanhood, and I also love men and masculinity. I write on a variety of subjects and yet rarely read about any aspects of my music other than its feminism.

Part of my daily life is catching men in the act of being schmucks and because I've written about that, like I've written about everything else that has happened to me, a red flag has gone up in the music business. "Steer clear of this one," it says, "she's trouble."

When rock gods jump around stages wielding their guitars like weapons and singing "do me, do me, do me baby, you look so fine, wanna be your daddy, wanna make you mine," people rarely belabor the masculinism of the music. And when folksingers sing labor songs, songs of working for the boss mans, of soldiers going off to war, or of their experience of loving someone, few people go on about the uniquely male frame of reference.

Robert Johnson, Bob Dylan, Billy Bragg, and Ice T can sing about their lives as men and not be labeled "men's music." It seems ludicrous to even try and imagine a label such as "men's music" because there is such a huge unrecognized bias in the way we think about music and all of life. Men's experience is considered universal and women's is not.

Rock and roll is just rock and roll and folk music is just folk music until a woman does it. Only then does gender awareness prevail. Suddenly, "political" is translated into "feminism" and the whole kit and caboodle is thrown into a box marked "women's music" to be opened only for special women's hour radio shows.

Women are 53% of history. We have 53% of all the heartbreaks, we have 53% of the fun, we make 53% of all the embarrassing blunders, and this business of pretending we are some special interest group is too weird.

It's not that I don't love women-only spaces, or appreciate the value of women's networking and solidarity. It's just that sometimes it feels as though our space is only rented from some sleazy guy who owns the building.

If women owned some concert halls, radio and TV stations, if we ran music festivals and record companies, women's hour would be longer than an hour, if you know what I mean.

The only way the double standard is going to disappear is if we make it disappear. More women have to flood the airwaves and the concert halls with their voices. We can't be afraid to write about our experiences in everything from relationships to working to walking down the street. We gotta get up in their faces. Women and men, together, have to insist on diversity and respect for women musicians, instead of patronizing tokenism.

How many women are reading this? Do you write music? How many people of any make and model are willing to put their butts on the line and risk being pigeonholed? I think that if enough of us did so, eventually there'd be no more pigeonholes.

In the meantime, this pigeonhole isn't such a bad place to be, given the alternatives – or should I say, the mainstream.

10.5 Songs of Rebellion

Yankee Doodle & Dixie

Songs have figured prominently in political movements since ancient times. Our own rebellion and revolution was to the tune of "Yankee Doodle," actually a much older melody with words adapted from a rhyme that was originally intended as an insult.

The Irish people have coped with the British occupation much in the way an oyster copes with a grain of sand. In the struggle to maintain a national identity and to keep faith with their ancient culture the Irish people have created many beautiful song-pearls. Music seems to be a suitable medium of transmission for the difficult emotions of national pride and hope, and the songs convey much of the strong current of human dignity.

All Over This World

Oh, Paddy dear and did you hear the news that's goin' round?
The shamrock is forbid by law to grow on Irish ground ...
You may take the shamrock from your hat and cast it on the sod,
But 'twill take root and flourish there though underfoot 'tis trod.

Traditional

Tommy Sands has written an eloquent indictment of the unending cycle of violence in Northern Ireland in his song "There Were Roses." At one point the song observes that we will continue exacting "an eye for an eye, until the whole world is blind." The chorus, which is very moving, is deceptively simple: "There were roses, roses, there were roses, and the tears of the people ran together."

The 15th Brigade, an international unit consisting of volunteers from twenty-five countries, fought against the fascists in the Spanish Civil War in the 1930s. That conflict left a rich legacy songs.

At times even a performance of Chopin's "Polonaise" was fraught with political implications.

"Sun City" protested the apartheid regime in South Africa.

Although it might be asserted that economic sanctions against the apartheid government of South Africa brought about the end of apartheid, the political will to enact those sanctions could be said to have been greatly affected by the expressions prominent in the popular culture, and the actions of some very public personalities.

The most prominent of the anti-apartheid demonstrations was the Sun City phenomenon. "Sun City" first appeared as a single record release at the New Music Seminar in New York. After creating a stir and generating support among musicians it grew into an album and showed up on Billboard's Top 40. The energy of the Sun City idea next became a video and then a paperback book.

"'Sun City' challenged musicians to consider the deepest implications of their work and success, taking thoughtfulness far beyond the tentative steps of Live Aid. Further, Artists United Against Apartheid – including Pat Benatar, George Clinton, Bruce Springsteen, Bonnie Raitt, Jimmy Cliff, Ruben Blades, Darlene Love, the late David Ruffin, Lou Reed, Bob Dylan, Miles Davis, Stanley Jordan, Peter Gabriel, Gil Scott-Heron, Nona Hendryx, and dozens more – openly challenged the audience to consider the world situation in light of specific policies and their effects. As an avowed educational campaign, 'Sun City' reached many people who otherwise would have remained ill-informed."
— NEAL ULLESTAD, *ROCKIN' THE BOAT*

Some of the best songs we know were created in answer to the need for a song to bring people of like mind together. To organize for a union, to confront a common enemy, or remember a truth arrived at through struggle and sacrifice. This is as much an aspect of good songwriting as rhyme, harmony and rhythm.

10.6 No Songs In a Minor Key, Please

Those of us who have written for this industry of music have at times confronted what amounts to company policy regarding the range of emotions that are deemed appropriate by the powers that be. I once was given a script for a children's television program for which I was to write two songs. A note attached to the script said, "No songs in a minor key."

I realized that with the best of intentions the producers were trying to keep the materials they presented on a bright, happy plane. But this kind of interference is like telling actors to smile *all* the time. It makes it impossible to do meaningful work.

It's Not Censorship, It's Just Demographics

There has been a recent rash of so called "consultants" advising radio broadcasting companies to cut out all portions of the symphonic repertoire that range into the darker side of the emotional spectrum. Freely chopping up the most revered classics, leaving out anything that isn't light and happy, they would create "Stepford wives" of whole orchestras. The misguided campaign by programmers to make music more format-friendly is like encouraging the French Impressionists to go in for "sofa-sized paintings."

Songs are real human emotions. It would be idiotic to deny that there are real problems in the world and that working with those problems is the process by which the emotions live. One of the first things that attracted me to folk music as a young person was that I sensed there was something lacking in the sterilized and deodorized material available to me in the media of the time. The traditional songs seemed to open a door to real things and real feelings. At the time I couldn't have told you this had anything to do with myth and human struggle. I only knew there was something there for me that was not to be found on *Your Hit Parade*.

There is plenty of room for songs that are pleasing, romantic, happy and sentimental. There is also room for and good reason for songs such as "AIDS It's a Killer" by the Areyonga Desert Tigers, an aboriginal Australian band with a serious stake in the education of their own people. It might be too much to expect that broadcasters would inflict these songs on their listeners even at 3 a.m. when they play the public service announcements, but the songwriter needs to live in the real world and write with his whole heart.

10.7 The Hard Issues & Real Life

It's not only that the experience of life contributes to the growth of the songwriter, but it may be that in that process of turning that experience into a song, another kind of growth takes place. It may be that writing is in itself a form of character building and by taking on the issues of one's life in the work, a new kind of work and a new kind of life are made possible.

... experience of life contributes to the growth of the songwriter ...

When we talk about inspiration, at first it seems like some shot-in-the-dark, bolt-out-of-the-blue sort of thing that just comes out of nowhere. As we begin to work with the issues of our life in our writing, inspiration takes on more of the character of a dialogue with our own spirit and that entity which could be described as the spirit of our community. Why should this be anything but easy?

"The artist's life cannot be otherwise than full of conflict, for two forces are at war within him — on the one hand the common human longing for happiness, satisfaction and security in life, and on the other a ruthless passion for creation which may go so far as to override every personal desire. ... There are hardly any exceptions to the rule that a person must pay dearly for the divine gift of creative fire."
— CARL JUNG

This "divine gift of creative fire" may cause us, like Prometheus, to risk getting our fingers burned. But it seems it has always been the province of the artist to boldly go into the difficult places. The best work has always been done by the few who developed the ability and the sensibility to be present and aware in the middle of a time of pain or trouble.

"I feel that art has something to do with the achievement of stillness in the midst of chaos. A stillness which characterizes prayer, too, and the eye of the storm. I think that art has something to do with an arrest of attention in the midst of distraction."
— Saul Bellow

10.8 "Courting the Muse" by Bob Franke

Why Write Songs?/ How Do You Write Songs?

The question "Why write songs?" is a valid one, and should be asked first. The question "How do you write songs?" will have different answers depending on one's response to the first question.

My reply to these questions rests in my own history, and the discovery that my own healing has been tied inextricably to my community, whether I've chosen to define that community in family, local, intentional, or religious terms. My own quest for fame had come to a screeching halt midway through the 1970s, as I prepared to leave street singing for what seemed a more "responsible" full-time job maintaining candy-making and candy-wrapping machines (my training for which was being a folksinger who'd had to learn how to maintain old cars to get from one gig to the next).

The advent of fatherhood demanded that I reexamine my life and make the appropriate adjustments. I prepared with some anguish and bitterness to turn my back on the idea of making music for a living, but in the process, some unexpected things happened. First of all, the process of reexamination revitalized my songwriting. Secondly, other artists, many of whom had played at the community coffeehouse I'd started in Marblehead, began to be attracted to my songs and started singing them. And because a lot of people my age were reexamining their own lives, the songs became popular in folksong-oriented communities. "Amateur" singers (etymologically, those who sing for love) began to sing my songs at important points of their lives (e.g. weddings and funerals), and through them my songs found a wide audience.

Since those days it's been clear to me that I write songs for my own healing, that of my community, and that of my culture, and that those circles of healing are much more interdependent than might at first be assumed. Song is such a powerful medium that being a songwriter is a tremendous responsibility as well as a great privilege. As long as one looks for the points of connection among one's own struggles, those of one's community, and those of the larger (if not greater) culture, faithfulness to the truth (a spiritual discipline in itself) can result in songs becoming artifacts that go out on their own and facilitate healing in unknown lives and on unknown levels. I am currently making music full time, and it's not so much an industry that supports me in this, but rather a collection of small communities. It's from those communities that I get direct support from people who tell me that my songs are important in their lives.

My advice to all songwriters, "amateur" or "professional" (and at this point I believe that these categories are irrelevant), is that they write songs for real audiences and real communities rather than imagined markets. "Amateurs" thus stand a chance of doing some good in the lives of those around them; the most vitality to be seen in any kind of American popular music is seen when that music is tied in to living cultural communities, whether urban or rural, whatever their ethnicity. "Professionals" can unleash creativity onto the media culture that may move it somewhat toward reality and health. It may take a while for the necessary risks of art to pay off to the business mind, but after a while they do. The money processes of capitalistic society tend to break up intentional artistic communities as they recruit their best artists for popular music, but new communities form.

The music industry is itself breaking up and reforming as risk-taking small companies move in to serve markets abandoned by the major labels. When the majors see the success of smaller companies, they occasionally modify their own behavior accordingly. Rather than waiting for this or courting it, the sanest course for the many brilliant young writers out there, I think, is to stick to the job at hand and look to the community (and other communities) for support. This country is loaded with small venues and public radio stations that need genuinely good work.

The personal computer is a great tool for accessing those venues and keeping in touch with a developing audience (and this, I think, is material for a whole other column). The alternative (spending lots of energy looking for a big contract) seems to me to be rather like staking your life on a lottery ticket. The risks of being an artist can and should be more properly broken up and taken one day at a time; the corresponding rewards are steadier and surer, and because they involve intimate contact with audiences, are more soul-nourishing as well.

10.9 The Healing Hand

Songwriting can be a healing art. The songwriter is the shaman of our media-oriented society. But even when the writer has no presence on the radio or the television he has the opportunity to be a nurturing presence in the community.

"*The community artist is the one type of artist at this point who has successfully resisted the values of the marketplace, offering up his skills in the service of the community. Only the community artist avoids the role of 'Sleeping Beauty,' to which other kinds of artists in our society are condemned since they are always waiting to be 'discovered.' Their whole mode of life is devoted to preparing for this discovery. By not waiting each day to be discovered, the community artist is able to use art to transform the experience of a community.*"

— Suzi Gablik

11.

Off the Deep End

" ... The individual may prefer to pay the price of incurring the haunting sense of futility which is the necessary accompaniment of not being oneself, rather than hazard the frank experience of frightened helplessness and bewilderment which would be the inevitable start to being oneself."
— R. D. Laing

11.1 Part-Time Songwriter, Full-Time Soul

Work & the Care of the Soul

"We move closer to the soul's work when we go deeper than intellectual abstractions and imaginary fancies that do not well up from the more profound roots of feeling. The more deeply our work stirs imagination and corresponds to images that lie there at the bedrock of identity and fate, the more it will have soul. Work is an attempt to find adequate alchemy that both wakens and satisfies the very root of being."
— Thomas Moore, The Care of the Soul

The Daimonic

In his book *Love and Will*, Rollo May talks about the primal and powerful forces below the line of conventionality and predictability tied up with hormones and irrational fears and torments – the daimonic. He writes about the strength that comes from our deeper understanding of these forces. Exploring these areas may bring us face to face with difficult issues: our own mortality, the tenuousness of relationships, and human traits which may be less than the idealized perfection we are always taught to emulate. But it is from this deeper place that our real strength comes.

"'In the beginning was the Word' is true experientially as well as theologically. For the beginning of man as man, in contrast to apes or the pre-self-conscious infant, is the potentiality for language. We find that some of the important functions of therapy rest on fundamental aspects of the structure of language; the Word discloses the daimonic, forces it out into the open where we can confront it directly. The Word gives a man power over the daimonic."

— ROLLO MAY

11.2 "Duende"

One of the themes of Garcia Lorca had to do with an old idea in Spanish letters and story. It is something called "El Duende." The title of an article he wrote on the subject is "Theory and Function of the Duende." Duende can be described as that quality in a story or musical performance or even a dance which suggests the presence of the dark understanding of death.

In *Women Who Run With the Wolves*, Clarissa Pinkola Estes says, "The trance-teller calls on El Duende, the wind that blows soul into the face of listeners." and ... "El Duende is literally the goblin wind or force behind a person's actions and creative life, including the way they walk, the sound of their voice, even the way they lift their little finger. It is a term used in Flamenco dance, and is also used to describe the ability to 'think' in poetic images. Among Latin storytellers, it is understood as the ability to be filled with spirit that is more than one's own spirit. Whether you are the artist or whether you are the watcher, listener, or reader, when 'el Duende' is present, you see it, hear it, read it, feel it underneath the dance, the music, the words, the art: you know it is there. When 'el Duende' is not present, you know that too."

"Very often intellect is poetry's enemy because it is too much given to imitation ..."

In his book *American Poetry – Wildness and Domesticity*, Robert Bly wrote that "Duende involves a kind of elation when death is present in the room. It is associated with "dark" sounds; and when a poet has duende inside him, he brushes past death with each step. ... Lorca mentions an old gypsy dancer who, on hearing Brailowsky play Bach, cried out, "That has duende!"

In the article Lorca writes, "Very often intellect is poetry's enemy because it is too much given to imitation, because it lifts the poet to a throne of sharp edges and makes him oblivious of the fact that he may suddenly be devoured by ants. ... The magical quality of a poem consists in its being always possessed by the deunde, so that whoever beholds it is baptized with dark water."

I wrote a setting for one of Garcia Lorca's poems, "La Guitarra." The first stanza of the poem is:

Empieza el llanto de la guitarra
Se rompen las copas de la madrugada
Empieza el llanto de la guitarra
Es inutil callarla, es imposible callarla.

Roughly translated it says:

Begins the crying of the guitar
It rends the chords of the sunrise
When the crying of the guitar begins
It is useless to hush it, it is impossible to silence it.

It cries monotonously like the crying of water,
The way the wind weeps over the snow.
It is impossible to silence it,
It cries for distant things.

The hot sand of the south
Thirsty for the white camellias *(a metaphor for peace)*
It decries the arrow shot wide of the target
   (the random destructiveness of war)
The darkening of the hour without the promise of morning.

And the first dead bird
Fallen from the branch. Oh, guitar,
Your heart cruelly wounded by five sharp swords.
   (the fingers of the guitarist)

Many poets have been influenced by these same ideas. Pablo Neruda seems to have imbued this poem with the Duende presence:

Ay, en ese minuto, corazon mio, un sueno con sus alas terribles te cubria.

Translated:

In that moment, my love, a dream with its terrible wings was covering you.

11.3 A Transcendent Vision

All songs have a spiritual component. That is because melody, harmony, rhythm, and language all have emotional attributes which speak directly to a very deep place in each of us. When there is the presence of an understanding on the part of the writer, and the intent to communicate soulfully, the effect can be very powerful and the song may take on a life of its own.

The "Spiritual" Song

Amazing Grace How Sweet the Sound

The famous song "Amazing Grace" was written by John Newton some time in the early 1860s. According to the story, he was the captain of a slave ship bound for America when he experienced a profound religious conversion. He turned the ship around and returned to Africa where he freed the slaves.

Sacred Harp & Shape-Note Hymns

In 1825 Benjamin Franklin White and his brother-in-law, William Walker, working in Spartanburg, South Carolina, compiled a music book and called it *The Southern Harmony and Musical Companion*. William Walker took the manuscript to New Haven, Connecticut, to have it published since there were no publishing houses in the South. Walker and the publisher, Nathan Whiting, changed the manuscript and published it without any acknowledgment to B.F. White for his contribution to the work.

White eventually moved his family to Harris County in Georgia and soon thereafter compiled a book to be called *The Sacred Harp*. He took the book to Philadelphia to be printed and bound and published the book in 1844. This book became the basis of the singing schools White established in Harris County and nearby.

In 1852, White became the editor of *The Organ*, the first newspaper in Harris County. *The Organ* was devoted to "art, science, education, morality, and the advancement of sacred music." Publishing articles about sacred music as well as songs, *The Organ* reached a large audience of singers and although the two books, *Sacred Harp* and *Southern Harmony* had been in competition, as the story of William Walker's treatment of his brother-in-law came to light, the book *Southern Harmony* fell from favor and the *Sacred Harp* was adopted as the official songbook for all sings and conventions in the Deep South.

The book, which has become an institution in itself, revised and republished by subsequent generations, first passed into the hands of Joseph S. James in 1906, and later, upon his death, became the property of The Sacred Harp Publishing Company organized by Thomas J. Denton in 1933. Revised once more, the book was republished in 1936 as the *Original Sacred Harp, Denton Revision*. It is said that next to the Bible, this is the most prevalent book in homes in the South.

The musical notation of the *Original Sacred Harp* is in the shape-note tradition. The book adheres to the system of the four shaped notes and what is called True Dispersed Harmony. The shape of the note tells the singer the note's tonal relationship to the scale. The first, fourth and eighth scale degrees are represented by triangular notes. The second and fifth scale degrees are represented by round notes, which look like whole notes tipped slightly. The third and sixth scale degrees are represented by square notes and the seventh scale degree is represented by a diamond shape.

These symbols give the singer an additional clue to the relationship of notes on the staff while singing. The shapes help to avoid the confusion that might occur with notes on adjacent spaces which could be either a minor third or major third apart depending on key and mode. Although still very popular with shape-note harmony singers all over the world, this system is a little cumbersome and has been left behind by the modern conventional musician.

In a section of the book devoted to basic terms and principles of music, harmony is described as the foundation of melody. "One is not complete without the other." When two or more notes are sounded at the same time and it is pleasing to the ear, it is harmony. "The notes which make harmony are concords, or chords, and the notes which sound disagreeable are discords."

The Cantor

Traces of folk song are to be found in biblical texts and in the Talmud. The earliest songs of the Jews dealt with the Sabbath, Elijah and the holidays. These are called "Zemirot." Songs were not entertainment in this context but were the spiritual expression of religious practice and community life.

Typically at a wedding, the "Badhan" or folk singer would sing about the bride and the groom and their families. Sephardic Jews from Spain and North Africa sing Ladino songs which date from before 1492 when the jews were expelled from Spain.

Traditionally, biblical cantillations and prayer chants were passed along orally from generation to generation. Eventually young cantors would apprentice themselves to individual synagogue-cantor-composers. In about the mid-1800s, formal training and a movement toward creating a printed repertory began to find support. By the 1880s, cantorial schools were established in Eastern Europe and in Great Britain by the early 20th century.

Cantillating of biblical texts settled on a system of notation called "te'amim," a term derived from ta'am, which means "to sense" or "taste." A system of manual signs was used to indicate the rise and fall of the voice. Leonard Bernstein's first symphony, "Jeremiah," is fashioned on the cantillatory motives, the Haftarah chant and fragments of Ekha, the book of lamentations chanted on the ninth day of the Jewish month Ab. Similar influences can be heard in Maurice Ravel's "Chanson Hebraique" and Aaron Copland's "Vitebsk."

11.4 Spiritual Materialism –
The Sincerity Issue

Tibetan Buddhists, among them Chogyom Trungpa Rinpoche, have written about the issue of "spiritual materialism." If we are to ask for the gift of creative thought to be given to us we need to examine the nature of our desire. The belief is that with enlightenment comes responsibility. The aspiring artist must be a respectful candidate for inspiration.

"As the artist works, some portion of his creation is bestowed upon him ... along with any true creation comes the uncanny sense that 'I,' the artist, did not make the work ... religions often prohibit the sale of sacred objects, the implication being that their sanctity is lost if they are bought and sold. A work of art seems to be a hardier breed; it can be sold in the market and still emerge a work of art ... but it may be possible to destroy a work of art by converting it into a pure commodity ... I do not maintain that art cannot be bought and sold; I do maintain that the gift portion of the work places a constraint upon our merchandising."
— Lewis Hyde, *The Gift*

Is the great songwriter truly without guile, or is he just better at it? Very few artists can point to work they have done and claim that it is without artifice, but with a healthy respect for the issues involved any writer can foster his own growth and approach his highest potential. Pablo Picasso made the following statement along these lines. I think he was being overly hard on himself but it gives us a glimpse of the way he thought about the best in art.

"Today I am famous and very rich. But when completely honest with myself, I haven't the nerve to consider myself an artist in the great and ancient sense of the word. I am a public entertainer who has understood his times. This is a bitter confession, mine, more painful indeed than it may seem, but it has the merit of being sincere."
— Pablo Picasso

Songwriters have no hourly wage. It seems that we're always paid far too little or far too much when we do get paid. When the lightning of notoriety strikes one of our songs, it is very hard to connect the success with the work we did. It's very hard to sit down and try to do it again. This whipsaw effect can be very disorienting. For this reason alone, a writer must find the way to keep the doors open and the lights on regardless of how long it has been between credits.

By indulging in the practice of manipulation and using devices calculated to have an effect on the audience rather than looking within and reaching more deeply for something of our own, we cheat ourselves. The only songs we will want to be remembered for are the ones which capture some aspect of grace and preserve it for time. This is hard to do by calculation. The real magic of a song may only be arrived at with the aid of some unconscious process which defies manipulation. It invariably requires some investment of honest wonder.

"Neurosis is the way of avoiding nonbeing by avoiding being."
— PAUL TILLICH

11.5 To Be Present, To Be Here Now

"To be here now" has been a popular slogan among practitioners of the New Age. It has not lost its relevance. It raises the question of the quality of perception and awareness and speaks to our tendency to race ahead of or lag behind ourselves. Often this turns out to be an issue of anxiety. To really stop and smell the roses we've got to be sure that we can let down our guard for a minute at least. We've also got to let go of the past, which may mean that we have to deal with its unresolved questions.

"Guilt is the call of being for itself in silence."
— HEIDEGGER

We have so much today, but the tempo of our lives has risen to accommodate the many layers of things going on all at once. Through meditation and relaxation techniques we can lesson our speediness, but a vague sense of guilt or feeling lost may still suggest the need for further soul searching. Choices may have to be made between comfort and effort, between having and the have nots, between sensation and being.

"The art of archery is not an athletic ability mastered more or less through primary physical practice, but rather a skill with its origin in mental exercise and with its object in mentally hitting the mark. "Therefore, the archer is basically aiming for himself. Through this, perhaps, he will succeed in hitting the mark – his essential self."
— HARRIGEL

In time, all writers come to a place where there is no longer room or reason for self-delusion in any form. Not all writers take the same approach to this issue, some don't seem to be any more cognizant at the end of their lives than when they began. I believe William Butler Yeats, who is someone whose creative life spanned more than sixty years, put it pretty well when he wrote:

Though leaves are many, the root is one;
Through all the lying days of my youth
I swayed my leaves and flowers in the sun;
Now I may wither into truth.

The Second Presence

Much has been written in the field of poetic criticism about the Chinese concept of the second presence. The first presence, of course, is the voice of the poet. The poet seeks to free his work from the service of ego and desire and to let it speak from the best place he can. He tries to clarify his personal issues so as to allow for the expression of the voice of a deeper truth. This is what is referred to as the "second presence."

In Chinese poetry, the second voice is the "voice" of nature. This may be another way of saying that we and all of the natural world are one organism and one spirit. It's my belief that nature is the only sane model for our ideas about the world. Man has constructed a world which is so much in reaction to his fear and obsession with control, that the man-made world can almost be described as an edifice to man's frailty.

Rather than be limited by the ill-fitting armor of conflict and competition tailored for us by others, I feel it is best to spend as much time as possible in as natural a place as possible or at least to try to maximize the "natural" qualities of the place we find ourselves in.

The Métis Indians of Canada talk about the quality of "Atoyocan," the essence or "isness" or central characteristic of living things. The thing that makes the bird the bird, the "treeness" of the tree. They have great respect for the sanctity of all living things and participate in the dialogue between them.

If nature can be said to have a voice, and I believe this voice can be heard in some of the poets, then let us seek to promote an atmosphere in which we can be aware of this presence and be guided by this awareness, this "nature-consciousness." It may be something that can be found in the work of others, but it remains for each of us to interpret this consciousness for ourselves.

12.

The Funny Bone

Humor has been a challenge for songwriters since the first wrong note. Anyone trying to sing more than two songs for an audience knows the value of comic relief. Writing funny songs turns out to be an exercise of many of the same techniques for writing effective songs of any kind. The same questions of character, clarity, melody, rhyme, and scansion all apply.

In addition, writing funny songs – more so than writing songs for other emotional territory – seems to be a matter of formula. The usefulness of card stacking is more obvious in comedy songs. You've got to get all the elements of the joke in and in the proper order or you don't have a punch in the punch line.

The old vaudeville writers had a formula which I have been trying to track down for years. It went something like "whipper, snapper, topper, capper" and it decreed that a good comedy bit had to set up the joke and then snap the laugh or punch line and then if it is a good bit, top the laugh with another level, and if it's to be a truly great bit, cap it off with a really big laugh. It brings to mind some of the old routines like "Slowly I Turned."

12.1 Exaggeration, Hyperbole & Tall Tales

Many of the earliest funny songs rely on tall tales. In many cases it's just a matter of taking the hero story to a ridiculous extreme.

The Darby Ram

In this traditional tall-tale song, the Darby Ram was so big that ...

One of this ram's teeth, sir, was hollow as a horn.
And when they took its measure, sir, it held a bushel of corn.

The Bragging Song

One of the best of all time is "I Was Born About Ten-Thousand Years Ago."

I saw Satan when he looked the garden o'er
I saw Eve and Adam driven from the door
When the apple they were eating I was 'round the corner peeking
I can prove that I'm the guy that ate the core.

The Cat Came Back

Harry S. Miller, who wrote songs for minstrel shows in the last part of the last century, wrote an extremely popular tall-tale song known as "The Cat Came Back." The song details an increasingly unbelievable sequence of episodes in which a man tries to get rid of his cat. The cat survives drowning, dynamite, a train wreck and even though almost everyone else is lost, the cat always comes back.

If It Weren't So Painful ...

Sometimes the sad sack approach is funny. I remember a song about a man born in the last day of the year, the last hour of the day, the last minute of the hour and the last second of the minute. "I tell you folks," he declares, "I almost didn't get here at all."

Funny situations which could almost occur in reality have made funny songs for many generations. "I'm Henry the VIII" is about a man who is the eighth husband of a woman who has been married to seven Henrys before him. The fact that there was a king of England by the same name and title is just a silly coincidence.

"I'm My Own Grandpa" is a wonderfully convoluted story song written by Dwight Latham and Moe Jaffe. It's about a man who marries a widow with a grown-up daughter while his father marries the daughter. His son becomes his dad's brother-in-law and so becomes his own uncle. His dad's son, his own grandson also becomes his uncle and brother to his daughter who is also his stepmother. His wife, as the mother of his father's wife, is also his own grandmother and as husband of his grandmother, he is, inescapably, his own grandpa. By the fourth verse the audience is confused and delighted.

12.2 Comedy Songs

There is always room for at least one good funny song on the charts. In former times, the fifties, for instance, there would be many vying for radio time. Songs about flying saucers ("The Purple People Eater"), the epic "Stranded In the Jungle," "Beep Beep" (the song about the race between a Nash Rambler and a Cadillac), "The Itsy-Bitsy, Teeny-Weeny Yellow Polka Dot Bikini" and dozens of other "novelty" songs.

George Jones' career song until the recent "He Stopped Loving Her Today" was "White Lightning," a song extolling the effects of the corn liquor of the same name. Ray Stevens has delighted country audiences with clever and silly songs like "Ahab the Arab," "Guitarzan," and "The Streak." A recent song on the country charts by David Frizell warned "I'm Gonna Hire a Wino to Decorate Our Home." In the song, the wife is notifying her husband that she is going to do the house over with the decor of the neighborhood bar so that he'll feel more "at home."

Writing funny songs seems to require a sense for the really absurd things that we all either do or have seen others do.

Lou and Peter Berryman have hit the mark with many excruciating and wonderful songs. In "A Chat With Your Mother," the mother describes a series of rough characters and ends each verse with "It's from them I would expect to hear the "F" word, not from you." Here's the last verse:

There's unsavory musicians with their filthy pinko lyrics
Who destroy the social fabric and enjoy it when they do.
With their groupies and addictions and their poor heartbroken parents,
It's from them I would expect to hear the "F" word, not from you.

Their albums are filled with songs like "Your State's Name Here," "Come Smell Our Dairy Air" and "The Speculator," a song about a device that sits on the dashboard and helps to figure out the meaning of things seen along the road.

Christine Lavin really gets inside the heads of characters with the trepidations we all go through in dating and other difficult social situations. In a daring song about adult sexual paraphernalia, she writes, "Our love is being kept alive by artificial means." One of her songs warns about the danger of saying the wrong name at a sensitive romantic time. She advises, "Never call your lover by his name." She then lists many nonspecific and increasingly hilarious names of endearment like, "Motor hips," etc.

In a song called "Fly On a Plane" about a fly which inadvertently gets aboard an airliner in Houston on a flight to San Antonio, Christine has written this clever bridge:

When I get to San Antone I'm gonna make a lotta new fly friends.
When I tell them that I am from Houston, their eyes'll bug out and they'll
    say, "Come again?"
Don't tell us no Texas tall tales, how did you get here? I'll say I flew.
All those San Antone flies'll say, "Man alive, we've got immense respect
    for you!

Nancy White's recent album "Momnipotent" enumerates the wonders and horrors of parenting. "Daughters Of Feminists" observes that no matter how liberated the mother, daughters still insist on being frilly and feminine. She says, "Daughters of feminists think they'll get married to some wealthy guy who'll support them forever, daughters of feminists don't bother voting at all!" Later on in the same song: "they say, Mommy, can I do the dishes," or "Let's make a pie for my brother." "Are they sincere, are they crazy or are they just trying to stick it to mother?"

In another of my favorites, Nancy is trying to explain to her 2-year-old what happened when the stock market crashed and the share in a mutual fund her grandmother bought her was wiped out. "Oh oh, sad today, Suzie money gone away."

Mark Graham has explored a sort of pseudoscientific vein of humor. He has written, "I've Seen Your Aura and It's Ugly," "Working On the Food Chain," "Festival Love" and "Their Brains Were Small and They Died," (a song about the once proud and passionate dinosaurs). One recent lyric he adapted from the Greek classic "Oedipus Rex." A line which sticks in my memory is "He killed his pa and he married his ma, they don't even do that in Arkansas."

Years ago Billy Rose wrote the song that asks the musical question "Does the Spearmint Lose its Flavor On the Bedpost Overnight?" The song, of course, appeared more recently as a big hit by Lonnie Donegan. Rolf Harris, an Australian, had a hit record in a similar busker style with a song called "Tie Me Kangaroo Down, Sport."

Certain timeless jokes have ended up in song. One that comes to mind is about the Scotsman who falls asleep by the side of the road. Two women who happen by can't resist settling the age old question of what a Scotsman wears or doesn't wear under his kilt. After resolving the question to their satisfaction they decide to leave a behind a little blue bow tied in a sensitive place as their little joke. Upon waking to natures call, as the song says, the Scotsman can't help but notice the bow. He says with pride, "Well, my friend, I don't know what you've been up to but I see you won first prize!"

Peter Schickele (a.k.a. P.D.Q. Bach) is a Juilliard graduate and a fine symphonic musician who seems to have had a lot of fun spoofing the classics. For his recordings and live performances he has created side-splitting arrangements and musical jokes on some of the most revered sacred cows of the symphonic pasture. As if that weren't enough, he has come up with many equally irreverent titles for these opi. Some of his well known pieces have titles like "Hornsmoke" (A horse opera for brass quintet), "Concerto for Piano vs. Orchestra," "Grand Serenade for an Awful Lot of Winds and Percussion," "Hansel and Gretel and Ted and Alice," "Overture to the Civilian Barber," and "Concerto for Horn and Hardhart."

Schickele has listed as an early influence the music of Lindley A. "Spike" Jones. "Spike" Jones and his City Slickers were a well-known band of musical misfits popular through the '30s and '40s with many hit recordings. At one point they had their own television show. They did popular gag versions of "The Tiger Rag," "Cocktails For Two," "Chloe," "My Old Flame," "You Always Hurt the One You Love," "Der Fuehrer's Face" and many others.

Many writers of humorous songs acknowledge the influence of Tom Lehrer. Lehrer is a former Harvard mathematics professor who wrote on the piano and did parodies of many of the more florid musical forms like Gilbert & Sullivan as well as the chestnuts of the piano bar. A song which must have come out of his experience in the academic world about a famous Russian mathmetician named Nikolai Ivanovich Lobochevski exhorts the listener to "Plagiarize, don't shade your eyes, that's why the good Lord made your eyes, so plagiarize, plagiarize, plagiarize."

12.3 The Bizarre

Lehrer's sense of humor has it's ghoulish aspect. One of his early songs, "I Hold Your Hand In Mine," describes a man holding a severed hand, tenderly singing, "I hold your hand in mine, dear, I clutch it to my lips. I take a healthy bite from your dainty fingertips" and concludes with the line "So 'til they come to get me I will hold your hand in mine."

Another of his classics describes a maid who murdered each member of her family in a different way. "She not only did everyone of them wrong, she did every one of them in, them in, she did every one of them in." Early Tom Lehrer fans still request "Poisoning Pigeons In the Park."

Writing for the British music hall, R.P. Weston and Bert Lee wrote the wonderfully gruesome, "Ballad of Anne Boleyn," better known as, "With Her Head Tucked Underneath Her Arm."

Jonathan Swift wrote what has become a textbook example of the use of irony. In an article called "A Modest Proposal" about the potato famine in Ireland, Swift suggested that the situation could be relieved if people would just eat the children. While not exactly humorous, it's true that it's possible to bring the listener or the reader to a realization about a difficult issue with irony or misdirection and that approach is often more effective than confrontation.

I borrowed from Swift for a song called, "Let's Eat the Old Folks" with much the same issue in mind. The chorus goes;

Let's eat the old folks, the homeless and the poor
If the four food groups are not enough, let's just add one more
Let's eat! Let's eat the old folks, don't let 'em go to waste
Let's show 'em we appreciate their style and their good taste.

I won't brutalize you with the whole song, but needless to say it was fun to think of ghoulish plays on words. My favorite part is the bridge:

Folks say my plum pudding is the best they ever had.
It's because I add that special touch, three fingers of Old Grand Dad!

12.4 What About Dirty Songs?

Too Blue to Sing?

The famous song "Rum and Coca-Cola" began life as a calypso song and enjoyed popularity (if a song can enjoy popularity) with many night-club audiences. There are dozens of suggestive and highly suggestive verses that have been sung to this song over the years. One of my favorites is:

Billy Rose said to Sally Rand,
"Why don't you dance without your fan?"
Sally danced without her fan,
Billy rose and Sally ran.

I remember hearing Chuck Berry complain that his song "My Dingaling" had eclipsed "Johnny B. Goode" in popularity and that he was afraid that he would be remembered for a song that he wrote as a gag.

12.5 Satire & Parody

Stan Freberg, one of the creators of the *Time For Beanie* and later, *The Beanie and Cecil Show,* produced many song parodies. One of the first was a wonderfully clever record with a man and a woman's voices saying "John" and "Marsha" alternately with different inflections each time. She would say "John?" as question with rising inflection, and then he, seeming to be angry, "Marsha!" This is followed by her pleading "John?", then him consoling "Marsha," again her more conciliatory "John," him, romantic, "Marsha," her giggling, "John," and so on. The effect, though difficult to describe, was truly hilarious.

Freberg did spoofs on Harry Belafonte's "Banana Boat Song (Day-O)," "Saint George and the Dragon Net" a parody of *Dragnet*, a very funny treatment of Lawrence Welk's television family, "Turn Off the Bubble Machine," and many other vicious takeoffs. Eventually Freberg made a whole album based on early American History. It was one of the first "concept" albums and made good fun of Christopher Columbus, George Washington, Ben Franklin, and Betsy Ross. The album, called,

The United States of America, was a big seller and many of us, as teenagers, had memorized every word.

More recently a group from Washington, D.C., known as The Capitol Steps has kept audiences laughing with songs that parody political developments. In the old tradition, they have taken familiar songs and adapted them to the issues of the day. On the health care crisis, one song advised, "Examine Yourself, At Home" to the tune of the Broadway song "Consider Yourself At Home." Their clever tongues in their cheeks seem to bring a new life to old issues and the older songs they use as well.

Another master of satire is Tom Paxton. When Ronald Reagan as president suggested mandatory drug testing for all federal employees it seemed only a matter of minutes before Tom had a song about "filling little bottles for Ronnie." When Republic airlines damaged Tom's guitar in baggage and refused to take responsibility for it, Tom smiled and wrote "Thank You, Republic Airlines" and sang the whole story to thousands of sympathetic fans upon whom the irony was not wasted.

12.6 Interview with Tom Paxton

I'll start by just asking you about your own creative process, how you work, and what you're trying to do in terms of being funny and relevant.

Tom: When it comes to being funny, I think I've spent the first thirty years trying to be as funny as Tom Lehrer and the last part will be trying to be as funny as the Berrymans. They don't come any funnier than that, but when it comes to the process of song, I'm a big believer in what I heard – I can't remember where, but it would be nice to chase this quote down – that most of my ideas come after I begin to work, rather than before.

"I have come to believe that waiting for the muse ... can be a long wait."

So I have come to believe that waiting for the muse is, well, it can be a long wait. You really have to go looking. I think of it as my job, it's what I'm supposed to be doing: writing songs. By writing songs, that means writing. You have to start from somewhere, and usually it's with a blank page.

Do you have a structured way of working each day, a certain amount of time?

Tom: Not a certain amount of time, but I try to make it the first thing I do. I get up and make the coffee and have a little breakfast and watch maybe 15 minutes of *Good Morning America*, try to catch the news portion of it, check the weather, turn it off and come upstairs and sit down with the coffee and a notebook. I work in spiral notebooks and I have stacks of them here, and I like to leaf through the last couple of them to see what ideas, what songs aren't finished but might deserve a little more work, and then I might strike out on the first blank page in the current book and try to settle myself and try to think of what I might be after now, try to think, was there was anything that jumped on me during the day before that might be ready to go?

Just this morning I was looking through the books from last July and I found that I actually wrote two separate songs on the trial of Lorena Bobbitt, before I wrote the one that I'm singing. And neither one of them really came alive.

Are many of the elements of the first two in the newest one, or are they completely different?

Tom: The new one is totally unlike the first two. Once again, I think I'm borrowing a philosophy when I say that I think that most humor is based on despair. I think when you write a song about a woman in response to marital rape severing her husband's penis, you're not talking about something that's funny. It's not funny, it's terrifying and awful, that first of all so much marital rape happens, and secondly that it can drive someone to the point of a sexual mutilation.

So how does it turn into a funny song? It's kind of mysterious to me. I know that there are things, there are subjects that I would never dream of approaching from a humorous point of view. So, I guess this was so horrendous that it lent itself to humor. There were so many jokes about it anyhow. I mean it's every man's worst nightmare, so I suppose it was kind of a safety valve.

What about the big fears, war, nuclear annihilation, the political situation?

Tom: When it comes to that, I think that the humor is in the politicians ever trying to make it acceptable somehow. So the humor is about the insanity of it. As if getting under a school desk was worth doing. As if evacuation plans could even begin. Since what we now know is that a nuclear explosion is going to destroy the electricity of any engines. No cars would start! Get out of here with your evacuation plans ...

I know you have to be responsive to what's happening right now, each day, but are there certain themes that are always with us?

Tom: I think there are. I think the theme of greed, I think stupidity is always there, malfeasance in high places is always happening. And there always needs to be ... eternal vigilance is what we need to bring to that. These people are always going to try to get over. That includes all of us, except for me and thee and I'm not so sure of thee.

Part of what I'm hearing, too, is that there's almost a shamanic function in what you do, in that someone has to burst those bubbles or cut through the hypocrisy.

Tom: Well, it turns out that the emperor really doesn't have new clothes. And that includes all emperors. Of course the world has made progress. We have a vaccine against polio. We have new medical techniques, and we have at the same time an appalling medical system, a health care system that is unfair and this is at the same time that medicine is advancing and making some truly awesome breakthroughs. I haven't done anything on the health care crisis. But I feel the absence of it, it's something I should be working on. ... I guess I'm kind of temporarily stymied right now about whether to try to write a serious song or a satirical song. I haven't been able to find my way into it. And that happens. There have been songs that I've tried to write, and just could not get a handle and had to give up.

Do you feel that there's still some benefit to that work though, even if nothing comes of it right now?

Tom: I'm not sure whether that might not be a romantic view. I think sometimes you have genuinely wasted your time. I think it's a rationalization to say, well you know, I wrote nothing but crap today, but at least it's out of my system. I think I'm going to have to let go of that. I think that there are days when it really has just not happened and that you just might as well have gone fishing.

You've also written a lot of songs for kids, like "The Marvelous Toy."

Tom: Just to fill in the history of it, the first keeper that I wrote was "The Marvelous Toy." I don't even remember anything I wrote before that. It's the first decent song I wrote. And other early songs were "Going to the Zoo" and "My Dog's Bigger Than Your Dog." I finally did a children's album in 1974 called *The Marvelous Toy*. You're right, in recent years I've written more specifically for kids, but actually right now I'm not doing that at all. All the work I'm doing right now is toward the next regular album, and I'm allowing myself the luxury of all the time I need to do it. A couple of the things I've written in the last year are children's songs, but I've kind of left them in the notebook in sort of unfinished form and I just want to put all my energy into doing the next regular record. Having said all that, I really like singing for kids. It's fun. It's different, but it's fun.

Do you write for your own children the way A.A. Milne wrote the Winnie-the-Pooh stories for his, or do you find that you're writing for a sense of a universal kid?

Tom: I think I'm writing for the universal kid. I'm going through Pete Seeger's new book, *Where Have All the Flowers Gone*, and he's got some songs in there he wrote for his kids when they were kids, and they're delightful. I didn't write much directly [to sing to] my kids, although I wrote the songs FOR them, each of them, when they were very young. The song "Jennifer's Rabbit" and the song "Katie" were written when each of them was around 3. But I think I'm writing more for universal kids than I am for them.

You're someone who I think of when I think of "a writer's life." Your life and your work and your presence are really inseparable from that sense of the writing. I think it's an inspiration to a lot of people to know that they can be a writer and be known as a writer and live as a writer and not have to be beholden to the corporate establishment. Is there anything that you'd like to add?

Tom: The only thing I would add is that, in my naiveté, I thought a time would come when writing would get easier, but instead it gets harder all the time. But it truly is the most rewarding thing.

13.

Who Am I?

13.1 Empathy & Compassion

"A human being is part of a whole, called by us Universe, a part limited in time and space. He experiences himself, his thoughts and his feelings as something separated from the rest; a kind of optical delusion of his consciousness.
"This delusion is a kind of prison for us, restricting us to our personal desires and affections for a few persons nearest to us.
"Our task must be to free ourselves from this prison by widening our circle of compassion to embrace all living creatures and the whole of nature in its beauty."
— ALBERT EINSTEIN

13.2 "Courting the Muse" by Mary McCaslin

Songs Are Like Old Friends

Songwriting is like pulling teeth, it does not come easy to me. But in order to pass oneself off as a songwriter, the writing of an occasional song does become a necessity. And when words and music come together, this creative process is one of my life's most fulfilling pleasures. How wonderful to work out a new arrangement and how much more wonderful to perform this new creation for an audience!

Not being prolific, I've usually been lucky to write a song or two a year – and there have been as long as two years between compositions.

Twice in my life I have gone through genuinely fertile periods when a few months' time has yielded a trove of workable compositions.

The most recent of these fertile times was late 1989 through spring of 1990. Six songs came out of this period, practically poured out! Since songwriting for me is usually a struggle, even when my idea of what I want to say is clear, it had been a long while since I had even attempted to write, let alone completed an endeavor.

Usually, the melody was the first to come, maybe developing from a guitar lick or a chord progression, either in standard tuning or one of the alternative tunings I use. The words were always the hardest to make come out right.

There are some songs it has taken me literally years to write! I had always wanted to write a song about a ghost train and had tried to do so many times. "Ghost Train" finally came out right in early 1990. I have other ideas and song fragments that I'm carrying around and will probably do so for years ...

Sometimes, you can be too close to a subject, making it much harder to write about, and causing it to take a long time to put your feelings into words and melody.

I am adopted, and for years I've wanted to write a song about hoping to find my birth mother and father, or at least know their names. At the same time, I didn't want to hurt my adoptive parents, who to me *are* my parents. I finally wrote a song about this very emotional subject. The last verse was quite a challenge and kept changing. I wanted to say how much I love my adoptive parents and that I know they love me, but that something is still missing. I think I finally have the last verse, and I'm satisfied with it.

I have never found a way to teach songwriting. I don't believe it is a technical skill. Yes, you can listen to certain styles of songwriting. You can figure out where the verses, choruses and bridges usually go, and try to follow the format only to have your endeavor turn out as dull as dishwater. Then you happen to turn on the radio and hear something like Marty Robbins' "El Paso" or Dolly Parton's "Coat of Many Colors" which broke all the rules. Novelties? Yes. Hits? Yes again!

I've been flattered by three wonderful artists who have recorded my songs: David Bromberg recorded "Young Westley" around 1977. Kate Wolf recorded "The Ballad of Weaverville" around 1980 (Jim Ringer wrote the lyrics; I wrote the melody and arranged it). Cris Williamson recorded "Circle of Friends" in 1991 as the title track of her new CD. None are what anyone I know would consider commercial, so you just never know what will grab someone's ear.

I have yet to receive any recognition from the truly commercial sector of the recording world. To grab any ears there, I would have to submit material far different from any of the above songs. I don't try to write commercial songs, in fact I don't really think of myself as a songwriter. I'd been performing professionally for years before I wrote my first song. I write strictly for my own self-expression. I feel the same way about singing and playing the guitar.

I wrote my song "Old Friends" right around my 30th birthday. I was staying at my dear friend Betty Glasser's house in Long Beach, California. It's hard to believe that over fifteen years have passed since I wrote "Old Friends." It has remained one of my most requested songs.

In spite of the last verses, I actually had not had anyone close to me die; I had no one in mind as I was writing. A legacy of the years since is that now I can call plenty of people to mind: Doug McLaren (who played the beautiful piano on "Old Friends"), Kate Wolf, Merle Watson, Steve Goodman, Stan Rogers, Gamble Rogers, Logan English, Peter Bellamy, and Lena Spencer. These are some well-known people who I knew and cared for personally. There are others, too, who have passed on but were not public figures, yet were dear to me. I think what has made "Old Friends" touch people is its universal theme. We all will lose dear ones along the way.

> "Melody and lyric are gifts that come out of all of life's experiences and they're with us every day."

One final thought: Melody and lyric are gifts that come out of all of life's experiences and they're with us every day.

13.3 "Courting the Muse" by Ferron

Sentimental Education

The process of writing can catch us like wind in a sail. It can surprise us, like the funny little tune we find ourselves whistling after encountering a certain smell. Sometimes the same old road, or the new spring blossoms, or a stranger's head from behind can make us remember things we'd much rather forget. But, writer or not, we can't forget some things. We seem to be sponges for memories.

Memories can be physical or poetic, in time or out of time, but how we hold them to our selves reflects our individual humanity. Many years ago I read an article suggesting a time when computers would rule the world, and I said to a friend that to make a computer act like a human, they'd have to program *sentimentality* into it. I guess what I'm saying is: If you like the songs on *Driver* – if you don't mind going down the winding, two-lane road that runs through the middle of that recording – then you are probably comfortably challenged by sentimentality. That "two-lane road" is the question of not only learning what *makes* us human, but also learning to *cherish* what makes us human.

My early work took people and put them in exacting, yet unfulfilling human situations and watched what they did with just a few inadequate tools. In my own life, I suppose I have felt like an experiment waiting to turn, but by what ingredients? But now, for a moment, and after 25 years of writing, a kind of quiet acceptance of roads taken or not taken has graced this present body of work. I love the woman/mother in "Sunshine." I wept openly for weeks trying to write out her perspective. It was not readily my full perspective, but I learned something following hers all the way through. Are you surprised to hear me say that I was listening to someone talk? Check out the conversations that go on in your head while you are, for instance, driving. Notice the times that you think you don't know something and then it's as though it's whispered into your ear. As a songwriter, I bank on that internal conversation and feel admittedly lonely when it leaves me from time to time. And speaking of "time," sentimentality requires a sense of time – time passing, time spent, time coming, time wasted and time suspended. Time places us on specific coordinate points. Time allows us to decide if something has happened or is still possible or was worthwhile. In the song "Sunshine," the most heart-breaking moment for me is realizing the mother is slipping in and out of linear time. I am heartbroken for her, but more so for her daughter, who's destined to lose something in a process where she's not the chooser. Choice is a powerful tool and the mother's tools, powerful and refined, are definitely future-focused. "Cactus," on the other hand, approaches time by starting in one place and running somewhat past-focused, going simply from the present to various pasts, not slipping and sliding. These two songs are both weary and loving, but "Cac-tus," while ultimately becoming refined, suggests a future by acknowl-edging and holding sacred a clumsy past, bringing to terms all the possibilities born out of rough tools – the comings and the goings of a hungry heart, the hopings and the letting go that only a dreamer can manage, the aspirations of the soul set against the backdrop of the cheap dreams and sometimes cheaper promises. I don't think I learned how to love until I was so dry to the bone that I had to pull my water from within, and so, yes, I am the cactus. And no one was more sur-prised than I.

If we do not value pain as the primary growth process, can pain ease its pull on us? Does pain reflect the major rite of passage toward reflective experience? To know our pain is to know one corner of our limits, but sometimes, when I'm hanging with funny friends, I know humor to be another important limit and a most valuable corner. And do not forget courage. Or conviction. Understanding these things to be what gods and goddesses are made of, why not imitate the best? So, while I am not hired to write a specific song for a specific person, I do write to my best and worst selves. By default, I live myself into a knot and then must straighten it out. The song "Cactus" came from a challenge, be-tween Roy Forbes, Don Freed, Connie Kaldor and me, to write a song titled "Chinese Dinner Alone." I believe that Roy, Don and Connie had written their song. Mine was slow in coming. Finally, in a motel in up-state New York, with two days leave from shows, during a great foliage week with weather that kept me both warm and forlorn, on a street of strangers with not a decent cup of coffee to be found, I must have asked my self "What price freedom?" And so began a series of reflections and a way to, in a sense, *coordinate* myself in time.

I like to explore "the deal." It changes depending on the light. I found myself in a Chinese restaurant drinking really bad coffee and I was alone. Sometimes things just click. I pretended I was writing to someone I had loved who had left to do something else. I let them love me even though they'd left, meaning ... *I let all the players be good people.* I let the song be an opportunity to own up to some things I'd never heard myself say, hoping it would change me, help me become the person I longed to be. And, of course, I tried to rise to Paul Simon's challenge of "writing a spiritual tune by writing about the moon," and learned and accepted during that particular verse that, though I had often wanted to leave Earth and head for the moon, when it came to being wistful it seemed I could and would do it anywhere, so why waste the gas!

Even though I am willing to start a song without knowing where it's going, sentimentality needs something to hang on. In the opening lines of "Cactus," I'm hoping that you, the reader/listener will know it's twilight because of the presence of the hoot owl, but I don't need you to place *me* in twilight so much as let twilight be the light you start to listen with. I want you to end up listening with the brilliant desert light shining down on everything. As in "Sunshine," the direction is toward an honest, brilliant light, but it's not important that you listen with that in mind. Sometimes these things are fine enough just happening for the writer. For me, I was relieved to see the direction the light was heading in both of these songs, and later, after the last song for *Driver* was written and placed, I could see the "holy" light I refer to in the song "Maya" having to do with the desire to grow – to love, to nurture and protect, to cherish. And, of course, like the mother in "Sunshine," to know when to let go. When I was a child I did, indeed, hide in hayfields. Thirty years later, the light that shines down in the last song on *Driver* shines down on both mountains *and* humans indiscriminately. And I am left with the feeling of having a chance at something I had mostly only dreamed of – pure and honest love that might exist in the light of day.

These are songs about doing until it's done. And then figuring out how to live. So it seems important to talk a daily kind of language: to create a sentence out of a simple task or a basic longing. These songs are the voice of a character who chose the wrong door at least once in almost every situation but still lives to talk about it – and can talk about it in plain English. These songs are also about tenderness in rugged circumstances, and grace being present for no apparent reason or ulterior motive – just the way grace is. Both "Cactus" and "Sunshine" are about love finding its way home with loss, even if the only loss is the loss of pride (one of my favorite losses). The voice behind the words purposefully spills them out steadily as reflectors on the highway letting me know that I had "learned my lessons well."

You don't have to know that orange and blue are opposite on the color wheel, and therefore complementary, to put them next to each other. You just need too know that you like blue and orange together. Complementary opposites can make for a very good song. Bittersweet comes from this. Wistful comes from this. Wry can come from this. I use it in the verse in "Cactus" where I talk about trying hard to cross the great river, and learning that the trying was the very thing you needed to do to find out that you *were* where you were going. That verse also suggests a loner fighting a battle, only to finally get to the other side and make camp/village/town/city/culture with every other proud-eyed loner. Look at your own language and see if you have a loner, or a clown, or a sad sack, or a river, a secret, a hill, a light that shows up everywhere. I bet you do, and I bet you live by your belief in those things. Our lives are also symbols of our lives. That is how a sentence like "A thought is as good as a deed" can be true. And I guess I think that an attempt is as good as an event for learning. I guess I think that our lives are backdrops for learning attempts. How's that for bittersweet?

The muse often plays hard to get. She has to. If she doesn't, then we don't think we've made something nice. We feel fraudulent. We feel like we cheated, and in art, we songwriters like to think we have very high standards. But whether it comes easily or if it draws blood, it is very important to realize that while the song won't make or break you, not caring might. Sometimes I think that I don't have a single song left in me, and then I hear the neighbor's radio, or I listen to music real low (loud enough to guarantee that I could never go to sleep but low enough not to hear the words), and then my words start tumbling around. The best part is when I'm interested in all the words that bounce around. But sometimes I make like I'm not. Must be my way of playing hard to get back!

"I have received many poetic interpretations of my songs from listeners whose ideas and connections I wish I'd made."

Ultimately, songlistening, like songwriting, is a private passage. I have received many poetic interpretations of my songs from listeners whose ideas and connections I wish I'd made. It would have lightened my load sooner. My intention with every song was to write something that might incite me to hang on through a rough day, to remember that weird and wonderful things have already happened and, therefore, have every possibility of happening again, and to remind myself that I am not alone. Say you were having a rough day, and you happened to remember to put on music that you loved. And, say it happened to be my music, and you chose *Driver*. An image I did not use, but intended, is that of a thick rope strong enough to swing any one of us over to the other side of a troubled moment. Writer or listener, we work for each other's love. Now how's *that* for sentimentality?

14.

Fun & Games

14.1 Children's Songs

Writing for children is a different kind of challenge. Most of the people who do it successfully have found a way to tap into their own child-like selves. Tom Chapin is one of the best. With kids of his own he seems to have tuned into the perfect wavelength, never talking down to his listeners and never failing to enchant us. He seems like the kind of dad who would be fun to be around.

His albums are filled with songs that glimpse the child's world. In one song he begs "Don't Make Me Go To School Today" to the dirge-like drones of Dvorak's Symphony no. 9 in E minor. In another song, "Oh-oh, Accident" he hammers his thumb, "Oh-oh, acci-dumb" and swallows the soap, "Oh-oh, acci-dope."

Larry Penn is a retired million-mile trucker and train buff who makes toys and writes songs for his grandchildren. One of his songs, which has been sung by many children's entertainers, goes:

I'm a little cookie, yes I am.
I was made by the cookie man.
And on the way from the cookie pan,
I got a little dent in me.

I got a little dent in me, uh huh,
I got a little dent in me, uh huh.
But I can still taste just as good as any other cookie can.

Peter Alsop, who sings the cookie song, has written many wonderful songs of his own. One of his most famous and most requested songs attempts to put some of the anxieties about the differences between boys and girls in the proper perspective. The song is evocatively titled "It's Only a Wee-Wee."

Malvina Reynolds wrote many children's songs. Most had a another level of understanding which would connect with older listeners as well. She wrote "The Pied Piper," her own version of "The Little Red Hen," and "You Can't Make a Turtle Come Out." Even her "adult" songs like "Little Boxes" are popular with children.

Rex Benson and I had the chance to write several songs for the Disney Cable Channel versions of *Winnie-The-Pooh* and *Dumbo's Circus*. There were about a dozen writers waiting to take a turn at a script but about 200 episodes of each were produced so there was plenty of work for all. Each script called for two songs and although it was a great honor to put the words in those illustrious characters' mouths, the songs all seemed to be due within a day or two.

We wrote songs for every conceivable situation, about forty all told and some I can hardly remember. One which I still sing has to do with hunting for buried treasure. The bridge says:

It might be the crown jewels of some forgotten kingdom,
Or a hundred pieces-of-eight or gold dubloons.
It might be a diamond, there's no way of tellin'
Or a ruby as big as a melon,
Or a box of chocolate-coconut macaroons!

14.2 Wordplay

Still fun but a little more challenging are the adult versions of word games. Get a little handle on some of the following ways of expression and see what an effect they can have on your writing.

14.3 Oxymorons

Oxymoron means literally "pointedly-dull." An oxymoron is a combination of two incompatible words or thoughts that can have the effect of making the whole idea seem preposterous. Some are fun. Here are a few examples. Think of more.

Jumbo Shrimp	Hard Water
Ordinary Sex	Benevolent Dictator
Bitter Sweet	Laborious Idleness
Important People	Politely Insulting
Deafening Silence	A Little Large
Cruel Kindness	Moderately Extreme
Pretty Ugly	Clearly Confused
Make Haste Slowly	Increasingly Little
Cheerful Pessimist	Monosyllabic
Harmonious Discord	Dry Wine
Terribly Pleased	Simple Arithmetic

14.4 Anagrams

An anagram is a word or phrase which can become another word or phrase if the letters are used in a different way. Usually all the letters must be used and the second phrase must make as much sense as the first. Sometimes this may be a bit of a stretch.

Two plus eleven = One plus twelve
Western Union = No wire unsent
A stitch in time saves nine = This is meant as incentive
Ronald Wilson Reagan = Insane Anglo Warlord
William Shakespeare = I am a weakish speller
Mother in law = Woman Hitler
Intoxicate = Excitation
Parishoner = Hire parson
The Morse code = Here come dots
Circumstantial evidence = Can ruin a selected victim
Victoria, England's Queen = Governs a nice quiet land

14.5 Palindromes

A palindrome is a word or phrase which is the same when read in both directions. Here, again, some leeway must often be given. Some of the more famous Palindromes are:

Able was I ere I saw Elba.
Sex at noon taxes.
Madam, I'm Adam.
Sums are not set as a test on Erasmus.
Was it Eliot's toilet I saw?
A man, a plan, a canal, Panama!
Too far, Edna, we wander afoot.
Are we not drawn onward, we few, drawn onward to new era?
Norma is as selfless as I am, Ron.

14.6 Tongue Twisters

Tongue twisters are fun to work with unless you are a singer trying to work your way through a tricky song lyric. It's a good idea to learn about the properties of tongue twisters if only to learn how not to create them. Here are few:

Six slippery seals slipping silently ashore ...
A blue bucket of ebullient blue blueberries
Some shun sunshine.

Literally literary literature.

Does the wristwatch shop shut soon?

I never felt felt that felt like that felt felt.

Tuesday is stew day ... stew day is tuesday.

It's just a question of repression.

I can't stand rotten writin' when it's written rotten.

The sinking ship sunk.

Lemon liniment.

Six slim slick slender saplings.

Sixty-six slick chicks.

Yellow yo-yo's

A noisy noise annoys an oyster.

A skunk sat on a stump. The stump thunk that the skunk stunk...the skunk thunk that the stump stunk!

I have a can opener that can open any can that any can opener that can open any can can open.

Beautiful Bonnie Bliss blows blissfully beautiful bubbles.

Dimpled Dina dances in a dainty dimity down the dunes.

The cows who graze in droves on grass which grows in grooves in groves.

The intrepid tracker who tracked and tricked and trapped the tricky tricycle tricksters.

The wizened wives who whistle while weaving wide white worsted waistcoats.

14.7 A Pride of Lions

The naming of groups of animals in colorful language is a tradition going back to a time long before Shakespeare. Often referred to as the game of venery, these terms demonstrate a certain worldliness on the part of the user. Some of these names seem archaic but most are wonderfully descriptive.

We've all heard "a gaggle of geese," or "a school of fish." How about "A leap of leopards"? Many of these examples are from James Lipton's *An Exaltation of Larks*, and C.E. Hare's *The Language of Field Sports*.

A Skulk of Foxes	A Husk of Hares
A Pod of Seals	A Labor of Moles
A Cowardice of Curs	A Bale of Turtles
A Sloth of Bears	A Dule of Doves
A Gang of Elk	A Shoal of Bass
A Covey of Partridges	A Drift of Hogs
A Fall of Woodchucks	A Trip of Goats
A Wedge of Swans	A Charm of Finches
A Party of Jays	A Sort of Mallards
A Colony of Penguins	A Tiding of Magpies

A Rafter of Turkeys	An Ostentation of Peacocks
A Business of Ferrets	A Cast of Hawks
A Crash of Rhinoceroses	A Bouquet of Pheasants
A Beige of Herons	A Congregation of Plovers
A Gam of Whales	A Paddling of Ducks
A Richness of Martins	An Unkindness of Ravens
A Host of Sparrows	A Building of Rooks
A Descent of Woodpeckers	A Bevy of Roebucks
A Spring of Teal	A Knot of Toads
A Route of Wolves	A Mustering of Storks
A Sounder of Swine	A Dray of Squirrels
A Hover of Trout	A Shrewdness of Apes

Lipton retells the famous joke of the four Oxford dons, each of a different school or area of expertise. Their path is crossed by small but conspicuous group of prostitutes. The quickest don mutters, "A jam of tarts." The second, obviously a fellow in music, ripostes, "No, a flourish of strumpets." From the third, apparently an expert on nineteenth-century English literature, "Not at all ... an essay of Trollope's." The fourth offers, "An anthology of pros."

He points out that, although clever and fun, these are not really examples of the same poetic principle we find in the list above. "What we are admiring is verbal dexterity and ingenuity; what emerges is not poetry but a joke, not revelation but a chuckle."

14.8 Interesting Word Pairs

Charles John Quarto teaches this exercise for discovering some of the magic in nouns and adjectives. Fold a piece of lined paper into two columns. Choose a list of nouns at random from the dictionary and put them down on the right. Then randomly chose adjectives and drop them in on the left. When you have filled a page, go through and look and listen for the unexpected.

ADJECTIVES:	NOUNS:
Striped	Pensioner
Watchful	Skillet
Patchwork	Idol
Vernal	Mascot
Incandescent	Wave
Denim	Charlatan
Complaining	Freight
Massive	Culvert
Insinuative	Limerick
Drunken	Bomber

Birth	Bed
Floral	Subsidy
Nubile	Inquisition
Shining	Noggin
Grievous	Bludgeon
Giddy	Replica
Noisy	Swagger
Perfidious	Umlaut
Scrupulous	Litmus
Blowzy	Conversant
Bluebird	Metaphysics
Slapdash	Fatback
Astigmatic	Repartee
Grandiloquent	Charade
Enameled	Ramekin
Shotgun	Spinster
Superogatory	Grasshopper
Supernal	Spicule
Airmail	Interface
Portuguese	Kegler
Agreeable	Grasswidow
Rented	Raison D'etre
Rampant	Grapnel
Repetitive	Replication
Sunlit	Grandson
Airsick	Grandmaster

All of these examples were generated randomly. Some are really surprising. My favorites are "Patchwork Idol," "Denim Charlatan," "Complaining Freight," and "Drunken Bomber." Try the adjective after the noun and see what happens. Some of these that work are "Pensioner's Stripes," "Limerick Insinuation," "Metaphysical Bluebird" and "Inquisitive Nubile."

14.9 The Names of the Full Moons

It almost goes without saying that the moon plays so many roles in the folklore and songs of the world. The moon has an effect on the romantic aspects of any situation. Moonlight on the snow, on the water, the moon rising through the trees, or crossing the sun in an eclipse is compelling. The moon has been a physiological and psychological force to be reckoned with through the ages and has had a myriad of symbolic attributes.

This list of the names of the full moons is from the Farmer's Almanac. Although this list is particularly useful to songwriters, the Almanac contains a wealth of other amazing and informative stuff. Many these names date back to the Algonquin tribes of the Northeast.

January:	The Wolf Moon, also called the Full Old Moon
February:	The Snow Moon, or The Hunger Moon
March:	The Worm Moon, or The Crow Moon, Sugar Moon or Sap Moon
April:	The Pink Moon, or Sprouting Grass Moon, Egg Moon, or Fish Moon
May:	The Flower Moon, Corn Planting Moon, or The Milk Moon
June:	The Strawberry Moon, The Rose Moon, or The Hot Moon
July:	The Buck Moon, The Thunder Moon, or The Full Hay Moon
August:	The Sturgeon Moon, The Red Moon, or Green Corn Moon
September:	The Harvest Moon (The Harvest Moon is always the full moon closest to the autumnal equinox. If this occurs in October, the full moon in September is called The Corn Moon)
October:	The Hunter's Moon, Travel Moon, or Dying Grass Moon
November:	The Beaver Moon, or The Full Frost Moon
December:	The Cold Moon, or The Full Long Nights Moon

A "Blue Moon" is the second full moon in any month.

14.10 "Courting the Muse" by David Massengill

Someone once asked Jimmie Rodgers what kind of songs he wrote. "I write two kinds," he answered. "Fast songs and slooow songs."

I like to think I have at least that in common with the singing brakeman. Besides my fast songs and slooow songs, I further divide my work into three main song types: the ballad or story song, the variation on a theme (saying the same thing over and over and over again) song, and the weird song. It's important to have weird songs, but I find that a little weirdness goes a long way.

I admire the ballad form most of all. Stories are irresistible. I've always had a passion for stories, the endings being of particular importance. One reason is that *Wagon Train* was my favorite TV show as a boy, but I rarely saw an entire episode. My bedtime was 8:30 and the show lasted until 9:00. I learned to beg at an early age, but to no avail. I was an unfortunate child: Both my parents were older than me. The logic of my arguments was apparent to all my contemporaries but failed to impress my parents. I survived to *write* the wrong by going to bed and constructing an ending in my head for that week's *Wagon Train* episode.

When I was 4 our 5 years old, my parents allowed me to freely visit Aunt Eula's house a block and a half away. Her children were slightly older and had collected a shelf full of comic books. Research. No Aladdin ever felt so in awe of hidden treasure. Even before I could read, I "read" my cousins' comic books by following the pictures and making up the dialogue to suit myself. Little Lulu and Uncle Scrooge were the Thackeray and Proust of my childhood.

For hours and hours, I would tirelessly devour these masterworks of literature, a child obsessed. My dear mother learned to accept my frequent disappearances and cut short any frantic search by simply telephoning Aunt Eula to see if I was there "reading" comic books. Time for dinner.

TV and comic books. I'm not sure Homer would approve my methodology, but then again Homer was blind. Which is a fine reminder that stories were primarily verbal to begin with. Before there were cave paintings, stories were told over generations. We tell each other thousands of stories in the course of everyday life. As Yogi Berra might posit, stories are 50 percent visual and 90 percent verbal.

My memory is my greatest resource. Until I left home for the world, my brother Mike and I shared the same room. Our beds were within jumping distance and we would leap from one to the other, using our pillows as shields and thudhumpers. When we finally lay down to bed he would ask me questions about nothing and everything. How come the milkman whistles? Does the Easter bunny know Santa Claus? What do you think happened in the rest of *Wagon Train*? I was always explaining the world to Michael. I often think that's why I do what I do now. I don't write for myself or the greater good; I write for my brother.

Folk music has expanded its base these last 30 years. Now subject matter can range through peace, love, environmental awareness and the pros and cons of inny and outy belly buttons. These are all worthy topics, but I prefer the more traditional folk themes of murder, lust and betrayal. Maiming is always good in a pinch. For more graphic examples of folk imagery, I recommend the movie *Pulp Fiction*.

I use three main tools in writing: instinct, hard work and dumb luck. Dumb luck is missing a train and, while you wait for the next one, writing a key word, line or verse. When this happens often enough you begin to believe in Fate.

I give myself the luxury of time in shaping a song. It's very common for me to work three months or more on a single song. Plotting takes time and effort, for there are many false turns. I fill up pages and pages with my mistakes, thereby eliminating them. Eventually a trail is broken through this mountain of mistakes. Sometimes it's as easy as putting eggs in a basket; other times it's like trying to pound a ton of sand into a diamond.

I work on the melody as hard as I work on the lyrics and I work best as I walk the streets of New York City. Just like any other New

Yorker, I'm not shy about talking to myself. Humming, too. I usually write the first line of melody and lyric simultaneously – the story in miniature. From then on I let the song inform me. Where does it want to go? Valhalla? Detroit? Bucksnort? Once you've grabbed the big toe, the body will follow.

I like to tell the whole story, which can make for some epic renderings. There are a couple of little tricks I use to keep the listener's interest: (1) I vary the melody every other verse or so, thereby shifting the emotional tone; (2) I sneak in the unexpected; (3) I update, postdate, prorate and fibulate all kinds of familiar stories. I'm not too proud to steal.

When I'm really going good, I work on two songs at the same time. I find it helpful if the songs are of different types so my brain is not overtaxed. I figure one side of my brain is good for stories, the other side for saying the same thing over and over and over again. Weirdness just seems to seep out of its own accord. Call it brain leakage.

I tend to write in different voices, differing styles. Who am I this time and what am I dancing? I'm also somewhat bloodthirsty. There can't always be a happy ending. Sometimes the hero must die, or at least be given a good talking-to.

Speaking of endings, I recently saw an entire episode of *Wagon Train* on a cable channel. I recognized the beginning from my childhood. Frankly, I thought my ending was better.

15.

Taking Care of Business

Not every writer is interested in earning money from his songs, but every creative work has the potential to generate income. The idea of "intellectual property" may seem to some like a contradiction in terms. You may wish to declare your work free and for the benefit of all without royalties or restrictions. Even this may require a knowledge of how things are done. It's best to get sensible about the money issues as early on as you can.

With care, you can create a catalog of songs that will provide for you and your loved ones for many years to come. Or, if you prefer, you can see that money earned by your songs will go to a worthy cause. You can let your song become part of the "public domain," that is, not owned by anyone, but even then you may want to be sure that nobody else claims authorship or ownership of your creation.

15.1 Basic Information About Copyrights

What Is A Copyright?

Copyright is a form of protection provided by the laws of the United States to the creators of "original works of authorship." The filing of a copyright application with the Library of Congress is a legal formality which publicly records the basic facts concerning the authorship, publication, ownership, or transfer of a song, dramatic work, pictorial or sculptural work, motion picture or sound recording. Even computer programs and maps are protected by copyright.

How Long Does It Last?

A work that is created after January 1, 1978, is automatically protected from the moment of its creation until fifty years after the author's death. Work copyrighted before the new law went into effect on January 1, 1978, is still protected for the original term of twenty-eight years, renewable in the twenty-eighth year for an extended term of forty-seven more years.

How Much Does It Cost?

Applicants must submit a properly completed application form, a fee of $20.00 for each application, and one or two complete copies of the work, depending on whether it is a new work or a previously published work. It is possible to register several songs in unpublished form if they are combined in a collection all by the same author, or, if more than one author, then one of the authors must have contributed to each song, and the collection must be registered under one title identifying the collection as a whole.

How To Do It

Write to the Register of Copyrights, Library of Congress, Washington, DC 20559, to request the proper application forms. If you wish to copyright a song you need form PA, for a sound recording you want form SR, and for a non-dramatic literary work, form TX. For a detailed explanation of all the forms ask for circular R1c. You may request forms by phone at (202)707-9100. This is a voice-mail request line. If you wish to speak to someone about copyright information call (202)707-3000.

15.2 Getting Paid

Royalties

Songs may earn money in many ways. Songs can be written for hire for a flat fee or for a royalty, which is an ongoing fee for the use of the song. Songs written for radio or television themes are paid royalties for their use during one season, usually thirteen weeks, and earn again, although at a different rate, if used in reruns. Songs written for commercials earn in a similar way and the amount is determined by how many times the commercial is played and in how many markets.

Mechanical Royalties

Recorded songs earn money in two main ways. When the song is "pressed" onto a record or reproduced and sold in any mechanical or electronic device, a royalty is paid based on the number of units sold. The device may be a CD, cassette, even a musical toy. This "mechanical" royalty is calculated currently at 6.25 cents per song per unit sold. So if you have co-written a song on an album which sells 1 million copies, your share, or the "mechanicals," would be a portion of the total royalties of $62,500. Ten songs would earn ten times this much.

The Publishing

Generally the publisher of the song gets a 50% share and the writers split the other 50%. In this case your share would be one-quarter of the total or $15,625. It's easy to see why songwriters want to publish their own songs. The publisher's jobs are to keep the books, collect the money and to help get the song used on records and in films. If the publisher is doing his or her job, it's worth the 50% of the song's earnings that they get. Often, however, it is the songwriter who gets the song recorded and if he can have an "administrator" do the paperwork for a smaller fee, he has rightfully earned the lion's share of the income.

Airplay Royalties

The second main way that recorded songs earn money is from airplay, or performance on radio and television and to a lesser extent live performances of the song. Broadcasters pay for the use of songs and this money is pooled and paid out to the writers roughly in proportion to the amount of play the song gets during a given royalty period. Performance royalties are collected by what are called "performance rights societies" and are paid directly to the writers and publishers in quarterly statements.

Airplay royalties on the album cut in the example above might be a few hundred to a few thousand dollars, but if the song is a Top 10 single it may earn many times in airplay what it earns in mechanical royalties.

15.3 Performance Rights Societies

There are performance rights societies in virtually every country of the world. Through international agreements, royalties are paid for the use of songs worldwide. The typical foreign royalty statement will show your song earning tiny amounts and sometimes not so tiny amounts in far flung and exotic places.

In this country there are three primary societies, ASCAP, BMI, and SESAC. Each will claim that it is unique and the premier organization in its field and will list famous songs in its catalog and famous stars on its roster, but for the purpose of our discussion they are pretty much the same. A writer "joins" and his songs are registered with only one society and this society sends statements of the songs' domestic and foreign earnings to the writer(s) and publisher of the song for each quarter of the year.

The money comes from radio and television broadcasters, concert promoters, coffeehouses, restaurants, bars, theme parks, riverboats, casinos, stores and public buildings where music is played and people spend money. There are still some unresolved questions and bills in Congress regarding the use of recorded music and live performances by people doing their own songs, as well as the difficult issue of traditional and cultural songs which may be unfairly penalized by the forces of the marketplace.

No one is keeping track of each time the song is played on each radio station everywhere. This would be too big a job. Instead, a sampling is done of perhaps sixteen stations at a time for a period of two weeks. During this time, songs that are "logged" earn royalties in proportion to the number of times they are played. Each society uses elaborate formulae and complicated statistical analysis to arrive at royalty amounts. If a song is "hot" and is played a lot, it will be rewarded with a "bonus" of double, triple, or quadruple royalties and special cash awards.

Obviously, there are a few people earning an awful lot of money in this process. As much as 100-million dollars will be collected and dispersed in a single year by just one performance rights society. The organizations admit that their sampling tends to favor commercially active songs. They also tend to make the mistaken assumption that if a song is being sung live, it must be one of the songs that is popular on the radio. Many kinds of programs are not logged. Folk music and public radio performances are not surveyed because they are "specialty" programs.

Not every writer is interested in earning money from his songs, but every creative work has the potential to generate income.

Many small presenters – coffeehouses, house concerts and folk music societies – have complained that they are being forced to pay for songs that are not performed there, although they don't dispute that writers should be paid for the use of their songs. Conversely, they point out that the money never goes to the writers who are performing their own songs if they are not part of the "big-time" music industry. In Europe and in Canada, performers are asked to file lists of the songs performed. With this system a more accurate accounting can be made. Eventually this procedure may be instituted in the U.S. as well.

Despite these unresolved issues, the performance rights societies do provide many services to the songwriters and publishers they represent. Although they are based in the three major music industry cities of New York, Los Angeles, and Nashville, they offer information and encouragement wherever you may be and can help you when you plan to go to these music marketplaces. If you are near one of these cities they offer writers workshops, song evaluations, talks by well-known professionals and guidance in pursuing your own music goals.

You can reach ASCAP at:
1 Lincoln Plaza
New York, NY 10023
(212)621-6160

You can reach BMI at:
320 W. 57th Street
New York, NY 10019
(212)586-2000

You can reach SESAC at:
156 W. 56th Street
New York, NY 10019
(212)586-3450

You can reach the Canadian performance rights society, SOCAN, at:
41 Valley Brook Drive
Don Mills, ON MB3 2S6
(416)445-8700

15.4 Publishers

As has been mentioned, the publisher provides much-needed ser-vices to the songwriter. Many publishers work very closely with the writer to help improve the quality or the commercial viability of the songs. Active publishers keep track of who is recording and when and who is producing their records. This amounts to a full-time competitive cam-paign to get the "cuts" and promote the singles that are the lifeblood of their business.

The writer-publisher relationship may be a lifelong arrangement with the publisher taking a real paternal or partnership role in the life of the writer. The publisher may arrange for advances to attract a writer to the company or to help the writer get through an occasional rough time. Even after the writer's death, the publisher often will provide for the surviving family by continuing to work the songs.

15.5 Staff Writing

Staff writing is often the first position that is offered to a writer by a publisher who recognizes potential in his work. It is a way for the writer to begin to earn a living from his songs even before they earn royalties. It also gives the publisher the opportunity to work closely with the writer. The staff writing job represents a salary which is advanced by the publisher against future royalty earnings.

Many times an offer of a staff position will come after the writer has achieved a lucrative recording of his or her song and the publisher can see that an investment of a year or two of salary will likely be earned back by the recording. Even though the songwriter is giving up a portion of the songs' earnings that he could collect eventually even without the help of the publisher, he or she may feel it is worth while to begin receiving payment right away. In cases like this it is not unusual for the publisher to offer a sizeable cash advance at the beginning of the contract in addition to the salary. In any case, a staff situation will only be likely to continue if it is justified by the earnings of the songs.

15.6 Advances

The whole question of advances is a tricky one. The thought of getting paid for work you haven't done yet seems too good to be true to some and causes dread in others. If your songs are not earning money yet, it is a wonderful help to have someone support you as a songwriter while you grow in your craft.

If your songs are earning money, and all advances are paid back it is good for your peace of mind to be able to live on current earnings and even save a little, knowing that somebody is there to give an advance against future royalties if it is needed in an emergency. If you have been a staff writer for several years, it may take quite a while to pay back this money and get outfrom under. Many professional writers have gone from one staff deal to another for years and have maintained homes and families in the process.

Years ago, David Mackechnie and I wrote a song called "Sweet Melinda," which was recorded by John Denver. When John's producer, Milt Okun, contacted us to tell us that the song would be on the next album (J.D.), they had already recorded the song. Part of Milt's reason for calling was that he wanted to discuss the publishing of the song and was willing to give us an advance for permission to put the song in their catalog.

Usually all the details of permission are worked out long before any recording takes place. In this instance we realized that we had a good bargaining position and while not wishing to overplay our hand, we supposed that the size of our advance might be influenced by the expense it would take for them to start all over again with another song. At this point we began to window shop for the new tape recorder and microphone we'd been wanting.

In addition to the fact that they had already recorded the song, Milt confided in us that he and John thought that our song might be a likely single. He intimated that this would be more likely if the song were in their publishing company and very forthrightly suggested that he would even give us his assurance that the song would be released as a single if we agreed to assign the publisher's share of the song to their company.

Needless to say this was an unusually good situation for us and since their efforts had done so much to enhance the value of the song we felt very good about letting them have the rights to publish the song and have never regretted it. "Sweet Melinda" was released as a single and made it to the mid-40s on the Billboard charts. We received enough advance to buy the equipment we wanted and used it to demo subsequent songs.

15.7 Assignments

Writing on assignment is a challenge often encountered by the professional songwriter. You may be given an assignment under a variety of different circumstances. Your publisher may just have heard that a top-selling recording artist is going back into the studio to record one last song to finish off his new album and is looking for a song about the recent disastrous train wreck. Or, you may be asked by the gang at the office to write a song for the secretary who is being promoted.

You may find yourself writing for a prominent radio series as Nancy White does for the CBC, or like Len Chandler did for *The Credibility Gap*. It may be that your assignments come to you at the last minute over the wire service as the news stories are reported. I always recommend that your response be, "Of course I can. How much time do I have?"

Your assignment may be very specific as to the type of song, the length of the song and so forth, or you may be able to use more of your own judgment and ideas as to what kind of song you write. The main thing is not to panic. It's really just a matter of applying the same basic songwriting principles discussed in this book in a timely way.

Writing on assignment is a challenge often encountered by the professional songwriter.

There is always time for walking. This is the best way to get the issues of the song to fall into place. If you are really stuck, you might think of a well-known song that conveys a similar emotional energy to the song you want to write and write new words to its melody or new music to its words until you feel you have a good start. If there is time for a little break before you take a final look at it, that is often worthwhile. "I'll just go get an ice cream and then look the song over one more time before I put it down on the cassette."

15.8 Commercials & Jingles

"Like a Rock"

Many professional songwriters have relied on writing commercials and jingles to generate extra money or to tide them over a rough patch between royalty checks. Many have found it to be a lucrative career in itself.

The biggest drawback of writing commercials is in the area of compromise. There are the compromises which may be necessary to satisfy the client, but the more basic compromise is in using a medium which has been the expression of the highest potential of the human spirit to serve the commercial purposes of the highest bidder.

In some cases you don't have to do any new writing at all. Many commercials are based on existing work. Carly Simon was paid 50 thousand dollars for the use of her song "Anticipation" for a ketchup commercial. Other songs which have been recycled for commercials are:

"Like a Rock" by Bob Seger for Chevy trucks
"Let's Have Another Cup of Coffee"
"In My Merry Oldsmobile"
"Try a Little Tenderness" for Perdue Chickens
"Bake Someone Happy" from "Make Someone Happy"
"Wessonality" from "Personality"
"Sound Off for Chesterfield" from "Sound Off"
and "Help Me Honda" from "Help Me Rhonda" by the Beach Boys.

Some commercial jingles are settings of the sponsor's words to a familiar tune which is from the public domain and as such doesn't earn any royalties. A good example is "Pepsi Cola Hits the Spot."

You might find yourself writing for a singing toilet mop, or a dancing thumb, or a talking sweater. You may have to satisfy some Maalox-crazed ad person. "That doesn't sound like tomato juice to me." You might be laboring in the trenches of obscurity working for the local car dealer or bowling alley or you may join that illustrious group of immortals with "hits" like:

"I'm Chiquita Banana"
"Use Ajax, the Foaming Cleanser"
"Have It Your Way"
"Double Your Pleasure"
"You Deserve a Break Today"
"It's the Real Thing"

On a recent episode of *The Simpsons*, Grandma was trying to promote a family songfest and the only songs that anybody could think of that the whole family had sung were commercials. They sang spirited versions of "What kind of kids love Armour hot dogs," and "Chicken Tonight." Sad.

If you just want the money, you might rather give blood. You may not make as much money as you would from a commercial, but at least you would be performing a public service.

15.9 Publishing & Self-Publishing: Pros & Cons, by Fred Koller

I have spent over twenty years trying to support myself as a professional songwriter. There have been good years and there have been those years when I wished I'd chosen a second career to fall back on like taxidermy. When I first went to Nashville, every successful songwriter that I know was employed by a publisher. I pictured long rows of desks like a big city newspaper and a publisher gathering the writers around him every morning. "OK boys, George Jones needs a drinking song." The songwriters would then each create what they hoped would be the next George Jones single.

It took awhile before I found a publisher who could hear past my grumbled vocals and bluesy guitar style and even then, instead of being a bureau chief, he turned out to be another songwriter who helped shape my roughest ideas into polished songs.

In most work situations, one wants to please the boss. My publisher was a sucker for story songs and I found myself slipping away from the blues-based songs I'd first played for him. I believe I spent two years writing the kind of songs he wanted to hear. It wasn't until I started performing again that I realized how much my music had changed.

It wasn't all that bad. I found that having a publisher who provided a meager income in the form of a weekly draw against the future brought me a lot of time to practice the craft of songwriting. It was no longer a hobby and each song got a little better. I learned what it was like to hear others interpret my songs and I learned what it was like to get a song I really believed in turned down again and again.

This piece is supposed to be about the pros and cons of working with a publisher. Woody Guthrie had a publisher; Bob Dylan worked with various publishing companies who, I assume, helped to exploit his catalog. One can buy the time one needs to be creative by signing away part of your copyright to a publisher. There are some very good publishers who work with their songwriters and have been very instrumental in their success. There are also situations where a writer with a unique style starts writing songs that they know the publisher will like, losing their own identity in the process. I don't believe that publishing is for everybody.

Your publisher becomes the judge and jury of every song you create. Some songwriters are only allowed to demo songs that their publisher feels warrant the expense. I've had too many strange songs recorded to play that game. I doubt that some of my former publishers would have spent a penny on a song like "Let's Talk Dirty In Hawaiian."

Take a close look at where you are with your songwriting. Can you readily accept someone else's suggestion on how to make your song more "commercial"? There's that dreaded word. Can you remain true to your own vision and not "sell out" in hopes of putting more interesting groceries on the table?

Publishing one's own songs is relatively easy but you find yourself wearing a lot of different hats. One day you're a songwriter trying to be at your creative best; the next day you're waiting for hours in hopes of leaving a tape for someone who's never heard of you. Your time for songwriting diminishes as your catalog grows. If you're only writing a dozen songs a year and plan to record them yourself, you might not need a publisher unless they can get your songs to an audience you yourself could never reach. Like I said earlier, the money can also buy you the time to write. A string of hundred-dollar gigs across five states in the dead of winter makes any of us long for a little mailbox money.

Talk to writers you know who've been to a music center like Nashville. Take a trip down yourself. Get out of the small pond and jump into the ocean. Some days the water's fine. It's a love/hate thing. I know what the ideal publisher would be like and they know what the ideal songwriter would be. It's like a marriage – we are often disappointed looking for something we thought would be there. If you feel you are ready to work with a publisher, good luck, may they serve you well. You can always publish your own songs until the right opportunity presents itself.

I've tried it both ways and it usually feels better to know that I have a team of people believing in me. I will admit that there are still days when I find myself wanting to censor myself to please a publisher but it's a price that one pays.

Read the many books now available on publishing. Learn what a good publisher should do before you sign anything and save yourself a lot of disappointment in the long run. You are taking on a partner and partnerships unfortunately aren't for everyone. It's a personal decision and it's a tough call. Follow your heart. That's where the best songs come from.

16.

With Other Songwriters

16.1 "Courting the Muse" by Steve Gillette

Songwriting Together

Collaboration in songwriting helps in many ways. Working with one or more friends can improve a writer's productivity and skills and can even create access to the business side of music faster than anything else I know of. Some of us have a hard time getting started, some have a hard time finishing a song. Some of us only write lyrics, some only music. Some of us are great at thinking of titles, some preponderate in the left brain, some are lost in the right. I live in Vermont, one of my collaborators, Charles John Quarto, lives in Nashville, another, Rex Benson, lives in California. Many write by mail or phone or modem. In this age of the cassette (and the fiber-optic cable) we can work together anytime.

The benefits of partnership far outweigh the occasional angst of compromise, but a writing team, like any relationship, is built on respect and communication. It may take a period of adjustment to begin to learn a little of each other's vocabulary and perceptions about music and what it is for, and to develop the trust to be open to each other's vision and contribution. There must be a willingness to be subject to each other. It's got to be OK to uphold one's own values and work within one's limits. In this way there is the opportunity for true growth.

Unlike a marriage though, a songwriting collaboration may be an uneven partnership with one writer seen as the junior or senior partner depending on experience or position in the industry. This may change with the issue at hand or the song in progress.

Each new collaboration represents an initiation and gives each writer a new voice. It's also perfectly OK to maintain several writing partnerships at once.

One area of difficulty has to do with inspiration. Most writers I know have a protective outlook on their personal relationship with the muse. It can be hard to take one's most precious dreamings into the glaring light of the workroom. "What happened to that little ache? You know, the thing that got me started on this song idea in the first place." Or, "How can I keep my inspiration from being swept away?" The only answer I know of is to work with the idea as long as it takes until you have enough of it to show to someone else, without the fear that he will fail to see the merit in it. If it still doesn't hold up, work on it alone or with someone else.

The idea that "first thought is best thought" comes to us from Eastern teaching. Every writer must develop some way of getting back to this "first thought" moment even after many second thoughts. This is in the same category as trying not to think of monkeys. I usually set up the tape recorder and do at least a half hour of a running first draft just to get some of the kinks out and to selectively forget what I can go back and evaluate later. It's good to do this in a place where you don't need to apologize if you moan or cry or laugh out loud.

A weekly co-writing session can keep the new work coming and provide a chance to bounce ideas and discuss things in general. Some people are really able to be creative at these times and a shared inspiration with one good idea after another in true rejoinder is very gratifying.

> **Solitude is one of the most important aspects of writing ... even in collaboration.**

I must admit that I still need time at home in my own space to steer by my own very tiny internal compass. Solitude is one of the most important aspects of writing, even in collaboration. Time together can be well- spent in fleshing out the song idea and considering who might sing it. "I hear this as a kind of a Delbert McClinton kind of a thing with a little bit of Reba." Or, "That line is still awkward for me but since your dad's producing the picture, I guess I can work with it."

With my co-writers, we do a lot of sending drafts back and forth. It's the next best thing to the oral tradition. Each subsequent version retains what one writer feels are the best lines and ideas, but attempts to solve problems he has perceived in the version before it. On the side of the cereal box it says, "Contents may have settled during shipping." Well, this settling in is a very important part of the writing process, too.

This can all take quite awhile, but if the listener is going to give us three whole minutes of his or her time, two or three months is not too much to spend on a good song. You might get the impression, listening to the radio, that songs don't have to be very good. Don't be misled by this. Songs may be recorded for a variety of the wrong reasons, but you are the only one who can write or not write what you are capable of and you have a lifetime to get there.

Compromise may not be comfortable or even workable. You may need tosay, "We haven't yet found a resolution I can live with. Let's put the song aside for a while." Or, "If you don't mind, I'd like to take the idea back and work with it on my own." In most good collaborations there is a some leeway. All any writer really wants to do is work on the most promising and productive ideas. Again, communication is the key. If you only write words or music, don't be content to let it stay that way. And don't be too willing to rely on another person to realize your version of the song. Aspire to your own.

When the song is finished and you get out into the marketplace with it, you may encounter the unexpected or even unwanted collaborator. One well-known country artist had a notorious rubber stamp with which he wrote himself in on songs he agreed to record and/or publish. "I like that song you did at the club last night. I'd like to co-write that one with you." A glance at the charts or the credits of a few top-selling albums will reveal an assorted plethora of writers and publishers dividing songs up like sides of beef. Not a pretty sight, but there are times when even a five-person honeymoon may be worth considering.

This brings up another thorny issue of writing and co-writing for the music business, the question of the publisher's share (usually half of the income of the song). My sense of this is that each writer retains his half of all rights to the song and that each is free to allocate his share to anyone he chooses. Or, to keep these rights for himself in the event that he has or wants to have his own publishing company.

When it actually comes down to getting a major recording on the song, there may be some incentive to give up the publishing, but the writer's share should always be sacred. By being a part of more songs by virtue of collaboration, you can more than make up for the smaller share of earnings. Even if your goal is not getting songs recorded, sharing the writing can get you on down the road and in out of the cold.

Who is more fortunate than he who benefits from a productive and salutary association in the pursuit of art? It's harder to be cynical or bitter or caught up in reaction to the vagaries of the business when there is someone else there. It's easier to be in good faith, to help each other toward the high road, and to foster a transcendent vision.

The songs I really care about I care about mostly because I like to sing them. Even if you don't sing, I think you must know what I mean. Good work is good work and there is satisfaction in doing good work together.

16.2 Swapping Songs

It seems as if songwriters don't have to be told to get out there and show their work. If anything, the artists and producers and record companies have had to adopt measures to give themselves some distance from the ubiquitous songwriter. This has made the atmosphere a little colder, but perhaps has served to generate all sorts of alternative pathways for the writer.

16.3 Festivals

There are many international song festivals which present the most illustrious songs and songwriters and artists and give kings' ransoms in awards. These seem to be primarily centered on the handful of "big" songs and are actively sought after by the large corporate music entities. Still they are all worth attending and certainly worth aspiring to.

By contrast, almost every regional and traditional music festival has now made some provision for emerging songwriters to present their songs. Some offer awards while some just provide a place and an audience and no other formal recognition. One example of an established song competition is the "New Folk" segment of the Kerrville Folk Festival held every spring in Texas. Begun at the suggestion of Peter Yarrow in 1972, "New Folk" has recognized six outstanding songwriters every year and has had such well known participants as Nanci Griffith, Tish Hinojosa, Hal Ketchum, Lyle Lovett, John Gorka, John Ims, Chuck Pyle and David Wilcox.

16.4 Contests

In addition to the festivals, song contests have been initiated in many places throughout the country. Most offer serious prizes, cash, studio time, even record deals. It's important to note that not all writers feel that songs are to be created for competition. There are many spiritual aspects to the process and to the effects of good songwriting and some may not wish to subject this to the materialism and competitiveness that is inevitably a part of song contests. Each writer must make his own choice in these matters.

Even if you don't enter, there is a lot of information about songs and the music industry to be gained by being aware of the major song competitions. Lists of contests are published often in the songwriter magazines and the many songwriter organization newsletters. Some these are listed in the Kerrville Directory (see the bibliography for the address).

16.5 Showcases

Len Chandler & the Los Angeles Songwriters' Showcase

I wanted to ask you about your work with the Los Angeles Songwriter's showcase. Over the years you have really given a lot of writers a chance to be heard within the music business establishment. How did that get started?

Len: Well, my focus was more selfish from the very, very beginning. My partner John Braheny and I had first wanted to have an opportunity to show our own songs. So when the Songwriters Showcase started, I would also be singing every week and the idea was that we would bring in record company people and publishers and we would show them songs ... instead of singing to them over their desks while they're taking telephone calls and all that and to do it in front of a live audience so that they could see the real magic that a song created.

So then we broadened it and put this thing on called the "two song hoot." We figured we could broaden our reach to include songs from people we didn't know and we thought we could bear two songs from anybody! Well, that wasn't true ... because some people's songs would be absolutely horrendous ... and then the record company guys would leave. So they told us that if this thing was really going to be functional, we couldn't have any bad songs. We'd have to screen everything and be sure that the songs were of good quality.

What had started out originally as a thing that might take a couple hours a week to organize then became a serious, labor intensive auditioning process. Two times a week we would be seeing a different person every half an hour from 12 until 6. And that became so busy that if you called up to get an appointment it might be a four-month wait. So we had to keep elaborate records and we had to start taping the auditions so we could remember who we had heard.

We had to design record sheets so that we could tell was a song better for a male or a female, was it slow, medium or up-tempo, could it be done by R&B, country, rock, crossover, all those categories, and we'd have to give our evaluation of the song as far as music and lyric content and other points of criticism.

I remember filling out those evaluation forms when I was the guest writer/ critic of the week. I remember some very talented people and I've wondered, you must have had some real success stories.

Len: There were many people that had a great deal of success there were still so many songs that you would say, "Gosh, that was a wonderful song ... that never saw the light of day." People like Diane Warren has had so many hits now – she's had eighteen Top 10 hits in the last nine years. "Solitaire," "Rhythms of the Night," "Nothin's Gonna Stop Us Now," "If I Could Turn Back Time," "Love Will Lead You Back." Billy Steinberg, "Like a Virgin," "True Color." A lot of these writers got picked up through being in the showcase. Stephen Bishop, "On and On," Karla Bonoff, "Someone to Lay Down Beside Me." Allen O'Day, "Undercover Angel," "Rock and Roll Heaven," Alan Rich, "I Don't Have the Heart" written with a guy he met through the showcase.

You seem to have found a way to bring it all together, your experience and your contacts and a lot of creative people.

Len: In many ways that's true. In August it'll be the twenty-fourth year.

16.6 Workshops

One of the most rewarding things songwriters and songwriting teachers can do is to attend a weeklong retreat where they can rub elbows with each other and get to the bottom of this songwriting thing once and for all. At least until next year. These workshops take place in the mountains, the forest, on college campuses during summer vacation and any other place where people can gather for a few days.

The Puget Sound Guitar Workshop conducts a weeklong songwriting school on a lake south of Seattle. The Kerrville Festival has a three-day school midweek between concert weekends. The Swannanoa Gathering takes place in Asheville, North Carolina, in July. The Augusta Heritage Workshops convenes at Davis and Elkins College in Elkins, West Virginia. The Pinewoods camp is located in a forest in Connecticut. Many encourage the writing of a complete song under the tutelage of one or more successful professionals. And they all offer a memorable and nurturing experience.

16.7 Guitar Pulls

Anywhere that songwriters meet other songwriters there occurs what has been described as a "guitar pull." After listening quietly and respectfully to one songwriter's song, the other songwriters will reach for the guitar with such urgency that a lot of veteran songwriters have learned to leave their pre-war Martins at home. Guitar pulls and picking parties spontaneously erupt in bus depots and hotel lobbies at festival time and during Nashville's Fanfare week.

16.8 Campfires

There is a long tradition of campfire singing. Just about every cowboy movie silhouettes some harmonica player or saddle guitar player against the prairie sky. There is something about the crackle of the fire and the sky full of stars that brings out the best energies of a song. I once thought that my business card, if I ever had one, would say on it "Campfire Singer" because I was so impressed by that setting as the most perfect focus for the song.

16.9 Interview with Mike Williams

Mike, if I had to choose the "A" campfire – the granddaddy of them all – it would be your campfire at Kerrville. Can you tell us about it?

Mike: On a Saturday night at Kerrville I announced backstage, "There's an all-night picking party in the campground. C'mon down and wail!" I raced to the campground, built a roaring fire and arranged logs and stumps for people to perch on, and welcomed a hoard of pickers. At 3 a.m. under a Texas full moon, 20 musicians howled original songs in tequila harmony, while a couple of hundred onlookers crowded near and applauded until their hands hurt. The party raged past dawn ... then resumed at noon.

I keep that original big campfire going each year. It has grown into a magic ongoing hooha called Camp Quisine. Dozens of friends pitch tents in a big circle around that campfire, and gourmet chef Phil Fletcher brings a chuckwagon with a propane refrigerator and a full size pizza oven. We feast and sing way past all legal limits. In 1990, Agua Azul Records taped 60 hours of live campfire music at Camp Quisine and released a CD, *The Camp Quisine Tapes*, that features great raucous renditions of songs such as Jon Ims' "She's in Love with the Boy" (BMI 1992 Song of the Year).

You have instigated a similar gathering in Nashville haven't you?

Mike: Since I moved to Nashville last spring, that ongoing campfire "I gotta Pick!" energy has bloomed here into Kerrville-style picking parties in my living room. My weekly "6 Chair Pickin' Party" – six fine songwriters "in the round" with plenty of listeners and harmonizers joining in – has featured nearly 100 Nashville songwriters in 1993 (a drop in the bucket in this town) and many talented writers.

Like Camp Quisine, the "6 Chair Pickin' Party" always highlights the song and the moment, creating a campfire feeling you won't find anywhere except here and Kerrville. The party features new songs every week, and nobody shows any surprise when somebody hauls out a song that "I wrote on the way home after the last time I played here." Oh boy, let's hear it! Several out-of-town pickers have enjoyed it so much that they're cranking up similar picking parties in other parts of the country.

16.10 The Kerrville Songwriter's School & "New Folk" Competitions

The Kerrville Folk Festival is held every spring at the Quiet Valley Ranch south of Kerrville in the Texas hill country. The festival is a camping festival and a small community of Kerrfolk convenes each year in the meadow. Whole groups of campers return year after year and many traditions have been established. The campfires and gatherings where songs are shared and discussed have made Kerrville a special place among songwriters. Rod Kennedy is the founder and producer of the Kerrville Folk Festival.

Closing Words from Rod Kennedy

I guess if I had only a few moments to share with an emerging songwriter, I'd try to tell them how important their contribution can be to re-humanizing our culture.

One of the last bastions of originality and genuineness, the "folk writer" who writes from the heart (as against the imitative, lowest common denominator pop culture writer of some of today's hits) can again make us feel what is enriching and inspiring about humanity. It's rewarding and rehabilitating to share a festival weekend with these creative singers who fill us with thoughts of what we can be.

So while it is so important to have the heart to reach out in song to our fellow man, energizing that artistic heart is the creative capacity to learn and use the tools of the professional songwriter.

What Kerrville has been about since its inception was building bridges for original songwriters between them and an appreciative audience. A carefully and thoughtfully created environment, filled with sharing and learning opportunity has paid off. This "no star system" community has now gained its own momentum, what was once an annual retreat for 2,800 has become a haven for more than 28,000.

The Kerrville Folk Festival, its main stage and campfires, combined with its music foundation projects – "New Folk" competitions (our own farm team) and "Ballad Tree" song sharings – have validated and encouraged literally thousands of songwriters who perhaps previously suffered doubts, uncertain confidence in their own work, and considerable perceived isolation from the people around them.

Here suddenly (over more than 20 years!) was a songwriter community where everyone at every creative level could find acceptance and encouragement. Here songwriters could meet their peers, their heroines and their heroes in a mostly noncompetitive environment.

One of the really significant steps toward maturing that environment was the establishment, 15 years ago, of the three-day annual songwriter's school. Conceived and guided for more than a decade by Chicago's Bob Gibson, this school provided an opportunity for songwriting students to spend three days and nights talking, working, co-writing, re-writing, and singing together under the tutelage of a carefully balanced handful of some of North America's most loved and widely admired songwriters.

So have heart. Be unique. Express your human capacity to feel what can be, and gather the tools from the experience of your fellow craftsmen. Write as if tomorrow depended on it. For me, it does!

Bibliography

Secrets Of Successful Songwriting, Carl E. Bolte Jr., Arco Publications, New York, 1984 (Published in 1978 as *Sucessful Songwriting.*)

The Mother Tongue, Bill Bryson, William Morrow & Company, New York, 1990

The Hero With A Thousand Faces, Joseph Campbell, Princeton University Press, 1990

Musical Applications of Microprocessors, Hal Chamberlin, Hayden Book Co., Hasbrouck Heights, NJ, 1985

Songwriting: A Complete Guide to the Craft, Stephen Citron, William Morrow & Company, New York, 1985

Music and Imagination, Aaron Copland, Harvard University Press, Cambridge, MA, 1952

Hit Men, Fredric Dannen, Vintage Books, 1991

What The World Needs Now, Hal David, Simon & Shuster, New York, NY 1970

The Craft of Lyric Writing, Sheila Davis, Writer's Digest Books, New York

The Psychology of Music, Diana Deutsch, Editor, Academic Press, New York, 1982

Drawing On The Right Side Of The Brain, Betty Edwards, Tarcher, 1989

The Chalice And The Blade, Riane Eisler, Harper & Rowe, Publishers,Inc., New York, 1987

Writing With Power, and *Writing Without Teachers*, Peter Elbow, Oxford University Press, 1981

Musician's Guide To Copyright, J. Gunnar Erickson, Charles Scribner & Sons, New York

Spirituality Named Compassion, Matthew Fox, Harper, 1990

Writing the Broadway Musical, Aaron Frankel, Drama Book Specialists, New York, 1977

The Forgotten Language, Erich Fromm, Grove Press, 1987

The Recording Industry Sourcebook, Michael Fuchs, Editor, Ascona Communications, 1992

Rockin' the Boat: Mass Music & Mass Movements, Reebee Garofalo, Editor, South End Press, Boston, MA 1992

Lyrics On Several Occasions, Ira Gershwin, Alfred A. Knopf, New York, 1959

Writing Down The Bones, and *Wild Mind*, Natalie Goldberg, Shambala, 1986 Bantam, 1990

The Musician's Business and Legal Guide, Mark Halloran, Editor, Englewood Cliffs, NJ, 1991

The Craft of Musical Composition, Paul Hindemith, Associated Music Publishers Inc., London, 1941-42

Entertainment Industry Series, Walter E. Hurst, Seven Arts, (23 volumes)

The Gift, Lewis Hyde, Vintage Books (Random House), New York, 1979

Happy With The Blues – Harold Arlen, Edward Jablowski, Doubleday & Co., New York, 1961

Dramatic Imagination, Robert Edmond Jones, Rutledge, Chapman & Hall,1941

The Transparent Self, Sidney Jourard, Van Nostrand, Reinhold

Man And His Symbols, Carl Jung, Dell, 1968

If They Ask You, You Can Write A Song, Al Kasha & Joel Hirschhorn, Simon & Schuster, 1990

Protecting Your Songs and Yourself: Legal Guide, Kent J. Klavans, Writer's Digest Books, 1989

How To Pitch And Promote Your Songs, Fred Koller, Writer's Digest Books, Cincinnati, OH, 1989

How To Be A Successful Nashville Songwriter, Michael Kosser, Porch Swing, Nashville

The Silent Pulse, George Leonard, E. P. Dutton, New York, 1978

The Street Where You Live, Alan Jay Lerner, W. W. Norton, New York, NY 1978

Freeing The Natural Voice, Kristin Linklater, Drama Book Specialists, NY 1976

The Technology of Computer Music, Max V. Matthews, M.I.T. Press, Cambridge, MA, 1969

The Courage to Create, and *Love And Will*, Rollo May, W.W. Norton & Company, New York,1975

King, Warrior, Magician, Lover, Moore & Gillette, HarperCollins Publishers, New York, 1990

A Writer Teaches Writing, Donald Murray, Houghton, Mifflin, 1984

Music Publishing: A Songwriter's Guide, Randy Poe, Writer's Digest Books, 1990

In Their Own Words, Bruce Pollack, Collier MacMillan Pub. Co., New York

The Songwriter's Handbook, Harvey Rachlin, Funk & Wagnalls, New York, 1977

How Can I Help?, Paul Gorman & Ram Dass, Alfred A. Knopf, New York, 1987

How To Make and Sell You Own Recording, Diane Rapaport, Jerome Headlands Press, Jerome, AZ, 1993

Writing the Natural Way, Gabriele Rico, J.P. Tarcher, Inc., 1983

A Soprano On Her Head, Eloise Ristad, Real People Press, 1982

MIDI: A Comprehensive Introduction, Joseph Rothstein, A-R Editions, Madison, 1992

Songwriter's Market, Rand Ruggeberg, Writer's Digest Books, Cincinnati, OH

Being And Nothingness, Jean-Paul Sartre, Washington Square Press, 1983

This Business Of Music, Sidney Schemel, Billboard Publications, New York, 1979

Style and Idea, Arnold Schoenberg, University of California Press, 1950

Learning How To Learn, Idries Shah, Institute for the Study of Humanity, 1978

The Writer On Her Work, Janet Sternburg, W.W.Norton Press

The Poetics of Music, Igor Stravinsky, Harvard University Press, Cambridge, MA 1942

Listening Out Loud: Becoming a Composer, Elizabeth Swados, Harper & Rowe, New York, 1988

The Record Studio Handbook, John M. Woram, Elar Publications, 1985

The Right-Brain Experience, Marilee Zdenek, McGraw-Hill, 1983

The Kerrville Directory ($25), Kerrville Music Foundation, P.O.Box 1466, Kerrville, TX 78029. Lists of venues, radio, etc.

Appendix

The Contributors:

Rick Beresford: "Principles of Lyric Rewriting"

At age 12, Rick, with the purchase of his first Davy Crockett guitar, knew he would be a singer and a songwriter. After listening to *Blonde on Blonde* at 24 years of age, he wrote his first song, "Laundromat Blues." He's been rewriting it ever since. His singing and songwriting evolution continued in Austin, Texas, where he entered the Kerrville Festival's New Folk Contest and won in 1977.

It was at Kerrville that Rick found his Nashville connection, and he has been living in "Music City" ever since. He is the director of the Kerrville Songwriting School and workshop coordinator and teacher for the Nashville Songwriter's Association International.

Rick has had songs recorded by George Jones, Don Williams, John Conlee, Mickey Gilley, Tom Kimmel, the Everly Brothers, Brenda Lee, and many others. He is completing his soon-to-be best-seller, *Dancing in Song Town: An Intuitive Guide to Songwriting*.

Peter & Lou Berryman: "Courting the Muse" #4

Peter and Lou have been composing songs since 1963 through a series of musical groups and various genres. Their musical partnership survived a brief marriage, and the duo as it exists today was formed in 1975. Since then, they've produced eight albums of original songs, a few of which have found their way into the pages of *Sing Out!*, reflecting their wide variety of interests and experiences – always through the softening lens of humor. Their eight recordings, as well as their songbooks containing "almost all of our recorded songs," 85 of them, are available from their own Cornbelt Records, Box 3452, Madison, WI 53704, (608) 256-7331.

Reprinted from *Sing Out!* magazine, Volume 37, No. 3, ©1992. Used by permission.

Tom Bocci: "Writing for Films"

Tom was born in Michigan, but has lived most of his eclectic adult life in California, where he has taught guitar and poetry courses in junior college, appeared on the *The Tonight Show with Johnny Carson* as a singer/songwriter, headed the music publishing division of Walt Disney Studios, and founded an independent music supervision company. He has been responsible for the music in many feature films including six years with director Blake Edwards and composer Henry Mancini.

Most recently he composed songs and wrote the text for a CD-ROM entitled *Great Lives – Interactive Biographies of American Heroes* and as artist and producer will soon release the first album on his own independent label entitled *Vanishing Voices*, an instrumental world music record honoring endangered animals and birds in their natural habitats by blending indigenous instrumentation and the sounds of the species with original rhythmic melodies that reflect particular regions of the planet. Write: Blue Planet Records, 2899 Agoura Road, # 166, Westlake Village, CA 91361.

Len Chandler: "An Interview with"

Len is a well-known singer and songwriter who has recorded several albums of his own music. In the mid '60s he moved to California to work with radio station KRLA as the chief writer for *The Credibility Gap* a three times daily musical commentary on the news as it was unfolding.

With John Braheny, Len founded the Los Angeles Songwriter's Showcase and has given hundreds of songwriters the opportunity to perform their songs for music business professionals in the best possible atmosphere. Screening often hundreds of songs in a single week, the Showcase has been able to establish a high standard and consequently a high level of clout among record company producers and A & R people.

Ani DiFranco: "Courting the Muse" #5

Ani's jaw-dropping lyrics come out of her own "pleasantly furious" experience of existing as a woman in a man's world, but she'd be quick to point out, "There's nothing that's happened to me that hasn't happened to a million other women or people." Her unflinching musical observations on life may be too straightforward for some, and her percussive, thumping guitar style may not strike everyone, but her dramatic vocals and blunt honesty *will* get your attention.

She says, "I'm the type of person who likes to get in someone's face ... I find that writing is a way of telling myself something, where first I have to figure out what it is I want to tell myself, so I will be able to tell other people." At the tender age of 22, Ani has three recordings to her credit; she's working on a fourth, and she hasn't "hooked up with some big machine, some record company" to do it. Her recordings are available from her own label, Righteous Records, 429 Richmond Ave., Buffalo, NY 14222.

Reprinted from *Sing Out!* magazine, Volume 37, No. 4, ©1993. Used by permission.

Ferron: "Courting the Muse" #11

Canadian born, Ferron left her home as a teenager and worked a series of blue-collar jobs until finding her muse – professionally – with a series of gigs in a Vancouver coffeehouse. Her writing is thick with poetic imagery, and grabs the attention and heart of the listener. A pioneer in the field of women's music, Ferron has recorded for a number of labels. Her latest, *Driver*, is available on the Earthbeat! label (1144 Redway Dr., Redway, CA 95560).

Reprinted from *Sing Out!* magazine, Volume 39, No. 3, ©1994. Used by permission.

Bob Franke: "Courting the Muse" #3

Bob has been acclaimed by his peers as a songwriter's songwriter. Testament to that statement is the fact that his songs have been covered by a growing list of his contemporaries, and three of those much-loved songs can be found in *Sing Out!*

Bob has been honing his craft for nearly thirty years, beginning while still in college at the University of Michigan, where he was one of the first performers at The Ark, the ledgendary Ann Arbor folk club, and continuing, with brief interludes as an employee of a candy factory and a seminarian at the Episcopal Theological School in Cambridge, to compose songs containing disarming insights into human emotions, which have a way of touching responsive chords in every listener. He has five recordings, four of which are on the Flying Fish label.

Reprinted from *Sing Out!* magazine, Volume 37, No. 2, ©1992. Used by permission.

Steve Gillette: "Courting the Muse" #7

Since Ian and Sylvia first recorded "Darcy Farrow" in 1966, Steve's songs have been sung by legions of major artists including Garth Brooks, John Denver, Waylon Jennings, Gordon Lightfoot, Anne Murray, Linda

Ronstadt, Jerry Jeff Walker and Don Williams. He's written songs that have earned gold and platinum records, as well as songs that have entered into the folk tradition. He's written for the movie industry, and for the Disney characters, Winnie-the-Pooh, Dumbo and Jiminy Crickett.

Ralph Earle wrote that Steve "... always keeps his subjects in perspective, and by doing so refines the sensitivities of his listeners." Tony May said, "Steve's 25-year career has seen his songs recorded successfully by many a distinguished artist; small wonder as he's a legendary songwriter ... makes you hang on every word with rapt attention. Obviously his peers are in awe of him."

Steve's albums include: *Steve Gillette*, 1968, recently reissued by Vanguard; *Alone ... Direct*, Sierra Records, 1979; *A Little Warmth*, Flying Fish Records, 1979; *Ways of the World*, Compass Rose, 1992; and *Live In Concert*, the duet album with his wife, Cindy Mangsen, also on Compass Rose. A songbook with 44 of Steve's songs is also available from Compass Rose Music; P.O.Box 1501, Bennington, VT 05201. He wrote this book, too.

Reprinted from *Sing Out!* magazine, Volume 38, No. 2, ©1993. Used by permission.

Dick Goodwin: "Elements of Musical Composition"

Dick is a composer and arranger who lives in Columbia, South Carolina, and has been on the staff of Kerrville Songwriter's School for many years.

Butch Hancock: "Advice to a Young Poet"

Butch is a Texas songwriter who has generated a loyal and vocal following. Amazingly prolific, Butch recently did a five-day marathon concert series and sang over two hundred songs, never repeating a song in all five days. Butch travels in the U.S. and Europe and is a former member of the legendary Lubbock band "Flatlanders" with Jimmie Dale Gilmore and Joe Ely.

Jack Hardy: "Courting the Muse" #1

Jack has released ten albums on his own Great Divide label (178 W. Houston St., NY, NY 10014) Many of which were recorded live to two-track at the current Houston Street weekly meeting headquarters of the legendary Songwriter's Exchange, which he cofounded, along with the NYC Musician's Co-operative, which currently runs the Fast Folk Cafe in New York.

Jack's writing mixes the myth and folklore with the trademark NYC singer-songwriter melodic style which he helped crystallize over the last 15 years. His body of work is nothing short of brilliant, and his writing and approach have influenced many writers on today's contemporary folk circuit.

Reprinted from *Sing Out!* magazine, Volume 36, No. 4, ©1992, Used by permission.

Anne Hills: "Writing for Singers"

Anne began her music career in the fertile Chicago folk music scene, where her voice quickly brought her to the public's attention. That attention led to her work with Tom Paxton, Bob Gibson, and many others, along with seven recordings of her own, which are all available from Flying Fish. She tours internationally, solo, with trio partners Priscilla Herdman and Cindy Mangsen, as well as with soulmate Michael Smith. Anne now makes her home in Bethlehem, PA, where she lives with her daughter, Tamlyn, and her husband, Mark Moss, *Sing Out!*'s executive director.

Fred Koller: "Publishing"

Fred is a very successful Nashville songwriter. He is the co-writer of Kathey Mattea's #1 country hit "Going Going Gone" and many other chart records including "She Came From Fort Worth." He has written in collaboration with Shel Silverstein, John Prine, Pat Alger, John Hiatt, and many others. Fred is the author of the book *How to Pitch and Promote Your Songs,* available from Writer's Digest Books. A nationally touring performing singer-songwriter, Fred has released several albums of his own music and conducts songwriting seminars and workshops all over the country.

David Massengill: "Courting the Muse" #13

A native Tennessean, David has been living, writing and playing dulcimer in New York City for nearly two decades. His songs have been recorded by the likes of Joan Baez and the Roches, and his sole recording (this far), *Coming Up For Air*, was released by Flying Fish.

Reprinted from *Sing Out!* magazine, Volume 40, No. 1, ©1995. Used by permission.

Mary McCaslin: "Courting the Muse" #2

Mary moved to the West Coast at the age of 6, with visions of wide open spaces and cowboys and horses. Her parents' choice of Los Angeles didn't quite turn out to be like that, so she settled for watching westerns on TV and listening to country & western music, especially the western ballads of Marty Robbins. Her recordings on Philo and Flying Fish reflect these influences.

Her note about the songs on *Way Out West* seems particularly apropos in this book. "To me, songs do one or two things. They either take the listener to another place or time or else they hit home in some way and the listener identifies with that song or some statement in the song. Or, sometimes the song does both."

Reprinted from *Sing Out!* magazine, Volume 37, No. 1, ©1992. Used by permission.

Graham Nash: "An Interview with ..."

Graham, best known for his distinctive lead and harmony singing with David Crosby and Stephen Stills, has written some of the best and best-known songs to come out of the Woodstock era and beyond. Lending his energy to many social issues like the MUSE concerts (Musicians for Safe Energy), he has been a voice for social change and human responsibility. By licensing his song "Teach Your Children" and by other fund-raising activities he has raised over $600,000 for UNICEF.

Tom Paxton: "An Interview with ..."

Tom has written four books, released twenty-eight albums and written some of the most familiar songs in the folk idiom, modern standards such as "The Last Thing On My Mind," "Ramblin' Boy," "Bottle Of Wine," and "Whose Garden Was This." A living legend!

Charles John Quarto: "An Interview with ..."

Charles John is a poet and songwriter who lives and works in Nashville. His songs have been recorded by Michael Martin Murphey, Crystal Gayle, The Band, Hal Ketchum, Jerry Jeff Walker, Don Williams, and many others. He has made two albums of his own poetry, the first for Atlantic Records produced by Graham Nash and the second for RCA produced by Bill Halverson. Charles' chief collaborators have been Michael Martin Murphey, Fred Koller, Pete Wasner, Randy Handley, Steve Gillette and John Townsend.

Ann Reed: "Courting the Muse" #8

Ann is a Minneapolis-based songwriter and the "woman who aced Prince" for Artist of the Year at the Minnesota Music Awards, 1990. In July 1993, she walked away from MMA with Female Songwriter of the Year. Combining folk, blues, jazz, country, and soft rock in her songwritng style, her voice has been described as both "creamy-chocolate" and "smoky." Her performances, honed to a fine art over 18 years, include a wide range of material interspersed with comedic interludes. Of her craft, she says, "My songwriting is something I do to cope with the world, with whatever emotions are going on. So I don't consider it work. It's just who I am." Her recordings are available from Box 8240, Minneapolis, MN 55408.

Reprinted from *Sing Out!* magazine, Volume 38, No. 3, ©1993. Used by permission.

Suzzy Roche: "Courting the Muse" #12

With her sisters, Maggie and Terre Roche, Suzzy has been creating her own brand of eclectic, quirky contemporary folk for more than 15 years now. Since their groundbreaking self-titled 1979 Warner Brothers debut, *The Roches*, the Roche sisters have blended acoustic pop with the self-examination and personal voice that have come to be such integral parts of the repertoire of the modern-day singersongwriter. The Roches' latest offerings include a family album, produced by Suzzy and featuring guests such as brother David and daughter Lucy, entitled *Will You Be My Friend* (Baby Boom 3004 2/4; P.O. Box 62188, Minneapolis, MN 55426), as well as a brand-new Roches' recording, *Can We Go Home Now*, available from Rykodisc, Shetland Park, 27 Congress St., Salem, MA 01970.

Reprinted from *Sing Out!* magazine, Volume 39, No. 4, ©1995. Used by permission.

Michael Smith: "Courting the Muse" #6

Anyone who's frequented a local coffeehouse or attended a folk festival knows Michael Smith's songwriting. So many people have performed and recorded his compositions, you'd have to have been a hermit in Alaska for the past twenty years not to have heard at least one of his songs. Though his own recorded legacy over that period of time has been limited (*Love Stories*, 1987, *Michael Smith*, 1986, and two discs recorded in the '70s, one on Decca, *Juarez*, and one on Bell, *Barbara Barrow and Michael Smith*, both out of print), he hasn't been idle. He has written the music for several TV productions, a movie, and Steppenwolf Theatre's production of John Steinbeck's *The Grapes of Wrath*, for which he led the group of musicians as well.

A revue of Michael's songs, *Personals*, ran for two years in Detroit and was featured on the Today show. He co-wrote another revue, a collection of musical vignettes about the female influence, *Women in My Life*, with Bob Gibson. He has appeared in the Goodman Theatre's Writers Series and on the nationally syndicated radio shows, *Good Evening* and *The Studs Terkel Show*. That he has been so sought after is fitting tribute to his uncanny and woefully rare ability to depict with compassion, wit, and insight the universal trials of existence through slice-of-llife sketches. As *Chicago Magazine* put it, "He is one of best songwriters in the English language."

Reprinted from *Sing Out!* magazine, Volume 38, No. 1, ©1993. Used by permission.

Bill Staines: "Courting the Muse" #10

Bill, a New England native, still courts his muse in New Hampshire. He has been singing and writing songs for over 30 years and has more than 15 albums to his credit. Bill's songs have also been recorded by the likes of Nanci Griffith, Jerry Jeff Walker, Priscilla Herdman, and Grandpa Jones. His latest release, *Going to the West*, is on the Red House label (P.O. Box 4044, St. Paul, MN 55504).

Reprinted from *Sing Out!* magazine, Volume 39, No. 2, ©1994. Used by permission.

Nancy White: "Courting the Muse" #9

Along with her duties as *Sunday Morning* composer, single mother of two daughters, and shipping clerk, Nancy tours widely. In 1994 she's made it to St. John's, Vancouver, and Whitehorse, with many "nasty little places in between." She's also performed at lots of cabarets, coffee-houses and folk festivals. Her recordings are available from Mouton Records, Box 128, Station E, Toronto, ON M6H 4F2, Canada.

Reprinted from *Sing Out!* magazine, Volume 38, No. 4, ©1994. Used by permission.

Mike Williams: "An Interview with ..."

Mike is a Texas-born singer-songwriter of larger-than-life proportions of talent and energy. Now living in Nashville, he is the author of *The Hop of the Small Time Toad* a handbook for performers interested in booking themselves on the college circuit. Mike founded the record label "B.F. Deal" for his own projects and as a vehicle for other talented artists. He produced Nanci Griffith's first album for the label.

Index

Bocci, Tom 141
"Bone By Bone" 122
Bonoff, Karla 205
Borge, Victor 37
borrowed chord 30
borrowing 28
Braheny, John 205
breathing 43
bridge 31, 39, 87, 101
Bromberg, David 177
Brooks, Garth 136
Broonzy, Big Bill 137
Brown, Milton 136
Brown, Norman 122
Brown, Willie 138
Brueggemann, Walter 80
Bryan, Mary 122
Buddha 120
Burns, George 38
business 191, 201

C

cadence 41, 105
call and response 136
Camp Quisine 207
Campbell, Joseph 126
Campbell, Tom 76
campfire singing 206
Cantor, the 162
The Capitol Steps 172
"Captain My Captain" 123
card stacking 47
career management 90
Carroll, Lewis 115
Carter Family style 32
"The Cat Came Back" 167
catalog 196
censor 93
censorship 153
chain gangs 137
The Chalice and the Blade *127*
challenge 179
Chandler, Len 145, 197, 204
changes 14
changing tense 87
chaos 99, 155
Chapin, Tom 182
Chaplin, Charlie 115
character 46, 55, 84, 95, 114, 126
charts 100
children's songs 60, 174, 182
Chinese poetry 165
chord progressions 177
chords 15, 162
  altered 31
  augmented
    diminished 15
  borrowed dominant 20
  inversion 18
  major
    minor 15
  open 35
  Roman numerals 18
  seventh 16
  suspension 19

chorus 31, 38, 81, 87
Chute, B.J. 83
circle of fifths 13, 14
circle of fourths 13
civil rights movement 145
Clark, Guy 45
Clearwater 47
cliches 45, 69, 89, 125
"Closing Time" 90
Clustering 95
co-writing 202
coffeehouses 194
cognition 121
"cognitive dissonance" 113
"cognitive resonance" 114
Cohen, Leonard iii, 90
Coleridge, "Notebooks" 111
collaboration 76, 81, 123, 201
collective unconscious 111
Collins, Judy i
colorful language 45
Coltrane, John 138
comedy songs 167
commercial 103
commercial music 2
commercials 197
communication 201
community 155, 156, 208
competitions 208
complementary opposites 180
composition
  elements of 29
"conceits" 86
concentration 124
concords 162
conflict 154
conscious 111
conscious attention 120
consciousness
  112, 117, 122, 125, 164, 165
consonance 2, 55
consonants 51, 52, 74, 87
consumer mythologies 133
contests 204
conversation 46, 47
conviction 179
Copland, Aaron iii, 93, 162
copyright 191, 199
country blues 138
country music 135
courage 112, 179
"Courage To Create, the" 111
"Courting the Muse" 1, 6, 58,
    73, 89, 96, 107, 128,
      150, 155, 176, 178,
        188, 201,
cowboy poetry 135
cowboys 135
creative activity 2
creative process 2
creativity 85, 99, 111, 124
  left-brain 114, 115
  right-brain 114, 115
credibility 46
The Credibility Gap 145, 197

criticism 80
crooked tunes 67
Crosby, David 6
"cross-state retention" 104
culture 144
cycle of fifths 13
cycle of fourths 13

D

daimonic, the 158
"Daughters of Feminists" 89, 91
daydreaming 117
deaconing 137
"the deal" 179
death 127
Debussy, Claude 9
"Deck the Halls" 122
The Defender 137
Delta blues 138
demographics 133, 153
demos 199
depth 100
desire 165
detachment 99, 118, 119
detail 45, 86
determination 2
Dickinson, Emily 122
dictionaries of contemporary usage 70
Diddley, Bo 65
DiFranco, Ani 150
diminished fifth 15
Dion and the Belmonts 139
diphthong 50
disappearance 123
discipline 122
discords 162
dissonance 2, 26
distraction 117
distribution networks 145
Dixon, Willie 138
Dobkin, Alix 149
dominant 14
doo-wop 139
Dostoyevsky 110
dotted notes 31
double entendre 45, 68
double meaning 28
double sharps and flats 14
drafts 81, 113, 202
"Drawing On the Right Side of the Brain"
    115
dream state, the 117
dreams 110
drummers 62
Duende, el 159
Dylan, Bob ii, 7
dynamics 33
    crescendo 33
    diminuendo 33

E

earning money 191
echo 25, 64
ecstasy 112
editor 93

Edwards, Betty 115, 116
ego 93, 110, 112, 165
Einstein, Albert 115, 176
Eisler, Riane 127
elegance 112
Eliot, T.S. ii
Ellington, Duke 59
emerging songwriters 204
emotional expression 27, 140
empathize 84
emphasis 61
enlightenment 119, 130
Estes, Clarissa Pinkola 127, 159
Evans, Dale 136
exaggeration 166
exercises 78

F

fables 110
family 155
fantasies 94
"Fantasy" 110
fantasy 117
Farmer's Almanac 187
fashion 133
Faulkner, William 78
feedback 80, 95
feminism 150, 151
fermata 33
Ferron 178
fertile periods 176
festivals 204
Fields, W.C. 115
figure-ground 116
film. See movies: writing for
"Finnegan's Wake" 126
first line 47, 50
first presence 165
Fisher, Archie 72
Five Satins 139
fixation 95
flamadiddle 62
"flash art" 88
flats 12
flow 98
focus 120
folk movement iii
folk music societies 194
folklore 126, 187
Forbes, Roy 179
forced rhyme 74
Ford, Ford Madox 29
form 82, 87, 102
Forster, E.M. 77
Franke, Bob 155
Franklin, Benjamin 115
Freberg, Stan 171
Freed, Don 179
Freud, Sigmund 110
Frizell, David 168
Frost, Robert 79, 122
full moon 187
Fuller, Blind Boy 138
funny songs 173

Muses, the 6, 82
music
    Eastern European 57
    Middle-Eastern 57
    power of
        excitement of 3
    reading 18
    reasons for 5
    theory 9
music business 2, 94, 203
    limitations of the 2
musical styles
    adult & contemporary 134
    bebop 138
    country 135
    country blues 138
    Delta blues 138
    doo-wop 139
    hip hop 139
    rap 139
    rhythm & blues 138
    rock and roll 138
    soul 138
Muzak 73
"myth of separateness" 120
mythology 126
myths 126

N
Nachmanovitch, Stephen 93, 124
names of groups 185
Nash, Graham 134
Nashville 198, 207
"Nashville" Chord System 18
Nashville Network 141
natural 12
nature 165
nature-consciousness 165
"New Age" 125
New Music Seminar 152
Newton, John 161
Niles, John Jacob ii
Nolan, Bob 135
non-commercial songs 177
noncompetitive environment 208
nonsense syllables 76
Northern Ireland 152
notes
    accidentals 30
    blue notes 30
    dotted 22
    duration of 9
    musical 9
    tied 22

O
O'Connor, Flannery 75
O'Day, Allen 205
O'Malley, D.J. 135
onomatapoetic 62
"ontology" 125
open chord 35
oral tradition 28, 136, 144, 202
originality 27, 82
Orioles, the 139

Otis, Johnny 66
outlook 201
outros 40
ownership 191
oxymoron 183

P
pacing 105, 123
painting
    influence on songwriting 103
Paley, Grace 125
palindrome 184
paradiddle 62
parody 74, 147
partnership 201
Parton, Dolly 143, 177
Partridge's Dictionary of American Slang 70
path 93
patting juba 137
Patton, Charley 138
Paxton, Tom ii, iv, 172
pedal points 32
Penguins 139
Penn, Larry 182
perception 116
perception of time 121
"perfect" intervals 15
performance 90
performance rights societies 193
    controversy 194
persona 111
personal unconscious 111
perspective 178
Peter, Paul and Mary ii
"Philadelphia" 123
phrases 45, 46
phrasing 44
Picasso 124
Picasso, Pablo 163
Pinewoods 206
pitch 2, 9, 29
plagiarism 28
plagiary 170
Plato 118
plot 85
Poe, Edgar Allan 122, 123
poems 73
poetic criticism 165
poetic interpretations 181
poetic terms 56
poetry 121, 159
political songs 173
politics 144
Porter, Cole 91, 142
post-production 143
premise 47, 50
presence 165
Presley, Elvis 21
Prestwood, Hugh 87
prewriting 79
process of writing 178
processes
    unconscious 5
productivity 106, 201
program your mind 120

progressions 18
pronouns 86
proprioceptors 107
prosody 60
psyche 111
psychodrama 95
psychology 110
public domain 191
public radio 194
publishers 193, 195, 199
publisher's share 203
Puget Sound Guitar Workshop 206
pulse 63
puns 70, 88

Q

Quarto, Charles John 85, 100, 186, 201

R

radio 50, 59, 100, 133, 151, 153
   consultants 153
   documentaries 146
ragtime 63
rap 139
ratamacue 62
Ravel, Maurice 162
"Raven, The" 122
Reavey, George 122
rebellion 140
recorded songs 192
Reed, Ann 58
Register of Copyrights 192
relaxation techniques 164
Renard, Jules 96
repetition 25, 74, 87, 88, 136
resolution 55
rests 21
retreats 206
rewrite 77
rewriting 29, 30, 85
Reynolds, Malvina 148, 182
rhyme 50, 55, 57, 83, 121
   AAAB rhyme 87
   approximate 90
   burying rhyme 88
   casual 51
   clustering 53
   compound 52
   don't rhyme 88
   double 50, 52
   feminine 50, 52
   inner line 52
   internal 89
   masculine 50, 52
   near 52
   single 50, 52
   slant 58
   sloppy 51
   soft rhyme 87
   triple 52
   True 51
rhyming dictionary 52
rhythm 31, 58, 103, 122
rhythm and blues 66, 136, 138
rhythm track 140

rhythmic character 59
rhythmic emphasis 30
rhythms
   cha cha 65
   dance 66
   huapango 65
   rhumba 65
Rich, Alan 205
right word 80
Ringer, Jim 177
Rinpoche, Chogyom Trungpa 163
risks 156
Robbins, Marty 136, 177
Roche, Suzzy 107
Roches, the 108
rock and roll 138, 140, 151
   leftist bias of 144
Rockwell, John 144
Rodgers, Jimmie 188
Rogers, Kenny 62
Rogers, Roy 136
romance 3
root movement 30
Rose, Billy 169
Ross, Diana 139
royalties 192, 196
   airplay 193
   mechanical 192
   performance 193
rules
   breaking and bending 1

S

s-count 74
sacred harp 161
sacred music 161
sales
   recordings 90
Sands, Tommy 152
Sartre, Jean-Paul 110, 124
satire 172
scale degrees 161
scansion 57
Schickele, Peter 169. *See also* Bach, P.D.Q.
Schlitz, Don 46
Schweitzer, Albert 119
Seattle, Chief (Stealth) 130
second presence 165
Seeger, Pete 5, 175
self 93, 111, 124
self publishing 198
self-consciousness 93
self-delusion 164
self-expression 1
self-hypnosis 121
self-justification 94
sentimentality 178
service 119
Service, Robert W. 123
SESAC 193
setting poems to music 122
setting the scene 47
Settle, Mary 77
settling in 202
sexuality 140

BECOME A MEMBER OF

Sing Out!

A not-for-profit tax-exempt organization formed to preserve the cultural diversity and heritage of all traditional folk musics; to support creators of new folk music from all countries and cultures; and to encourage the practice of folk music as a living phenomenon.

SUBSCRIBING MEMBERS receive
• Quarterly issues of *Sing Out!* magazine. Each 200+ page issue of *Sing Out!* includes 20 traditional and contemporary folk songs, along with feature articles, interviews, news, reviews and columns covering the a broad range of folk styles: singer-songwriter, blues, ballads, Cajun, world, old-time country, klezmer, and much, much more! Plus our indespensible comprehensive folk festival and camp guide! Don't miss future installments of "Courting the Muse"!

BASIC MEMBERS receive the above PLUS
• Access to the Sing Out! Resource Center. (a $15 value)
• A 10% discount on all Sing Out! Publications purchases (excludes bulk/box orders & special discounts).

SUSTAINING MEMBERS receive all of the above PLUS
• A $50.00 usage credit for the Resource Center (copies, print outs, longer searches, etc.)
• Your support helps Sing Out! increase the exposure of all forms of folk music, and create more opportunities for musicians to produce the music you enjoy.

To become a member, simply fill out the return card below and send it with your check or money order (or credit card information) to :
Sing Out Corporation, P.O. Box 5253, Bethlehem, PA 18015-0253
OR
Phone: (610) 865-5366   FAX: (610) 865-5129
TOLL FREE FOR ORDERS ONLY: 1-800-4-WE-SING
(Mastercard or VISA accepted)

---

the card is missing, simply send your name & address with your check or money order (or call, if you'd prefer to use a credit card!)

Subscribing Membership:
$18.00 1-yr.
$32.50 2-yrs.
$45.00 3-yrs.

Basic Membership:
$30.00 1-yr.
$56.50 2-yr.
$81.00 3-yr.

Sustaining Membership:
$50 or $100/yr.

Canada add $5 /year;
Overseas add $18/ year.
U.S. funds only!

Sing Out! Membership Order Form

Yes! I'd like to become a member of Sing Out!. Sign me up as a:

Subscribing Member: ☐1 yr. $18.00   ☐2 yrs. $32.50   ☐3 yrs. $45.00
Basic Member: ☐1 yr. $30.00   ☐2 yrs. $56.50   ☐3 yrs. $81.00
Sustaining Member: ☐$50 for 1 yr.   ☐$100 for 1 yr.
Institutional Membership: ☐$25 for 1 yr.
In Canada: Please add $5.00/year.   Overseas: Please add $18.00 / year (airdrop delivery)

Name: _____

Address: _____

City: _____ State/Prov.: _____ Zip: _____

Country: _____

This is a ☐ new   ☐ renewal membership

☐ This is a gift. Please send a gift card from: _____

Payment: ☐ Check or Money Order enclosed *Check from U.S. bank or U.S. Funds I.M.O. only, please!*
☐ Visa/Mastercard (circle one) Signature: _____
Card # _____ Exp. Date: _____

STCP   Sing Out!, P.O. Box 5253, Bethlehem, PA 18015-0253 (610) 865-5366
Toll Free for Orders ONLY 1-800-4-WE-SING

More Books from Sing Out!